QUIZ
QUEST

USA
NASA

QUIZ
QUEST
KINGFISHER

Kingfisher Publications Plc
New Penderel House,
283–288 High Holborn
London WC1V 7HZ
www.kingfisherpub.com

First published by Kingfisher Publications Plc 2006
10 9 8 7 6 5 4 3 2 1
1TR/0606/LFG/PICA(PICA)/140MA/C

Senior editor: Jane Chapman
Editor: Conrad Mason
Senior designer: Steve Woosnam-Savage
Picture research manager: Cee Weston-Baker
Artbank archivist: Wendy Allison
Production manager: Nancy Roberts
DTP co-ordinator: Catherine Hibbert

A CIP catalogue record for this book is available from the British Library.

ISBN-13: 978 0 7534 1384 5
ISBN-10: 0 7534 1384 1

Printed in China

Contents

How this book works

It's as easy as one, two, three! Option one: use the question panels to quiz yourself. Option two: turn the page to read all about the topic – numbered circles show you where to look to work out the answer for yourself. Option three: look up the answers at the back of the book. These are the three ways you can use *Quiz Quest*. Or you can just read the book all the way through!

1. The questions

Look at the question panel on the far right of each page. You will find the questions divided into three levels of difficulty. Level one questions are easy, level two are harder, and level three are real brain-teasers! Stumped? There are two ways to find the answer.

2. Read all about it!

You can turn the page and read all about the quiz topic. Look for the number of each question in the coloured circles – the answer will be somewhere inside the box...

3. The answers

...Or, you can look up the answers at the back of the book. Just turn to the topic and find out whether you got it right.

Picture clues

You can find clues to some of the answers in the pictures. Look at them to try to work out the answer.

Quick quiz

The answer pages have the questions too, so you can ask a friend to give you a quick quiz – another great way to use *Quiz Quest*!

QUIZ ONE

Nature

The rainforest
Ants
Dinosaurs
Snakes
Sharks
Sea creatures
Marine mammals
Sea birds
Birds
African herbivores
Lions
Polar animals
Farm animals
Horses
Cats
Dogs

QUESTIONS:

The rainforest

Level 1

1. Are frogs reptiles or amphibians?
2. Are reptiles cold-blooded or warm-blooded?
3. What 'A' is the world's largest river?
4. How often does it usually rain in the rainforest: daily, weekly or monthly?

Level 2

5. In which continent does the cinchona tree grow?
6. What type of animal is a boa?
7. Which plant has the largest flower in the world?
8. In which part of the rainforest do most of its animals live?
9. What do pitcher plants feed on?
10. What does the flower of the rafflesia plant smell like?
11. GREEN STEM can be rearranged to give the name of which group of tall trees?
12. Where in the world do poison dart frogs live?
13. Is a bromeliad an animal or a plant?
14. A poison dart frog's skin has enough poison to kill a person. True or false?
15. Where does the Atlas moth live?

Level 3

16. Are snakes more closely related to frogs or lizards?
17. How wide is the Amazon river at its mouth: more than 300km, more than 400km or more than 500km?
18. What illness is treated with quinine?
19. What part of geckos' bodies gives them grip?
20. Where do the plants known as epiphytes grow?

FIND THE ANSWER: The rainforest

Tropical rainforest is the richest of all natural habitats. More animals and plants live here than anywhere else on earth. The rainforest is well named – in most places it rains every day. The mixture of water and warmth is what makes this habitat so full of life.

Canopy 8 11

The canopy is like the roof of the rainforest, formed by the branches of the tallest trees. Most rainforest animals live here, eating leaves, flowers and fruit, or one another. Really tall trees, called emergents, rise above the top of the canopy.

Plants 13 20

Rainforest trees are themselves cloaked with other plants. Climbers such as vines and strangler figs grip their trunks, while ferns and bromeliads grow in their branches. Plants growing on other plants in this way are called epiphytes.

Insects 15

Rainforest insects include the world's largest moth – the Atlas moth, which lives in the rainforests of southeast Asia.

Reptiles 2 6 16 19

Reptiles are cold-blooded animals, which thrive in the warmth of tropical rainforests. Snakes such as boas and pythons hunt prey in the branches, while gecko lizards scuttle up and down the trunks, gripping with flattened toes, which act a bit like suction pads.

Amphibians 1 12 14

The dampness of the rainforest suits slimy-skinned amphibians such as the poison dart frog of South America. This type of frog has enough poison in its skin to kill a person.

Rivers

3 17

Almost all of the world's largest rivers flow through rainforests. Among them is the largest river of all, the Amazon. This massive waterway drains much of the continent of South America. Near its mouth in Brazil, the Amazon river is more than 300km wide.

Plants and animals

7 9 10

Rainforest plants use animals in unusual ways. Pitcher plants lure insects into their 'pitchers' with droplets of nectar. They then digest the insects as food. The rafflesia has the world's largest flower – 1m wide. It smells of rotten meat to attract flies to pollinate it.

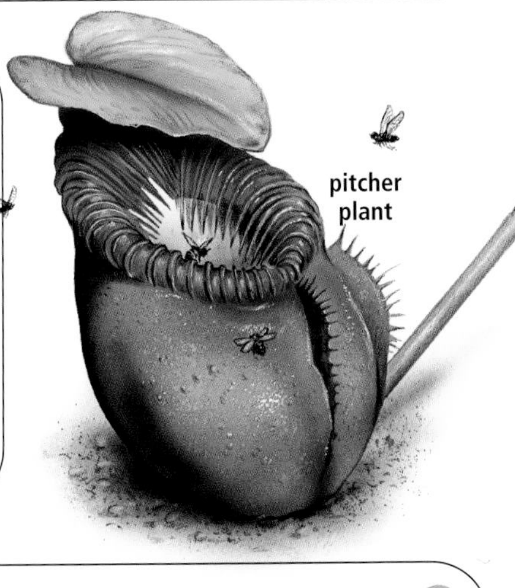

Water

4

Plants have adapted in different ways to the daily downpours of the rainforests. Many have shiny leaves with downward-pointing tips to channel water away. Some, growing in branches, have trailing roots to gather rain running off the trees.

Plant remedies

5 18

Many medicines were first discovered in rainforest plants. Quinine, for example, is used to treat malaria. It was first taken from the bark of the cinchona tree, which grows in the South American rainforests.

QUESTIONS: Ants

Level 1

1. Which have the stronger mandibles (jaws): worker or soldier ants?
2. What 'Q' is the large ant that lays all the eggs in a colony?
3. Are aphids worms or insects?
4. Are wood ants bigger or smaller than most other ants?

Level 2

5. Are there any ants that bring aphids into their nests?
6. Most ants build nests underground. True or false?
7. What do aphids feed on?
8. What is the name of the sugary substance that aphids produce?
9. Are honeypot ants most common in dry or wet places?
10. Do leaf-cutter ants live in warm or cold forests?
11. Do wood ants ever bite people?
12. What type of substance can some ants fire at attackers?
13. What do wood ants build their nests from?
14. Do ants ever attack birds?

Level 3

15. Do leaf-cutter ants eat the leaves that they harvest?
16. How many different types of ant are there in a colony?
17. What does the word metamorphose mean?
18. In what kind of forest do most wood ants live?
19. Do all of the workers in a honeypot ant colony store food in their bodies?
20. Name a continent in which both honeypot and leaf-cutter ants live.

FIND THE ANSWER: Ants

Ants live in huge communities of closely related individuals. Most ants are workers, collecting food and looking after the eggs and larvae (young). Soldier ants are slightly larger than workers and protect the nest from intruders. All ants are hatched from eggs laid by a giant ant called the queen.

Farming 3 5 7 8

Some ants farm smaller insects called aphids. Aphids feed on plant sap and produce a sugary substance called honeydew, which the ants eat. Some ants bring aphids into their nests to feed them, so they can eat honeydew.

Eggs 2 16 17

All of the eggs in an ants' nest are laid by the queen, and then taken away by worker ants to special chambers. Here they are tended until they hatch. The worker ants feed the newly hatched larvae until they are big enough to metamorphose (change shape) into adult ants themselves.

Leaf-cutter ants 10 15 20

These ants live in warm forests in North and South America. They gather leaves as compost to grow mushrooms (fungi), which they eat.

Tunnels 6

Most ants build their nests underground for protection from the weather and predators. They dig tunnels and chambers in soft earth.

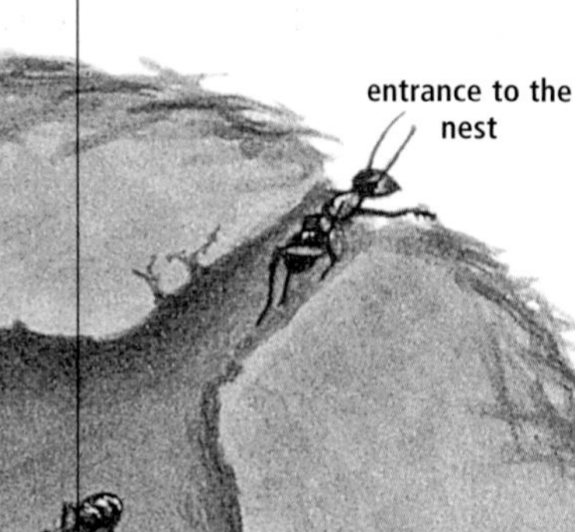

Attack and defence

1 12 14 16

Soldier ants are larger than workers and have stronger mandibles, or jaws, so their job is to protect the colony from attack. Worker ants join in if needed. Some ants also defend themselves by firing acid from the rear sections of their bodies. Ants are fearless and often attack much larger insects for food. They will swarm over birds or mammals if they threaten the ants' nest.

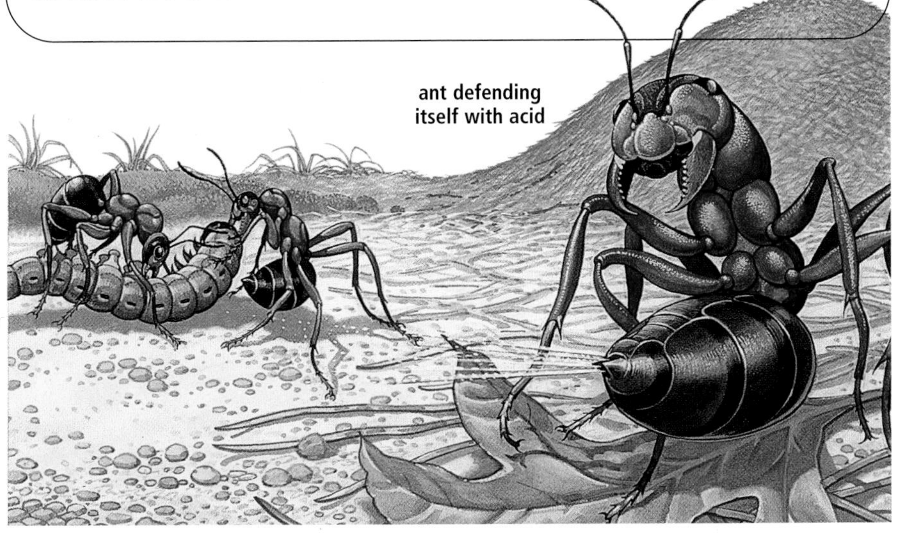

ant defending itself with acid

Honeypot ants

9 19 20

These ants use some of their workers as storage jars. They feed the storage ants with nectar, which is held inside their bodies for future use. Honeypot ants live in dry regions in North and South America, Africa and Australia.

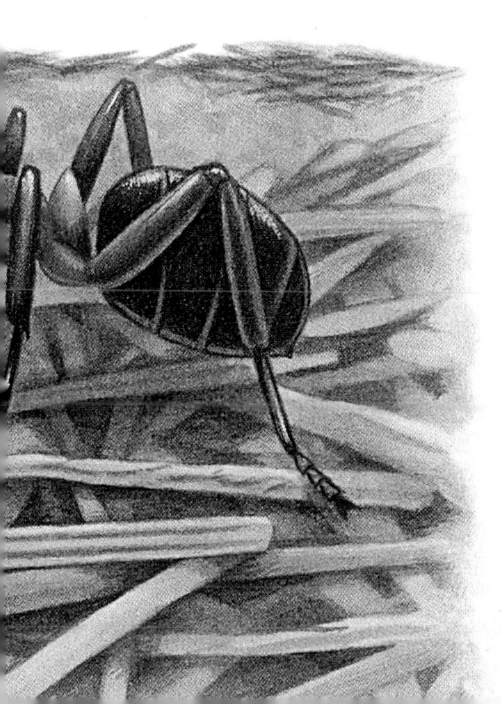

Wood ants

4 11 13 18

Wood ants live in pine forests and make their nests above ground. They build them from dried pine needles, which they collect from the forest floor. Their nests can be over a metre high. Wood ants are bigger than most ant species (types). Their mandibles are so large that they can give even people a painful bite if they are disturbed.

QUESTIONS: Dinosaurs

Level 1

1. What did *Spinosaurus* have on its back: wings or a sail?
2. What 'S' was the largest stegosaur?
3. Which dinosaur had plates on its back: *Kentrosaurus* or *Tyrannosaurus rex*?
4. Which had larger teeth: plant-eating or meat-eating dinosaurs?

Level 2

5. *Tyrannosaurus rex* teeth could be more than 10cm long. True or false?
6. Do fossils take thousands or millions of years to form?
7. Did sauropods have long necks or short necks?
8. Did any dinosaurs have beaks?
9. What did *Styracosaurus* have on its nose?
10. What did male horned dinosaurs probably use their horns for, apart from defence?
11. Which are more common: scattered fossil bones or entire fossil skeletons?
12. What type of dinosaur was *Kentrosaurus*?
13. How did a *Spinosaurus* cool down?
14. Where can you see dinosaur bones on display?

Level 3

15. What did *Tyrannosaurus rex* eat?
16. Which was bigger: *Seismosaurus* or *Stegosaurus*?
17. Are fossils made of bone or of minerals from rock?
18. *Styracosaurus* ate meat. True or false?
19. Is an *Apatosaurus* more closely related to a *Seismosaurus* or a *Styracosaurus*?
20. How many rows of plates did most stegosaurs have?

FIND THE ANSWER: Dinosaurs

a pair of *Pachycephalosaurus* fighting

Dinosaurs first appeared on earth 235 million years ago but were all wiped out suddenly 170 million years later, probably by a massive asteroid (rock from space), which hit the earth. Dinosaurs are the ancestors of modern reptiles and birds, and included the largest land animals ever. Some close relatives of dinosaurs also lived in the sea and flew in the air.

fossilized *Tyrannosaurus rex* skull

Food
4 5 8 15

Some dinosaurs ate meat, and others ate plants. Plant-eaters had small, peglike teeth, and some had horny beaks. Meat-eaters had large, sharp teeth for slicing flesh. A *Tyrannosaurus rex* tooth could be up to 15cm long!

Apatosaurus

Fossils
6 17

Fossils are formed over millions of years, when a dead dinosaur's bones are buried under mud or sand, and are slowly replaced with minerals from the surrounding rock.

Sails
1 13

The *Spinosaurus* had a large sail on its back. In hot weather, it could pump blood into the sail to cool itself down.

Defence
9 10 18

Many plant-eaters had horns to protect themselves from big meat-eaters. This *Styracosaurus* had one on his nose. Male horned dinosaurs may also have used their horns for fighting each other, just like male cattle and antelope do today.

Spinosaurus

Oviraptor

Stygimoloc

Styracosaurus

Panoplosaurus

Giant dinosaurs

7 16 19

The biggest of all dinosaurs were plant-eating sauropods like this *Apatosaurus*. Sauropods all had small heads on long necks. The largest, such as the giant *Seismosaurus*, could sometimes weigh more than 100 tonnes.

Skeletons

11 14

Most dinosaur fossils are just a few scattered bones, but sometimes complete skeletons are found. They can then be pieced together on metal frames, to be displayed in museums.

sauropod skeleton on display

Plates

2 3 12 20

Stegosaurs were plant-eaters with twin rows of plates along their backs. These probably worked in a similar way to a sail of a *Spinosaurus*, both for display and to help the dinosaurs cool down. The largest and most famous of the stegosaurs was the *Stegosaurus*. The *Kentrosaurus* was one of the smallest members of the stegosaur family.

Iguanodon

Kentrosaurus

QUESTIONS: Snakes

Level 1

1. Are pythons snakes?
2. Do snakes have legs?
3. Can snakes see?

Level 2

4. Are there any snakes that eat eggs?
5. Which snakes have a hood that they raise when threatened?
6. Where is a rattlesnake's rattle: in its mouth or on the end of its tail?
7. Are snakes vertebrates or invertebrates?
8. What are snakes' skeletons made from?
9. Do snakes' eggs have hard or flexible shells?
10. Are there any snakes that give birth to live young?
11. Rattlesnakes live in Africa. True or false?
12. Do cobras have solid or hollow fangs?
13. Do anacondas grow to over 50cm long, over 3m long or over 8m long?
14. Does camouflage make a snake harder or easier to see?

Level 3

15. What does a baby snake have on its snout to help it hatch?
16. Why do snakes flick their tongues in and out?
17. How do snakes move?
18. How do pythons kill their prey?
19. What does the African egg-eating snake use to break eggs?

FIND THE ANSWER: Snakes

Snakes are reptiles like tortoises, turtles and lizards. Reptiles are cold-blooded animals, which means that their body temperatures change with those of their surroundings. Because they need warmth to be active, most snakes live in hot countries.

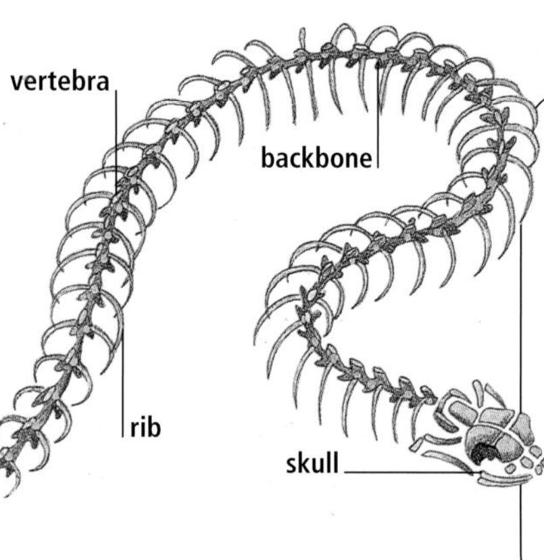

Skeleton (2) (7) (8) (17)

Snakes are vertebrates and have skeletons made of bone. Snakes have no legs, however, and move by rippling the muscles on the underside of their bodies. A snake's body is supported by its many ribs.

Eggs (9) (10) (15)

Most snakes lay eggs, although some give birth to live young. Unlike birds' eggs, snakes' eggs have flexible, leathery shells. Baby snakes have a sharp egg tooth on their snouts for breaking out of their eggs.

Food (4) (19)

Nearly all snakes are predators that catch and eat live animals. A few specialize in eating eggs. The African egg-eating snake dislocates its jaws to swallow birds' eggs three times larger than its head. The egg is swallowed whole and is punctured by sharp spines that stick down from its backbone.

coral snake moving by rippling its muscles

cobra

Cobras (5) (12)

These large snakes kill their prey with venom. They inject this poisonous liquid into their victims through their hollow fangs. Cobras can easily be told apart from other snakes by the hoods that they have behind their heads. When they feel threatened, they raise themselves up and spread their hoods outwards, just like this cobra is doing.

Senses

3 16

Snakes are able to see, but their senses of smell and taste are combined. Snakes flick their tongues in and out because they can taste the air. A snake's forked tongue can pick up particles given off by prey, and these are detected by an organ, called the Jacobson's organ, in the roof of the mouth.

Jacobson's organ

rattlesnakes

Rattlesnakes

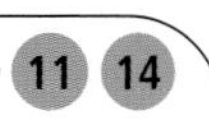

These venomous snakes live in North, Central and South America. They have rattles on the ends of their tails, which they shake to warn off larger animals and also to prevent themselves from being trodden on. Like many snakes, they are well camouflaged, which makes it harder for other animals to see them.

Constrictor

1 13 18

Some snakes, such as boas and pythons, are called constrictors because they wrap themselves around their prey until it suffocates. Anacondas are constrictors from the Amazon region of South America. They reach more than 8m long.

garter snake

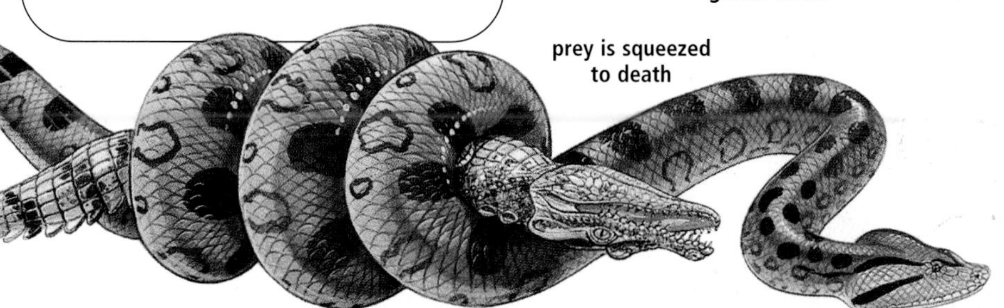

prey is squeezed to death

QUESTIONS: Sharks

Level 1

1. Are sharks fish or reptiles?
2. The whale shark is the world's biggest fish. True or false?
3. Do great white sharks eat lions or sea lions?
4. Is a shark's egg case called a mermaid's purse or a sailor's purse?

Level 2

5. Do sharks have the same set of teeth all their lives?
6. Do basking sharks live in warmer or cooler waters than whale sharks?
7. The biggest great white sharks can grow up to 6m long. True or false?
8. What is the name given to the tiny sea creatures that are food for whale sharks?
9. Which is bigger: the basking or the great white shark?
10. HE MADE HARM can be rearranged to give the name of which type of shark?
11. How heavy can a whale shark be: 11 tonnes, 21 tonnes or 31 tonnes?
12. Do all sharks lay eggs?
13. The teeth of an individual shark are all the same shape. True or false?
14. Which shark is more likely to attack people: the great white or the hammerhead?
15. Do sharks ever resort to cannibalism (eating each other)?

Level 3

16. What feature of a hammerhead makes it easier to follow a scent trail in the water?
17. What is the largest type of fish seen off the UK?
18. What is the largest shark to actively hunt prey?

FIND THE ANSWER: Sharks

dorsal fin

gill slits

The biggest fish in the world are sharks. Some can weigh more than an elephant and be as long as a bus. However, not all sharks are giants. Some, such as dogfish, are quite small, rarely growing to much more than 1m long. Almost all of the world's sharks live in the sea, although a few live in large rivers. Most sharks are predators, hunting and killing other creatures for food.

anal fin

pelvic fin

caudal fin

hammerhead shark pups

Hammerheads

10 16

Hammerhead sharks are named after their oddly shaped heads. Scientists think that the widely set nostrils help them find prey by making it easier to follow scent trails in the water.

hammerhead shark

Young sharks

1 4 12 15

All sharks are fish; some lay eggs and others give birth to live young. The egg case of a shark is known as a mermaid's purse. Baby sharks must feed and fend for themselves right from the start. Most sharks are predators, hunting other creatures for food. When they are young, they are eaten by other creatures, including other sharks.

great white shark

Teeth

5 13

Sharks go through thousands of teeth in a lifetime. As old ones fall out at the front, they are replaced with newer ones from rows behind. The teeth of an individual shark are all the same shape, but differ in size.

nose

great white shark

pectoral fin

Great white 3 7 14 18

The great white is the world's third-largest fish and the biggest shark to actively hunt prey. Some great white sharks grow to around 6m long, although most are smaller. Great white sharks hunt sea lions and other large prey. They kill and injure more people than any other type of shark.

Whale shark 2 8 11

Reaching 18m long and weighing up to 21 tonnes, the whale shark is the world's largest fish. It lives in warm, tropical waters and feeds on tiny sea creatures called plankton.

whale shark

basking shark

Basking shark 6 9 17

The basking shark is the world's second-largest fish. Like the whale shark, it feeds on plankton but it lives in cooler waters such as the seas around the UK.

QUESTIONS: Sea creatures

Level 1

1. How many tentacles does an octopus have?
2. Most of a jellyfish's body is made up of air. True or false?
3. What does SCUBA equipment help people to do?
4. Are seahorses fish or molluscs?

Level 2

5. What is the world's largest species of ray?
6. Are there more than 100 types of shark in the world?
7. How many tentacles does a squid have?
8. What do squid eat: jellyfish, plankton or fish?
9. What do jellyfish use to attack their prey?
10. Are squid invertebrates?
11. Which ocean habitat is home to the most types of fish?
12. How long can divers stay underwater for: 10 minutes or more, 15 minutes or more or 20 minutes or more?
13. What do the tanks in SCUBA equipment contain?
14. Are sharks more closely related to squid or rays?
15. Do squid spend most of their time in open water or on the seabed?

Level 3

16. What 'P' leave behind the hard, stony cases we see in coral reefs?
17. To which of these creatures are corals most closely related: jellyfish, giant clams or sharks?
18. What word is used to describe a tail that can grip things?

FIND THE ANSWER:

Sea creatures

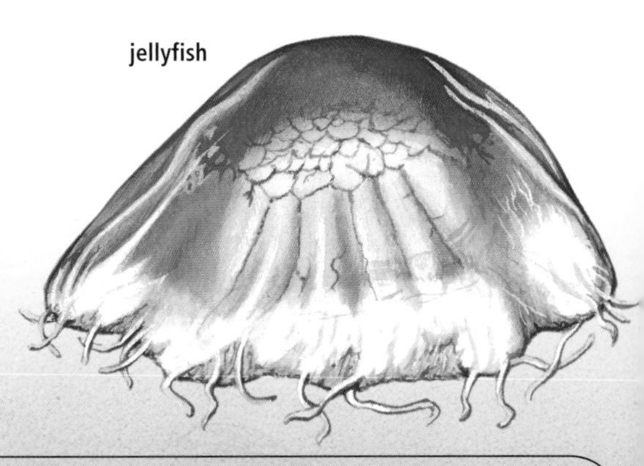

Most of the world's animals live in the sea. The sea itself covers more than two-thirds of the planet's surface. Sea creatures vary greatly in shape, size and form. Most, however, fall into two groups: vertebrates and invertebrates. Vertebrates are animals that have a backbone, like people do. Invertebrates have no bones at all.

Sharks

5 6 14

Altogether, there are more than 360 different species (types) of shark. Sharks are closely related to rays. The world's largest ray, a manta ray, can be seen in this picture just below the squid.

Jellyfish

2 9 17

Jellyfish are invertebrates with simple body structures, closely related to corals. More than 90% of a jellyfish is water. Jellyfish hunt other animals with stinging tentacles.

Squid

1 7 8 10 15

Squid swim in open water and hunt fish and small sea creatures. They are closely related to octopuses but, unlike them, have ten tentacles instead of eight. Both are cephalopods (a type of invertebrate).

hammerhead shark

great white shark

squid

Coral

16

Corals often crowd together to form reefs. The bits we usually see are hard, stony cases laid down by individual polyps: tiny sea anemone-like animals.

coral

starfish

giant clam

Diver

3 12 13

People can explore the world of sea creatures by using SCUBA diving gear. Tanks of compressed gas allow them to breathe underwater for 20 minutes or more.

marine biologist

Netting fish

4 11 18

This diver is catching fish for scientific study. More types of fish live on coral reefs than any other sea habitat. Among the strangest-looking fish are seahorses. Their prehensile (gripping) tails help them hold on to coral reefs.

net for collecting sea creatures

seahorses

manta ray

octopus

QUESTIONS: Marine mammals

Level 1

1. What is the biggest animal on earth: the elephant or the blue whale?
2. Do seals eat fish or seaweed?
3. By what name are orcas more commonly known: killer whales or seals?
4. Baby harp seals are born with grey fur. True or false?

Level 2

5. Which use echolocation to find their prey: dolphins or walruses?
6. What 'K' are shrimp-like creatures that humpback whales eat?
7. Seals give birth in the sea. True or false?
8. Do all walruses have tusks or only the males?
9. What 'P' is a group of killer whales known as?
10. Why are many large whales rare today?
11. Which marine mammals sometimes kill and eat whales that are larger than they are?
12. Do all whales eat large animals?
13. Which ocean surrounds the North Pole?
14. What 'S' do walruses eat?

Level 3

15. Where on a whale would you find its baleen?
16. What 'C' is the name of the marine mammal group that contains whales and dolphins?
17. Near which pole do walruses live: the North or the South Pole?
18. What part of a blue whale weighs as much as an elephant?
19. How long was the largest blue whale ever measured?

FIND THE ANSWER: # Marine mammals

blue whale's size compared to other animals

Mammals are warm-blooded animals that feed their young on milk. Most of them live on land but some, the marine mammals, live in the sea. Marine mammals include whales, dolphins, seals, sea lions and walruses. All of them breathe air but have adapted to life in the sea, having flippers instead of legs, for example.

Biggest animal

1 18 19

The blue whale is the biggest animal that has ever lived. Its heart is as big as a car and its tongue weighs as much as an elephant. The biggest ever measured was 33.5m long.

killer whale pod attacking a humpback whale

Killer whales

3 9 11

Killer whales, or orcas, live and hunt in groups called pods. By working together, they can overpower and kill much larger whales. Some orcas hunt small prey like seals and fish.

humpback whale

Humpbacks

6 12 15

Like most large whales, humpbacks feed on small fish and shrimp-like krill. They trap whole shoals inside their mouths behind plates of baleen, which hang down from their upper jaws.

whaling ship harpooning a humpback whale

Whaling

10

Most large whales are rare, because in the past they were hunted. Whalers killed them for their meat, considered a delicacy in some countries. It is now illegal to hunt most large whales, and the huge whaling fleets that once sailed the seas are a thing of the past.

Dolphins

5 

Like whales, dolphins belong to the mammal group called cetaceans. Dolphins use echolocation to find food, making loud clicks, then listening for echoes that bounce back. They often work together to round up prey.

bottle-nosed dolphins

Seals

2 4 7

Seals eat fish, but they haul themselves out onto ice or land to rest and to give birth to their young. Baby harp seals are born with white coats. Their mothers' milk is very thick and creamy.

baby harp seal with its mother

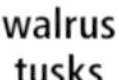

walrus tusks

Walruses

8 13 14 17

The walrus lives in the Arctic ocean, which surrounds the North Pole. It feeds on shellfish, which it collects from the seabed. All walruses have long tusks, although those of the males are bigger. They use these to spar for mates and also to defend themselves from polar bears. Walruses live together in large groups.

QUESTIONS: Sea birds

Level 1

1. Do puffins carry food in their mouths, their feet or their wings?
2. Do seagulls ever feed inland?
3. SNIFF UP can be rearranged to give the name of what sea birds?
4. An albatross is a type of sea bird. True or false?
5. What 'F' is the main food of most sea birds?

Level 2

6. Some sea birds carry food for their chicks in their stomachs. True or false?
7. Why do cormorants stand with their wings open after hunting in the water?
8. Do puffins use their wings or feet to swim?
9. Do boobies hunt by diving into the water from the air or by diving in from the surface?
10. Is a male frigate bird's throat-pouch red, yellow or blue?
11. Do cormorants use their wings or feet to swim?
12. Does oil float on water or does it sink?
13. Do frigate birds live in the tropics or near the North Pole?

Level 3

14. What 'G' is a sea bird that nests near the tops of cliffs?
15. What does the word regurgitate mean?
16. How do frigate birds get food?
17. Why do male frigate birds inflate their throat pouches with air?
18. What 'T' is a word for warm air currents that frigate birds use to lift them into the air?

FIND THE ANSWER: Sea birds

Many birds find their food in the ocean. Birds that do this are known as sea birds. Shore birds, such as the oystercatcher, live beside the sea and find their food on mud flats and beaches. Although sea birds spend their lives out over the ocean, they lay their eggs on land and return every year to coastal cliffs to breed.

Frigate birds (10) (13) (16) (17)

Frigate birds live in the tropics, and attack other sea birds in order to steal their food. Males have red throat-pouches which they inflate to attract females.

Colonies (14)

Many types of sea bird live and breed in large colonies on cliffs, to help protect each other from predators. The gannet, shown on the right, nests near the tops of cliffs.

Food (1) (5) (6) (15)

Most sea birds eat fish, and carry it back to their chicks. Some, such as puffins, stuff their beaks with food. Others swallow it and then regurgitate it (cough it up) when they return.

Hunting (3) (8) (9)

The booby dives from the air into the water to catch its prey. Other sea birds, such as puffins, land on the water and dive in from the surface, paddling with their wings.

Cormorant

7 11

Cormorants are large sea birds that hunt by diving from the water's surface and using their webbed feet as paddles. After hunting, they stand with their wings held open wide to dry out their feathers.

cormorant drying its wings

Using air currents

4 18

Some sea birds, such as frigate birds, use thermals (warm air currents) to lift them into the air. Others, such as albatrosses, use small updraughts that blow off the crests of waves to lift them upwards.

On land and sea

2

Some sea birds have become successful on land as well as on the ocean. Many seagulls, for instance, have learned to find food in bins and rubbish tips. They also follow fishing boats for discarded fish.

Pollution

12

Sea birds often suffer because of human waste and pollution. Whenever oil tankers sink, hundreds of sea birds die as the oil floats on water and clogs up their feathers. Only the lucky ones that are found on beaches and cleaned up, survive.

QUESTIONS: Birds

Level 1

1. Do birds have teeth?
2. Birds are the only animals in the world that have feathers. True or false?
3. Do birds flap their wings when they are gliding?
4. Can swans fly?

Level 2

5. A NEST FILM can be rearranged to give the name of what parts of a feather?
6. What is the world's largest bird?
7. Birds have elbow joints. True or false?
8. Are birds' bones solid or hollow?
9. GLEAM UP can be rearranged to give what name for the feathers that cover a bird?
10. Does a kestrel eat fruit, seeds or meat?
11. Which are usually more brightly coloured: male birds or female birds?
12. Which 'H' means to stay still in mid-air?
13. Which has the longer beak: a curlew or a robin?
14. How many times can hummingbirds flap their wings every second: seven times, 70 times or 700 times?

Level 3

15. What is the chamber between a bird's mouth and its stomach called?
16. How many sections does a bird's stomach have?
17. What do hummingbirds feed on?
18. What 'R' is a large flightless bird?

FIND THE ANSWER: Birds

Birds are masters of the air. Their ability to fly enables birds to travel long distances in search of food. Some migrate, flying thousands of kilometres each year to breed and take advantage of the abundance of food in spring and summer. All birds lay eggs with hard shells, and most make nests. Some birds sing to attract mates or show they own a territory.

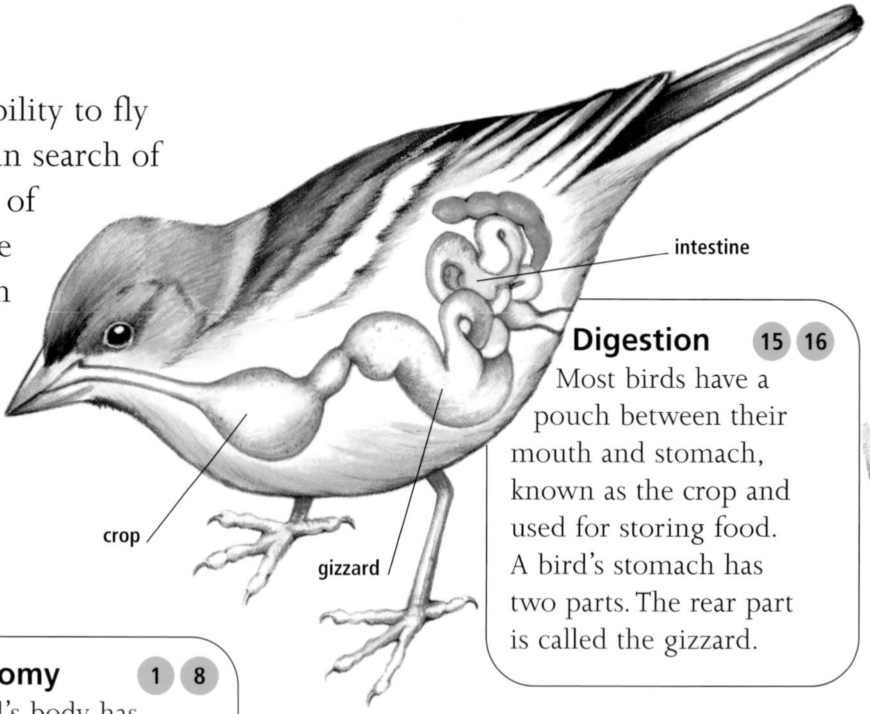

intestine

crop

gizzard

Digestion 15 16

Most birds have a pouch between their mouth and stomach, known as the crop and used for storing food. A bird's stomach has two parts. The rear part is called the gizzard.

Feathers 2 5

Birds are the only animals in the world that have feathers. Feathers are what enable birds to fly. They are lightweight but strong, made of many filaments held together by very small hooks.

filaments

hooks

Anatomy 1 8

A bird's body has several features to make it lighter and so make flight less of an effort. For example, its bones are hollow and therefore lighter than those of other animals. Birds also have beaks instead of teeth.

rock dove slowing itself down as it lands

Flight 3

Most birds fly by flapping their wings, using them to push down on the air and lift their bodies upwards. Some birds glide, holding out their wings and catching updraughts of air – this uses hardly any energy.

Wings 7

A bird's wings are like arms, with shoulder and elbow joints. Bones that formed fingers in birds' ancestors have adapted to form ends of wings.

Large birds 4 6 18

The largest flying birds are pelicans (left), bustards and swans. The largest bird of all is flightless – the ostrich. Other flightless giants include emus and rheas.

Plumage 9 11

The feathers that cover a bird are called plumage. Usually, male birds' plumage is colourful, to attract mates, whereas females have dull plumage to hide them when sitting on eggs.

wren

swallow

robin

greenfinch

kestrel

redshank

curlew

Beaks 10 13

A bird's beak is adapted for the food that it eats. The curlew's long beak is used for probing in the mud for worms, while the kestrel's hooked beak is used for tearing off meat.

Hummingbirds 12 14 17

Hummingbirds feed on nectar from flowers, and have long beaks and tongues to dip into the blooms. These tiny birds flap their wings over 70 times a second to hover (stay still in mid-air).

hummingbird

QUESTIONS: African herbivores

Level 1

1. Do zebras have spots or stripes?
2. Are rhinos larger or smaller than rabbits?
3. Are zebras more closely related to horses or sheep?
4. Whereabouts on an elephant's body is its trunk?

Level 2

5. What is the world's largest land animal?
6. What is the world's tallest land animal?
7. What 'B' is the word for a male elephant?
8. How can an elephant use its trunk to cool itself down?
9. African elephants can weigh more than a tonne. True or false?
10. How tall do male giraffes grow: 3m, 6m or 10m?
11. Rhinos have excellent eyesight. True or false?
12. Do giraffes feed mainly on grass, insects or leaves?
13. Which African predator can kill elephants?
14. How many species (types) of zebra are there: three, five or seven?

Level 3

15. What 'P' hunts elephants for their tusks?
16. How many species (types) of rhino are there?
17. What 'J' is a species of rhino that lives in Asia?
18. What are elephants' tusks made of?

FIND THE ANSWER:

African herbivores

Herbivores are animals that eat plants but do not eat meat. Many of the world's largest herbivores live on the plains of Africa. Here, there are vast amounts of grass and other vegetation for them to eat, so they exist in large numbers. Some herbivores live quite solitary lives, but most live in small groups or large herds.

Tough skin 13 15 18

Elephants' skin is thick and tough. This makes it hard for predators to kill them, although sometimes lions do attack and kill elephants. Unfortunately, poachers also hunt elephants for their ivory tusks.

Elephants 5 7 9

The African elephant is the world's largest land animal. Adult male, or bull, elephants can weigh up to 12 tonnes.

Trunks 4 8

An elephant uses its trunk to spray water on itself to cool down, and to pick things up. The trunk is formed from the nose and upper lip and contains thousands of muscles.

baby elephant spraying water from its trunk

Zebras

1 3 14

Zebras are members of the horse family and live only in Africa. There are three species (types) of zebra: plains zebras, Grevy's zebras and mountain zebras. All zebras have stripes and live in herds.

zebras

giraffe using its tongue to reach leaves

Giraffes

6 10 12

The giraffe is the tallest of all land animals, with adult males growing up to 6m tall. It lives only on the African plains. The giraffe uses its long neck and muscular tongue to reach leaves on the highest branches. It has to splay its legs apart to drink, so that it can reach the ground.

Rhinos

2 11 16 17

Rhinos are large, powerful herbivores that most meat-eaters leave alone. Two species (types) of rhino live in Africa: the black rhino and the white rhino. The three other species – the Indian, Sumatran and Javan rhinos – all live in Asia. Rhinos have very poor eyesight.

black rhino

QUESTIONS: Lions

Level 1

1. What is the name for a female lion?
2. RIP ED can be rearranged to give what name for a group of lions?
3. Which lions have manes: the males or the females?
4. Do male or female lions make up most of the pride?
5. Which are bigger: male or female lions?

Level 2

6. Which are the last members of the pride to feed at a kill?
7. Apart from hunting, what do the lionesses do in the pride?
8. Which members of a pride of lions do most of the hunting?
9. Do female lions stay with or leave the pride when they grow up?
10. Do lions usually hunt in groups or on their own?
11. Do lions ever fight to the death?
12. How long do lion cubs stay hidden from the rest of the pride: eight days, eight weeks or eight months?
13. What do lion cubs have on their coats that adult lions do not?
14. How many male lions usually lead a pride?

Level 3

15. What is the name of the area in which a pride of lions lives and hunts?
16. What do lions use to mark the borders of this area?
17. What do male lions do to keep others away?
18. How does a male lion take over a pride?

The lion is sometimes called the King of Beasts. It is a large, majestic creature, the second biggest of all the cat family after the tiger. Unlike most big cats, lions are social animals, which live and hunt in groups called prides. Most of the world's wild lions live on the African plains, but a few live in north-west India, in an area known as the Gir Forest.

Territory

15 16

Each pride lives and hunts in an area of land known as its territory. The edges are patrolled and marked with urine, droppings and scratch marks on trees.

Females

1 2 4 7 8 9

Female lions, called lionesses, make up most of the pride. They stay together throughout their lives. Daughters remain with their mother, aunts and sisters even after they have grown up. As well as caring for the young, they do most of the hunting.

two males fighting

Fighting

11 18

Rival males without prides may challenge another male for ownership of his pride. Such fights can be violent and even end in death.

lioness and her cub

Cubs

12 13

For the first eight weeks, lion cubs stay with their mother away from the pride. Unlike adult lions, lion cubs have spots, which gradually fade as they grow older.

two lionesses hunting

Hunting

6 10

Lionesses work together when hunting. When an animal is brought down, the kill is shared among the pride. Adult males feed first, followed by the lionesses and, lastly, the cubs.

Males

3 5 14 17

Male lions are much bigger than females and have a thick, shaggy mane. Each pride of lions is led by just one or occasionally two or three adult males, who mate with all of the females. Males roar to keep others away.

male lion

QUESTIONS: Polar animals

Level 1

1. Can penguins fly?
2. Can polar bears swim?
3. Polar bears can weigh over a tonne. True or false?
4. Do polar bears ever lie in wait for their prey?
5. Polar bears eat seals. True or false?

Level 2

6. In which season do migrating birds arrive in the polar regions?
7. Killer whales live in polar waters. True or false?
8. Why do some types of baby seal have white coats?
9. Do polar bears live near to the North Pole or the South Pole?
10. Penguins live in the Antarctic. True or false?
11. ALE BUG can be rearranged to give the name of which whale that lives in Arctic waters?
12. Which sense do polar bears use to find most of their prey: sight, hearing or smell?
13. How do penguins paddle themselves through the water: with their wings or with their feet?
14. What is the world's largest kind of penguin?

Level 3

15. Which bird flies all the way from the Antarctic to the Arctic and back again every year?
16. How can people protect baby seals from humans hunting them for their fur?
17. Do narwhals live near to the North Pole or the South Pole?
18. What word is used for keeping an egg warm until it hatches?

FIND THE ANSWER: Polar animals

The regions around the poles are tough places to live. In order to survive, animals need to be able to cope with extreme cold and sometimes go for long periods without food. Weather conditions are harsh. In the middle of winter, the sun never rises and it is dark for weeks on end, while in summer the sun is always in the sky, meaning that there are 24 hours of daylight.

Birds

6 15

Many birds migrate to polar regions in spring to lay their eggs. Every year, Arctic terns fly all the way from the Antarctic to the Arctic and then back again. By leaving each pole just before winter, they manage to completely avoid the coldest time of the year.

Polar bears

The polar bear is the world's largest land carnivore (meat-eater). Adult males can weigh over a tonne. Polar bears live in the Arctic, near the North Pole. Their large, padded feet act as paddles when swimming in water.

Life in the water

7 11 17

Many polar animals live in the sea. Seals hunt fish under the ice. Other mammals in the polar seas include killer whales, which live both in the Arctic and Antarctic. Belugas and narwhals are small whales that live only in the Arctic waters.

Hunting

4 5 12

Polar bears hunt on the open ice and find most of their prey by smell. They sometimes feed on walruses, but mainly on seals, chasing them when they are out of the water, or lying in wait beside holes in the ice.

seal

polar bear

Penguins

1 10 13

Penguins are flightless birds that live in the Antarctic. They are totally adapted to life in the sea. Their stiff wings act as paddles for their streamlined bodies.

penguins sliding on the ice

Winter wonder

14 18

Emperor penguins are the largest kind of penguin. The males incubate (keep warm) the females' eggs by holding them on their feet through the winter.

male emperor penguin

baby penguin

Seal hunting

8 16

Some types of seal are born with beautiful white coats to hide them in the snow. Unfortunately, some people like to wear clothes made from their fur, and many seal pups are killed for this reason. People try to protect the baby seals by spraying them with harmless dye, making their coats useless to the humans who hunt them.

spraying a ringed seal pup

QUESTIONS: Farm animals

Level 1

1. Are dairy cows kept for their milk or their fur?
2. Is a cockerel a male or a female chicken?
3. What animal do farmers keep to hunt down rats and mice?
4. Which farm animals produce wool?

Level 2

5. What 'K' is a baby goat?
6. Today, dairy cows are milked by hand. True or false?
7. On which part of a cow are its teats?
8. How many teats does a cow have?
9. Which have larger crests on their heads: male or female chickens?
10. Which animal is needed to make butter?
11. EAGER FERN can be rearranged to give the name of what kind of chicken?
12. Which farm animal does gammon come from?
13. What 'L' is a meat from sheep?
14. What 'F' is removed from a sheep by shearing it?

Level 3

15. What is the smallest piglet in a litter called?
16. How many teats does a goat have?
17. What is the most common kind of sheep dog in the UK?
18. What is a male pig called?
19. What is the name for chickens that are kept in cages?

FIND THE ANSWER: Farm animals

Some animals are looked after by people on farms. Most of them are kept to provide us with food, but some give us other useful products, such as wool. Farm animals are domesticated versions of creatures that once lived in the wild. Most of the world's sheep, for example, are descended from the mouflon, which still lives out in the wild in Europe and Asia.

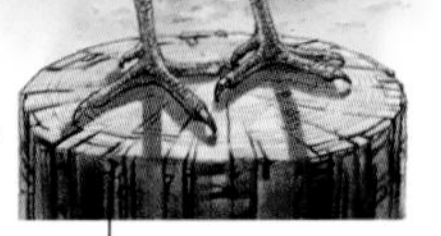

cockerel crowing at sunrise

Dairy cows 1 6 7 10

Farmers keep dairy cows for their milk. Farmers used to milk by hand, but today, machines gently squeeze the teats on the cows' udders to collect the milk. Milk can be used to make butter and cheese.

Cockerels and hens 2 9 11 19

Farmers keep chickens for eggs and meat. Male chickens (cockerels) usually have bigger crests and longer tails than females (hens), and also crow at sunrise. Free-range chickens live outside in the open, while battery chickens are kept indoors in cages.

Friesian cow

milking teats

feed bucket

farmer

Cats 3

Many farmers have cats to hunt down mice and rats. Unlike most pet cats, farm cats spend their lives outdoors and sleep in barns and hayricks. Some farmers have dozens of cats.

Goats 5 8 16

A female goat is called a nanny and a male goat a billy. Baby goats are known as kids. Goats' udders have two teats, unlike those of cows, which have four.

Sheep (4) (13)

Sheep are kept for their wool and also for their meat, which is known as mutton or lamb. Male sheep are called rams and usually have horns. Female sheep are known as ewes.

Sheep shearing (14)

Once a year, sheep have their wool cut off, a process known as shearing. The wool from one sheep is called a fleece. Sheep shearing is done by hand, using motorized clippers, and does not hurt the sheep at all.

Sheep dogs (17)

Sheep dogs help farmers round up their sheep from the fields. Most of these dogs are intelligent and easy to train. In the UK, the most common sheep dog is the border collie. The Alsatian was originally bred as a sheep dog.

Pigs (12) (15) (18)

Farmers keep pigs for their meat, which is known as pork, gammon or bacon. A male pig is called a boar and a female a sow. A sow may have ten or more piglets (baby pigs) in a litter. The smallest is called the runt.

mother sow with piglets

QUESTIONS: Horses

Level 1

1. What are baby horses called?
2. What do cowboys wear to shade them from the sun?
3. In showjumping, do riders try to jump over obstacles or crash into them?
4. Horses are used to pull ploughs. True or false?
5. What 'L' is the looped rope that cowboys use to catch cattle?
6. Are ponies larger or smaller than horses?

Level 2

7. Is an Exmoor a breed of pony or a breed of horse?
8. What is the largest breed of horse?
9. What is the main difference between the skeleton of a horse and the skeleton of a human?
10. When do male horses show their teeth and pull their lips back?
11. HEN CARS can be rearranged to give the name of what large farms on which cowboys work?
12. What is worn by jumping horses to protect their ankles from knocks?
13. BANDY HURDS can be rearranged to give the name of what item, used for removing dirt from a horse's coat?

Level 3

14. What 'C' is a type of pony from Iran?
15. How does a horse show aggression?
16. What is the name of the bones that make up a horse's spine?
17. What kind of brush is used to brush away loose hair on a horse?
18. What 'D' is a horse-riding sport, which tests obedience and rider control?

FIND THE ANSWER: Horses

rider

People have kept horses for thousands of years. Before the invention of the car and train, they were the main form of transport, carrying people on their backs or towing them in carts and carriages. Horses were also used by farmers to draw ploughs and by cavalry soldiers to carry them into battle. Today, most horses are kept for pleasure, although some are still used as working animals.

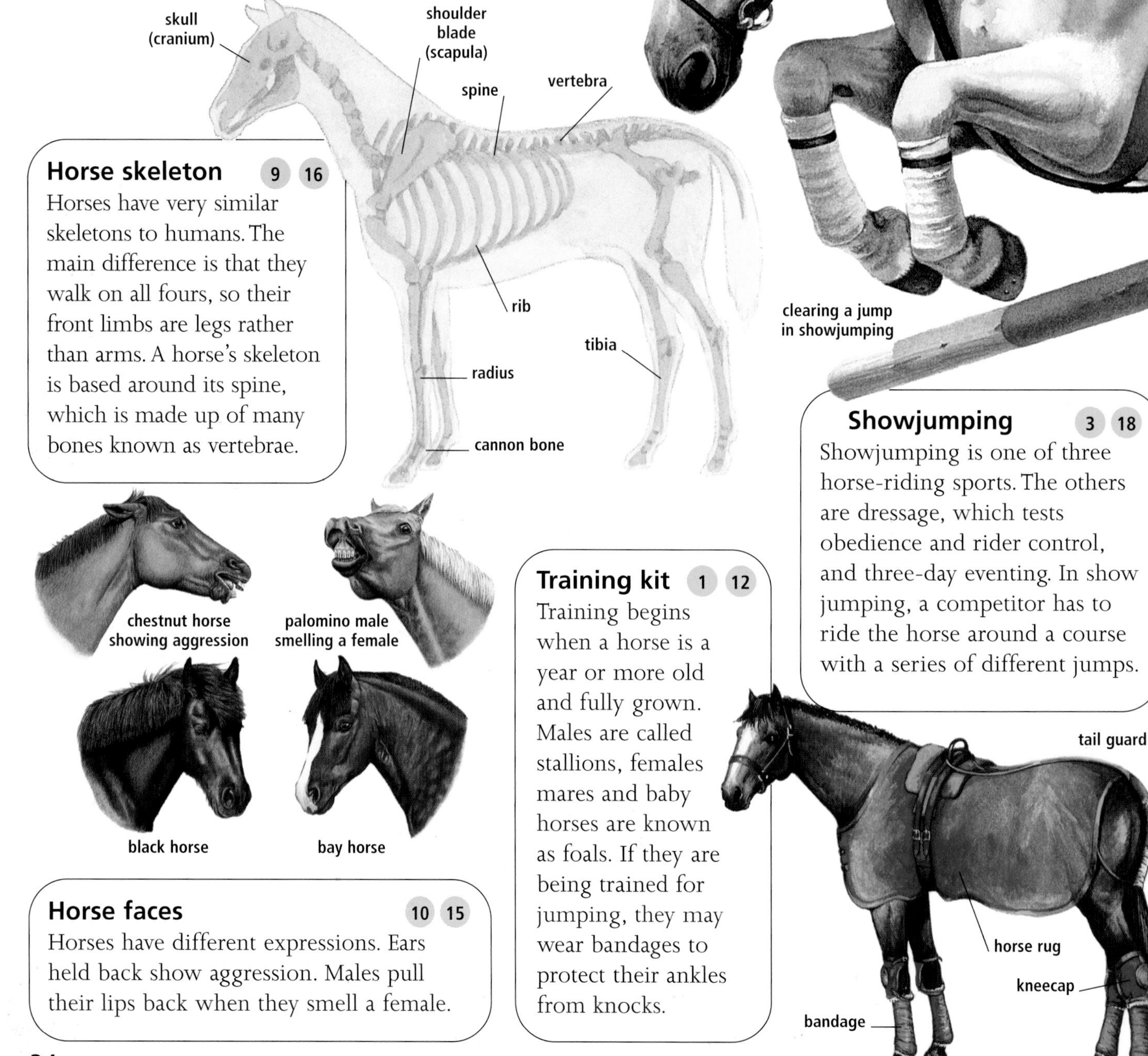

clearing a jump in showjumping

chestnut horse showing aggression

palomino male smelling a female

black horse

bay horse

Horse skeleton 9 16

Horses have very similar skeletons to humans. The main difference is that they walk on all fours, so their front limbs are legs rather than arms. A horse's skeleton is based around its spine, which is made up of many bones known as vertebrae.

Showjumping 3 18

Showjumping is one of three horse-riding sports. The others are dressage, which tests obedience and rider control, and three-day eventing. In show jumping, a competitor has to ride the horse around a course with a series of different jumps.

Training kit 1 12

Training begins when a horse is a year or more old and fully grown. Males are called stallions, females mares and baby horses are known as foals. If they are being trained for jumping, they may wear bandages to protect their ankles from knocks.

Horse faces 10 15

Horses have different expressions. Ears held back show aggression. Males pull their lips back when they smell a female.

Cowboys

2 5 11

Cowboys ride horses to round up cattle. Today, most work on ranches in the USA, which are like large farms. Cowboys catch cattle with a lasso, a looped rope. They wear wide hats to shade them from the sun.

cowboy with lasso

Working horses

4 8

Police on horseback are often used to control large crowds. Horses are also used to pull carts and ploughs in some places. The largest horse of all is the shire horse, which can weigh a tonne.

Ponies

6 7 14

Ponies are smaller breeds of horse. They are not as fast as large horses, but tougher, and can live outside in all weathers. Caspian ponies from Iran and Exmoor ponies from the UK live out in the wild.

Shetland pony

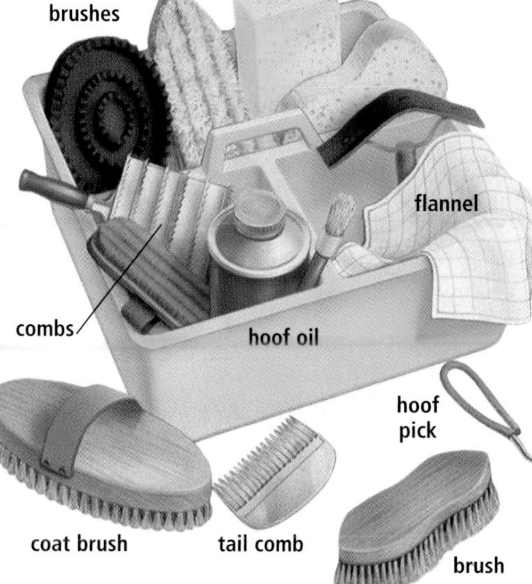

Grooming

13 17

Owners like to keep their horses looking nice and clean by grooming them. Dandy brushes are used for removing dirt, rubber curry combs brush away loose hair and mane combs remove tangles in manes.

QUESTIONS: Cats

Level 1

1. What are baby cats called?
2. Is catnip a type of plant or a type of animal?
3. Do cats creep up and pounce on their prey or chase it round and round until it is exhausted?
4. Do cat owners use brushes for grooming their cats or for feeding them?
5. Can cats climb?
6. Do young cats prefer playing with balls of wool or with knitting needles?
7. Are cats good at jumping?

Level 2

8. Cats have claws. True or false?
9. What is a scratching post for?
10. Do cats prefer to live on their own or in groups?
11. For how long do a cat's eyes stay closed after it is born?
12. How often should cats be fed?
13. Which fight more often: male cats or female cats?
14. What are male cats called?
15. Why is it a good idea to use a special dish for feeding a cat?

Level 3

16. What part of a cat's body can be retracted?
17. From which animal are domestic cats descended?
18. Why do cats spray and scent-mark things?

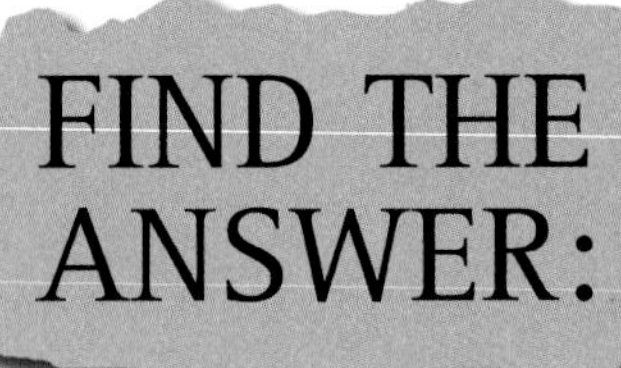

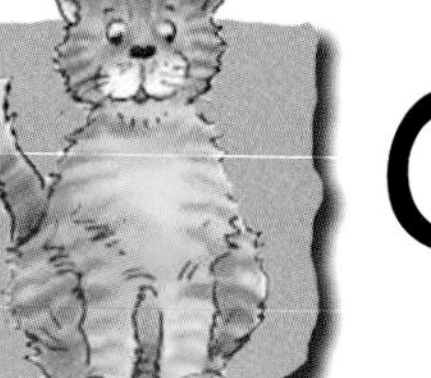

Cats

Cats are popular household pets. Unlike dogs, they do not need to be walked every day and they are quite happy to be left on their own while their owners are out at work. Nowadays, most people keep cats as pets or companions, but in the past they were mainly kept to kill mice and other vermin that got into peoples' houses.

kittens

The cat's body

Cats are muscular and flexible. They can jump long distances, and if they are dropped, they twist in the air to land on their feet. Cats are also good climbers. They have sharp claws, which they can retract (pull back into their paws) when not in use.

skull
tail
spine
humerus
femur
ribcage
fibula
tibia
metatarsals

Family

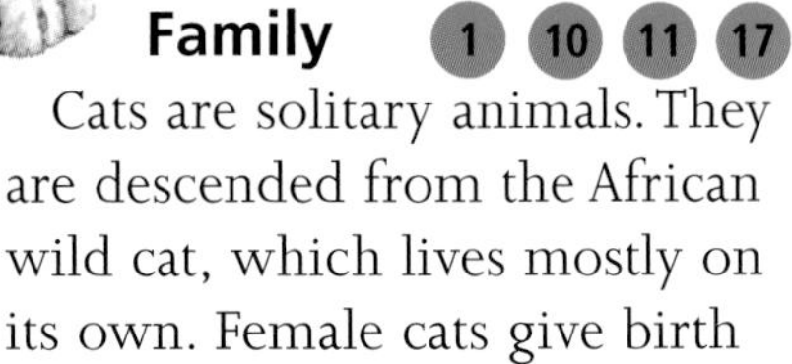

Cats are solitary animals. They are descended from the African wild cat, which lives mostly on its own. Female cats give birth to litters of several baby cats, known as kittens. Their eyes stay closed for the first week.

Cat accessories

2 4 9

Cats like to keep their claws sharp by scratching on a scratching post. They also like to play with toys and are fond of catnip, a plant. Owners use brushes to groom their cats and shampoo to wash them.

scratching post
catnip
shampoo
comb
brush
toy ball
toy mouse

Learning

3 6

Kittens enjoy playing with lots of objects and are fond of balls of wool. Playing helps them to learn and get used to how their bodies work. As they play, they learn how to hunt, creeping up on their toys before pouncing.

Feeding

12 15

Cats are fed at least once a day, either with dry food or moist food from tins or pouches. It is a good idea to put a cat's food in a special dish. Cats learn to associate the dish with feeding and come running when their owners approach it.

moist food

Territory

13 14 18

Both wild and domestic cats defend their home areas, or territories, from others. Male cats, or tom cats, in particular, will fight others that enter their area. Cats spray and scent-mark their territory as a warning to stay away.

defensive cat

scent-marking

cats fighting

QUESTIONS: Dogs

Level 1

1. What is a baby dog called?
2. Are most police dogs Alsatians or Dalmatians?
3. Were pit bull terriers originally bred for fighting or fetching slippers?
4. Are most Labrador dogs friendly or aggressive?
5. The terrier is the largest breed of dog. True or false?

Level 2

6. What is a group of related puppies called?
7. How long does it take for a puppy to grow into an adult: six months, a year or three years?
8. Which 'S' is a kind of dog often trained to be a sniffer dog?
9. How might a hearing dog help a deaf owner?
10. If a dog wags its tail, is it happy or angry?
11. Does a sad dog drop its tail or raise it?
12. Which wild animal is the ancestor of all domestic dogs?
13. EDGIER REVEL TORN can be rearranged to spell what breed of dog, often trained as guide dogs?
14. Which would make a better guard dog: a Rottweiler or a Labrador?

Level 3

15. How long should you wait before giving away puppies to new owners?
16. During which year of a dog's life is it easiest to train?
17. What is another word for cutting off a dog's tail?
18. How can you tell when a dog is frightened?
19. What type of dog was bred to hunt large animals?

FIND THE ANSWER: Dogs

People say that a dog is a man's best friend, and most dog owners agree that this is true. Dogs are friendly, protective and loyal companions. They are descended from wolves, which are pack-living animals, so a dog thinks of its owners as members of its pack. Unlike wolves, most dogs have been bred to be less aggressive and more friendly to humans.

Puppies (1) (6) (15)

A baby dog is called a puppy. Female dogs have a litter of several puppies at a time. Many people sell their dog's puppies to new owners. They have to wait until the puppies are a few weeks old and big enough to be away from their mother.

mother and litter

Growing up (7) (16)

Puppies take about a year to grow up into adults. This first year is the best time to train them, as their brains develop. (Adult dogs need more time for training.) Puppies are playful and enjoy wrestling.

adult golden Labrador

Learning (2) (8)

You can train dogs to do many things. The police train Alsatians to catch criminals and spaniels as sniffer dogs to find drugs and clues. You can train a pet dog to make it easier to control, using food treats as a reward.

Tails (10) (11) (17) (18)

A dog's tail may be straight or curly. A happy dog wags its tail, and a sad dog drops it. A confident dog holds its tail high, while a frightened dog holds its tail between its legs. On some breeds the tails may be cut off (docked) when they are puppies.

Dog breeds 5 12 19

All dogs are descended from wolves, but over the centuries many breeds have been created. Dog breeds are grouped by characteristics. Terriers, for example, are small dogs originally bred to hunt rodents. Hounds were bred to hunt larger animals.

Guide dogs 9 13

Golden retrievers and black Labradors are trained as guide dogs for blind people. They look out for obstacles on streets. Some dogs are trained as hearing dogs, alerting a deaf owner, for example, if there is a knock at the door.

Temperament 3 4 14

Dog breeds have different temperaments. Labradors are friendly and eager to please, making them ideal pets. Pit bull terriers and Rottweilers were bred to fight, so they make better guard dogs.

wolf

Alsatian

collie

basenji

basset hound

Dalmatian

bulldog

fox terrier

confident dog

straight tail

happy dog

QUESTIONS: Where in the world?

Level 1

1. Would you find a European bison in Poland or in Madagascar?
2. Do tigers live in Europe or Asia?
3. TAIPAN DANG can be rearranged to give the name of which animal that lives in the bamboo forests of China?

Level 2

4. Are tamarins types of monkey or turtle?
5. Which island off Africa is home to all of the world's lemurs?
6. Where in the world does the numbat live?
7. Which country is home to the Iberian lynx?

Level 3

8. What is the world's largest tree-living animal?
9. The Tasmanian wolf is another name for which animal?
10. What is the name of the largest bird in North America?

FIND THE ANSWER: Where in the world?

In many parts of the world, many species of animal have been disappearing at an alarming rate. Some have been hunted to near extinction by man, while others are threatened by damage to their natural habitats or by climate change. Endangered species include not only large mammals, such as the Asian elephant, but also countless birds, fish and insects.

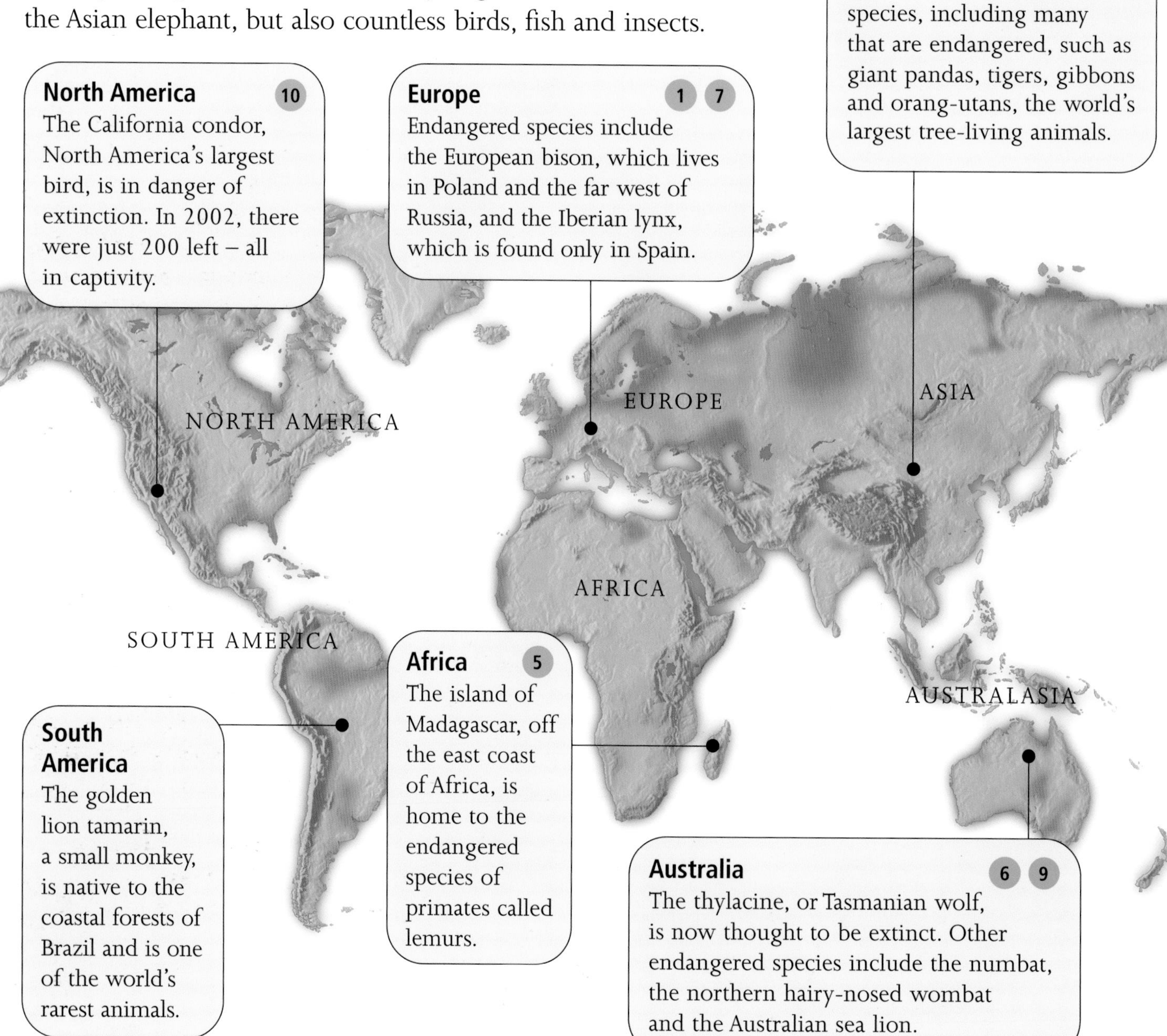

North America (10)
The California condor, North America's largest bird, is in danger of extinction. In 2002, there were just 200 left – all in captivity.

Europe (1, 7)
Endangered species include the European bison, which lives in Poland and the far west of Russia, and the Iberian lynx, which is found only in Spain.

Asia (2, 3, 8)
Asia has many unique species, including many that are endangered, such as giant pandas, tigers, gibbons and orang-utans, the world's largest tree-living animals.

South America
The golden lion tamarin, a small monkey, is native to the coastal forests of Brazil and is one of the world's rarest animals.

Africa (5)
The island of Madagascar, off the east coast of Africa, is home to the endangered species of primates called lemurs.

Australia (6, 9)
The thylacine, or Tasmanian wolf, is now thought to be extinct. Other endangered species include the numbat, the northern hairy-nosed wombat and the Australian sea lion.

Answers 1) Poland **2)**Asia **3)**Giant panda **4)**Monkey **5)**Madagascar **6)**Australia **7)**Spain **8)**The orang-utan **9)**The thylacine **10)**The California condor

QUIZ TWO

Geography

Continents

International community

Flags

Natural wonders

Coasts

Rivers

Deserts

The poles

QUESTIONS: Continents

Level 1

1. Where is the Nile?
2. Which continent lies to the east of Europe?
3. Is Asia the second-most populated continent?
4. Is Central America part of North or South America?
5. Which is the smallest continent?

Level 2

6. What is the world's largest country?
7. What divides Europe from Africa?
8. What population milestone was reached in 1802?
9. Is Sydney the capital city of Australia?
10. In which continent would you find the world's highest mountains?
11. What larger landmass encompasses Europe?
12. How many billion did the world's population reach in 1999: one, five, six or 11?
13. Are the Andes on the east or west coast of South America?

Level 3

14. How much of the Amazon rainforest lies outside of Brazil?
15. What are the names of the island groups of Australasia?
16. By how many million per year was the world's population increasing in 2004?
17. How many countries are in Africa: 47, 52 or 53?
18. In which continent is the world's largest freshwater lake?
19. How long is the Andes mountain range?

FIND THE ANSWER: Continents

Millions of years ago, the world's land was all connected in a 'supercontinent'. Over time the land shifted and settled into the seven continents we know today. This is known as continental drift. Antarctica is the world's only unpopulated continent because 98% of the land is covered in ice. It is also the coldest, windiest and driest continent.

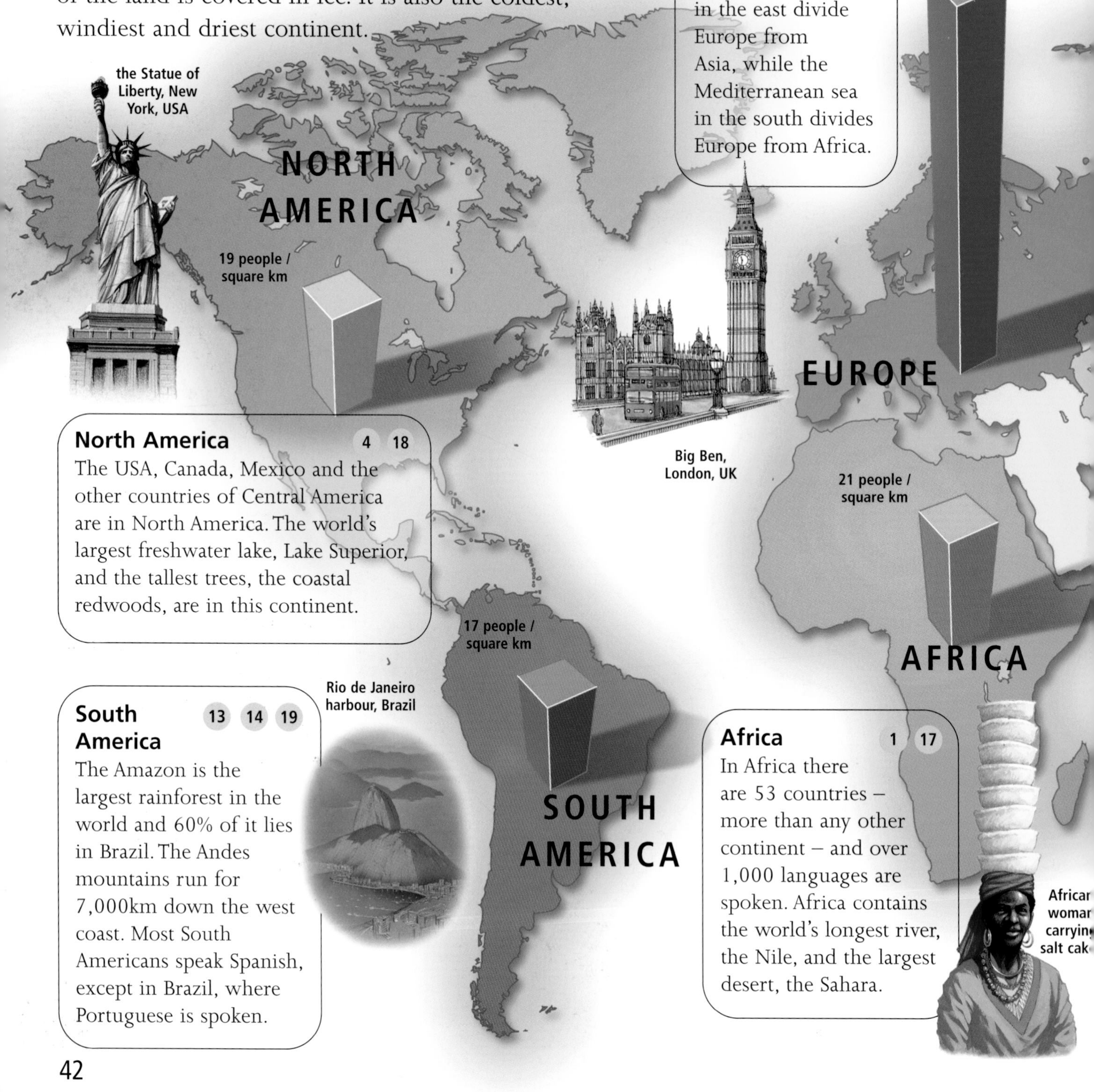

Europe 2 7 11
The continent of Europe is part of a larger landmass called Eurasia. The Ural mountains in the east divide Europe from Asia, while the Mediterranean sea in the south divides Europe from Africa.

the Statue of Liberty, New York, USA

NORTH AMERICA

19 people / square km

68 people / square km

EUROPE

Big Ben, London, UK

North America 4 18
The USA, Canada, Mexico and the other countries of Central America are in North America. The world's largest freshwater lake, Lake Superior, and the tallest trees, the coastal redwoods, are in this continent.

21 people / square km

AFRICA

17 people / square km

South America 13 14 19
The Amazon is the largest rainforest in the world and 60% of it lies in Brazil. The Andes mountains run for 7,000km down the west coast. Most South Americans speak Spanish, except in Brazil, where Portuguese is spoken.

Rio de Janeiro harbour, Brazil

SOUTH AMERICA

Africa 1 17
In Africa there are 53 countries – more than any other continent – and over 1,000 languages are spoken. Africa contains the world's longest river, the Nile, and the largest desert, the Sahara.

African woman carrying salt cak

Population increase 8 12 16

The world population has grown at an increasingly fast rate, even though birth rates have gone down in many countries. In 1802, the world reached one billion people, and by 1999 it had reached six billion. By 2004, the population increase was 75 million per year.

77 people / square km

ASIA

Asia 3 6 10

Asia is the largest continent and the most populated. It contains the world's largest country, the Russian Federation, as well as the Middle Eastern countries, the Far East and India. The world's highest mountains are in Asia, including 96 in the Himalayas.

a rickshaw bicycle, China

Australasia 5 9 15

The smallest continent includes Australia, New Zealand and Papua New Guinea, and the island groups of the south Pacific: Melanesia, Micronesia and Polynesia. Sydney is Australia's largest city, and Canberra its capital.

AUSTRALASIA

2 people / square km

the Sydney opera house, Australia

QUESTIONS: International community

Level 1

1. The United Nations was formed during World War I. True or false?
2. What does NATO stand for: the North Atlantic Treaty Organization or the North Antarctic Treaty Organization?
3. All peacekeeping units are armed. True or false?
4. What is the single currency of the European Union?
5. CRESS ROD can be rearranged to give the name of what organization that provides medical aid?

Level 2

6. Why was NATO formed?
7. What convention protects wounded soldiers and prisoners?
8. In what city is the UN headquarters?
9. How many countries are in the UN?
10. What treaty marked the beginning of European union?
11. In what building do member nations of the UN meet?
12. For what purpose can peacekeeping units use their weapons?

Level 3

13. In what year did the UN headquarters officially open?
14. What treaty led to the formation of the European Union?
15. What is the full name of the Red Cross?
16. How much money was donated to buy land for the UN headquarters?
17. What is the name of the central command of NATO's military forces?
18. Who first used the term 'United Nations'?

International community

The countries of the world have formed many organizations to help each other. These groups provide medical and military aid, as well as opportunities for trade. Many international committees try to make the world into a safer, more peaceful place.

United Nations (1) (9) (18)

The term United Nations (UN) was first used by US President F D Roosevelt during World War II, but the UN was not officially established until 1945. Since then, it has grown from its original 51 members to 191.

the UN flag

Peacekeeping (3) (12)

When armed fighting breaks out within countries, UN peacekeeping groups may be called in to help. They may set up refugee camps and help to maintain law and order. There are armed and unarmed UN groups. Armed groups are only allowed to use their weapons for self-defence.

Headquarters (8) (11) (13) (16)

The UN headquarters officially opened on 9 January 1951, on the banks of the East river in New York City. An American millionaire called John D Rockefeller Jr donated $8.5 million to buy the land. Member nations meet in the General Assembly Building.

UN headquarters

flags of UN member states

European Union headquarters

European Union (4) (10) (14)

The Treaty of Paris, in 1951, marked the beginning of European union. The European Community (EC) grew out of this, and the Maastricht Treaty, signed in 1992, led to the formation of the European Union (EU) and the single European currency, the euro.

5 euro note

NATO (2) (6) (17)

The North Atlantic Treaty Organization (NATO) was formed in 1949 to keep peace in its 26 member states. They all help each other if any of their states is attacked. Supreme Headquarters Allied Powers Europe (SHAPE) is the central command of NATO's military forces.

Red Cross (5) (7) (15)

The International Committee of the Red Cross and the Red Crescent Movement provides medical aid in war and peace. The Geneva Convention also helps to protect wounded soldiers and prisoners.

QUESTIONS: Flags

Level 1

1. What colours could a pirate flag be?
2. Where are navy flags used: at sea or in space?
3. In what kind of sport is a black-and-white chequered flag used?
4. What kind of flag do explorers plant on lands they have discovered?
5. Which has the oldest national flag: Scotland or the USA?

Level 2

6. Which sport uses flags: rugby, cycling or rowing?
7. What are navy flags called?
8. What event prompted the redesign of the French flag?
9. Are signalling flags used alone or together?
10. What is semaphore?
11. How many US flags have been placed on the moon: four, five or six?
12. Which colour is not used in navy flags: yellow, black or green?

Level 3

13. What do referees use flags to indicate in an American football game?
14. In semaphore, how is an 'R' signalled?
15. On a pirate flag, what does an hour glass symbolize?
16. What colour flags are used in semaphore?
17. In which century were pirate flags first used?
18. What displayed a US flag on Mars?

FIND THE ANSWER: Flags

Flags have been used for centuries both as identification and to communicate a message. In the Middle Ages, for instance, they were used in battle to identify leaders. Flags vary greatly in colour and style, but they all convey an immediate visual message.

China
Brazil
Sweden
Greece
Germany
Israel

National flags 5 8

National flags are used to identify individual countries. Scotland has the oldest national flag. Sometimes countries change their flags: the French flag was redesigned as the famous tricolour in 1794, after the revolution.

Navy flags 2 7 9 12

Ships at sea communicate with navy flags called signalling flags. These convey different meanings when used alone or together. They use colours that can be seen at sea: blue, white, red, black and yellow.

Sports flags 3 6 13

Flags are used in many sports, including rugby, rowing and cycling, to communicate with the sportsmen. Referees use flags in American football games to indicate an error. The chequered flag is used in auto and motorcycle racing to signal the end of a race.

chequered flag

Semaphore 10 14 16

One signalling system, semaphore, uses two square red and yellow flags held in different positions to indicate letters. Arms and flags straight out means 'R'.

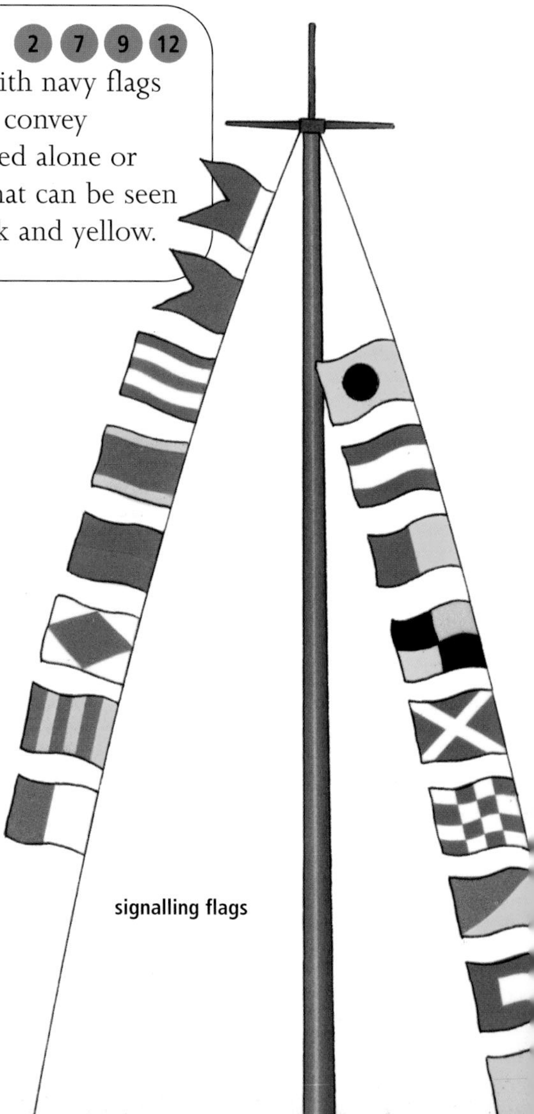

signalling flags

Pirate flags

1 15 17

A red or black pirate flag was meant to frighten, with images such as a skull, meaning death, or an hourglass, meaning time was running out. These flags were used by British pirates from about 1700.

Black Bart's flag

Christopher Moody's flag

Calico Jack's flag

Explorers' flags

4 11 18

Explorers often plant their national flag on the lands they discover. Six US flags have been placed on the moon. Each US space shuttle is given its own flag. The *Viking* lander displayed a US flag as it explored Mars.

US flag on the moon

QUESTIONS: Natural wonders

Level 1

1. What is the tallest mountain in the world?
2. What is the tallest waterfall in the world?
3. K2 is in Europe. True or false?
4. The Great Barrier Reef lies off the coast of which country?
5. The Great Barrier Reef can be seen from space. True or false?
6. Which is longer: the Grand Canyon or the Great Barrier Reef?

Level 2

7. Who were the first people to reach the top of Mount Everest?
8. How is the length of the Grand Canyon measured?
9. How many times higher is Angel Falls than Niagara Falls: 10, 15 or 20?
10. What is the Hillary Step?
11. How old are the rocks in the Grand Canyon?
12. In what continent is the widest waterfall in the world?
13. What is another name for *aurora borealis*?

Level 3

14. What causes the Northern Lights?
15. How much older are the Alps than the Himalayas?
16. How high is Mount Everest?
17. What is the Latin name of the Southern Lights?
18. What geographical feature is 10,783m wide?

FIND THE ANSWER: Natural wonders

oxygen cylinders

Spectacular features are found all over the world and include amazing waterfalls, fiery volcanoes and natural phenomena, such as the Northern Lights. Wind and water erosion has created some of these features, such as the canyons, while the movement of the earth's plates has created others, such as the world's highest mountains.

Mount Everest (1) (3) (15) (16)

Everest, the tallest mountain in the world, is part of the Himalayan mountain range in Asia. Its peak is 8,850m high. The second highest mountain, K2, is also in the Himalayas. The Himalayas are 60 million years old – younger than the Alps in Europe, which formed 75 million years ago.

Conquering Everest (7) (10)

In 1953, New Zealander Edmund Hillary and Nepali Tenzing Norgay became the first people to reach the peak of Everest. A steep section of the mountain has since been named Hillary Step.

angel fish

staghorn coral

harlequin tusk fish

jack fish

hard coral

fan coral

Coral reefs (4) (5) (6)

The Great Barrier Reef, off the coast of Australia, is over 2,000km long and is visible from space. Over 5,000 species of plants and animals live there.

Victoria Falls, Africa

Waterfalls

2 9 12 18

Angel Falls in South America is the tallest waterfall in the world, at 979m high. It is 15 times higher than Niagara Falls in North America. The widest waterfall is Khône Falls in Asia. It is 10,783m wide.

Aurora

13 14 17

The Northern Lights (*aurora borealis*) and the Southern Lights (*aurora australis*) are dancing displays of coloured lights in the night sky. *Aurora* are caused by high-speed particles from the sun colliding with gas molecules to create light.

Canyons

6 8 11

The Grand Canyon, in Arizona, USA, is the largest in the world. It is 446km long and 1,500m deep. The canyon's length is measured by the Colorado river that cuts through it. The oldest rocks there are 2,000 million years old, though the canyon itself is probably only about five or six million years old.

the Grand Canyon, USA

QUESTIONS: Coasts

Level 1

1. A tsunami is caused by the wind. True or false?
2. ACE VASE can be rearranged to give what name for a cavern in a cliff?
3. What is the wearing down of a headland called: erosion or erasure?
4. What two materials do waves deposit on beaches?
5. What 'W' causes waves?
6. HELLO BOW can be rearranged to give the name of what coastal feature?

Level 2

7. What is special about the Painted Cave?
8. What does the word 'tsunami' mean?
9. What causes water to gush through a blow hole?
10. The fetch is the material deposited on a beach. True or false?
11. A stack is a mound of sand. True or false?
12. Is sea water acidic or alkaline?

Level 3

13. Which is formed first: a cave or a blow hole?
14. How fast do tsunami waves move?
15. What coastal process do groynes prevent?
16. On what island is the Painted Cave?
17. How high can tsunamis be?
18. A stack is formed from which coastal feature?

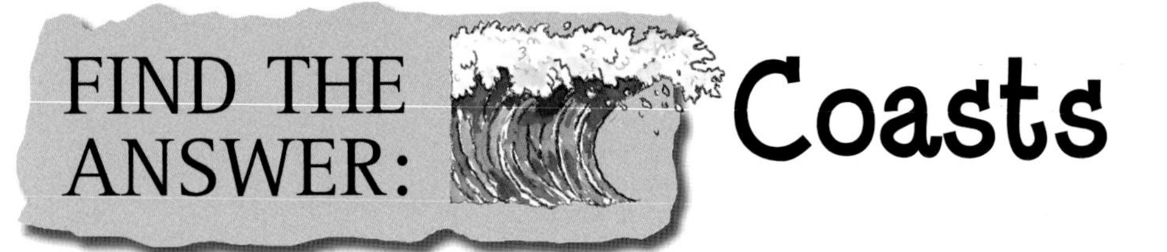

FIND THE ANSWER: Coasts

The world's coastlines are about 504,000km long, which is long enough to circle the globe 12 times. Primary coasts are formed by changes in the land, such as river deltas. Many of these coastlines were formed as the sea levels changed over thousands of years. Secondary coasts are formed by changes in the ocean, such as coral reefs.

Coastal erosion

3 12

Coastlines do not stay the same. They change continually as they are worn down by water throwing pebbles and rocks against the shore, a process called erosion. Sea water is also acidic, helping to wear down coastlines.

cliffs

collapsed arch

blow hole

sea cave

beach

Sea caves

2 7 16

A cavern in a cliff is called a sea cave. Sea caves are caused by water erosion. Faults or weaknesses in the rock will enable waves to break it down. The longest sea cave in the world is the Painted Cave on Santa Cruz Island, California, USA.

Blow hole

6 9 13

A blow hole is formed when erosion creates an opening between a sea cave and the land above it. Sometimes built-up air pressure forces water up through the hole, causing a gush at the surface.

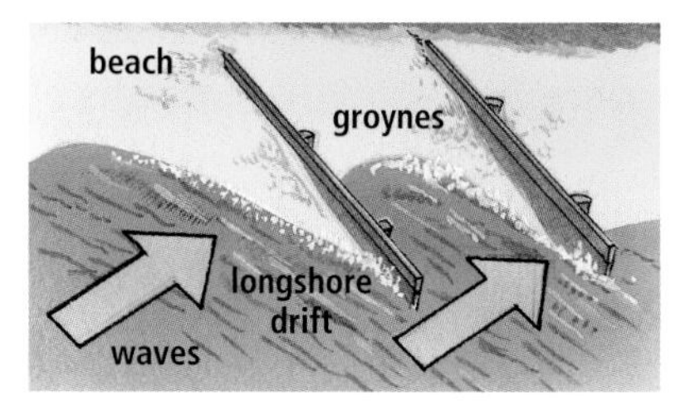

Longshore drift

Waves deposit materials such as pebbles and sand on beaches. If the waves approach at an angle, this material is pushed sideways (longshore drift). Sometimes wooden barriers called groynes are used to stop longshore drift.

crest

trough

breaking wave

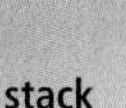

stack

Stacks

11 18

On a rocky headland, sometimes waves can erode through the back wall of a sea cave to form an arch. In time, the arch will collapse, leaving behind a pillar of rock, or a 'stack'.

Waves

5 10

Waves are caused by wind. The height, length and speed of a wave are controlled by the speed of the wind, how far it blows over the water (called the fetch) and for how long.

Tsunami

1 8 14 17

A tsunami (Japanese for 'harbour wave') is not a tidal wave. It is caused by an underwater earthquake or erupting volcano. Ripples of waves move at over 700km/h and form a 'wall' of water up to 30m high as they reach land.

wall of water

QUESTIONS: Rivers

Level 1

1. What is the beginning of a river called?
2. In what continent are the Great Lakes?
3. Do waterfalls flow over a ledge of hard or soft rock?
4. What is the name of the process by which water moves between the land and sea and back again?
5. What is the name of the area of flat land on either side of a river?

Level 2

6. What 'R' is precipitation?
7. What kind of lakes are created by ice sheets?
8. What is formed when a river floods shallow lakes or ponds?
9. Do tributaries increase or decrease the water volume of a river?
10. What happens to evaporated water?
11. What other name is used for an estuary?
12. Headwaters are the top of a waterfall. True or false?
13. What prevents water seepage in a marshland?
14. What forms at the bottom of a waterfall?

Level 3

15. What 'Y' is a waterfall in the USA, created by a glacier?
16. What name is given to fertile land formed on a flood plain?
17. What can form from sediment in an estuary?
18. How was Lake Tanganyika formed?

FIND THE ANSWER:  Rivers

A river is a flow of fresh water that travels downhill to another river, a lake or to the sea. The course that a river follows depends on rocks, soil and the amount of water it is carrying. The two most common patterns of river are meandering and braided. A meandering river twists and bends. A braided river has many different channels, which change constantly.

clouds meeting cool air

precipitation

clouds forming

sea water evaporates

The water cycle 4 6 10

Water is constantly moving from the land to the sea and back again. Water in the sea is heated by the sun and evaporates, condensing to form clouds. When the clouds meet cool air, precipitation (rain) returns the water to the river, which flows back into the sea.

source

tributary

headwaters

meander

River features 1 9 12

A river begins at a source (often a natural hollow in the ground into which water seeps) and flows downhill to end at the mouth. The streams at the source are called headwaters and are found at the river's highest point. Smaller rivers called tributaries feed into the river system and increase the volume of water.

Marshland 8 13

Freshwater marshes are formed when water from a river floods shallow lakes or ponds. They are common where there is granite, slate or quartz beneath, which stops the water from seeping into the earth. Grasses, reeds and shrubs often grow in them.

Waterfalls 3 14 15

Most waterfalls form where an area of soft rock lies in front of an area of hard rock (stage one). The soft rock is quickly worn away by the river, leaving a ledge of hard rock over which the water falls (stage two). The gushing water creates a plunge pool at the bottom (stage three). Other waterfalls, such as Yosemite Falls in California, USA, were made by glaciers.

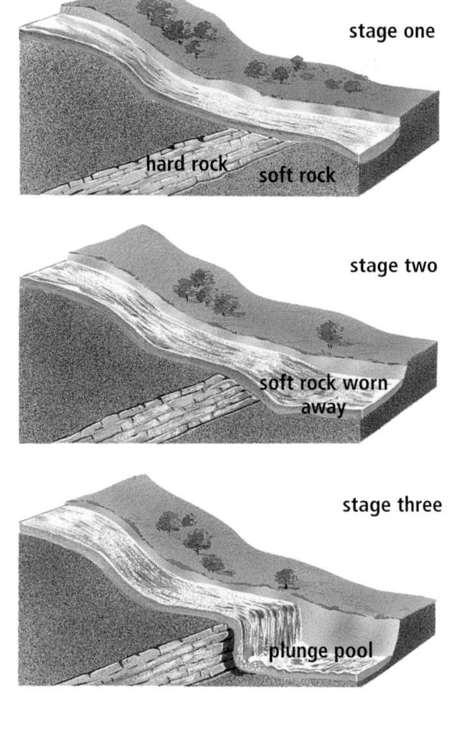

Lakes 2 7 18

Freshwater lakes, such as the Great Lakes in North America, are formed by glaciers or ice sheets. Other lakes, such as Lake Tanganyika in Africa, are made by earth fault movements.

Flood plains 5 16

Flat land alongside a river is called a flood plain. If the river overflows, it deposits sand and mud on the land. As the water drains away, this sediment forms fertile land known as alluvium.

Estuary 11 17

A river mixes with salty water from the sea to form an estuary, or harbour. A delta may form from sediment in the river.

QUESTIONS: Deserts

Level 1

1. What 'D' is a sandy desert feature?
2. Which animal is used to carry people and goods in the desert?
3. Sand holds water. True or false?
4. What plant with spines can survive in a desert?
5. What 'B' is the home of a meerkat?

Level 2

6. Is a Tuareg a type of sand dune or a member of a desert tribe?
7. What type of sand dune forms when the wind blows in all directions?
8. What is a one-humped camel called?
9. What is the name for wind carrying away fine sand?
10. What is the slope of a sand dune called?
11. Wind blowing in two different directions creates which type of sand dune?
12. Is a hoodoo: a type of sand dune, a rock formation or a desert rodent?
13. In which desert would you find a Tuareg?

Level 3

14. What desert plant can be over 200 years old?
15. What 'F' is a kind of fox that lives in the desert?
16. What is a barchan?
17. What substance is formed by cemented sand and gravel?
18. What features of a camel help it survive in deserts?

FIND THE ANSWER: Deserts

Deserts are dry areas of land with little rainfall or plant and animal life. The driest desert in the world is the Atacama desert in Chile, South America. Deserts may be hot, such as the Sahara in Africa, or cold, such as the Antarctic. Hot deserts can be cold at night because rocks lose their heat quickly and there is little humidity or vegetation to hold in heat.

hoodoo rock

Desert winds (9) (12)

The wind wears away rocks in deserts by deflation (carrying away fine sand) and abrasion (friction). These processes create arches, ridges, flat-topped mesas and pedestal rocks. They also create formations called hoodoo rocks, which look like giant mushrooms.

Nomads (6) (13)

Nomads are people who move from place to place. The nomadic Tuareg tribe live in the Sahara desert in Africa.

dromedary camel

Tuareg tribesman

Desert animals (5) (15)

Many desert animals, such as the fennec fox, are nocturnal (active at night). Others, such as the meerkat, live in burrows to keep themselves cool.

Caravan (2) (8) (18)

The Tuaregs use 'caravans' of camels to carry people and goods. Dromedary (one-humped) camels can go without water for days. Their thick, padded feet can walk on hot sand without pain.

Types of sand dune
7 11 16

A curved barchan dune forms when the wind blows in one direction. A star dune forms when the wind blows in all directions. A linear dune is formed when the wind blows in two different directions.

Sand dune formation
1 10

Dunes, or heaps of sand, form as desert sand is moved and shifted by wind until it creates a slope, called a slip face. A dune's shape depends on the wind speed and direction. Sometimes sand dunes migrate, blown along by wind.

slip face
wind

Soil
3 17

In deserts water seeps through sand, but can be trapped by soil and rock. Hard layers of cemented sand and gravel (calcrete) are found in many deserts.

sand
soil and rock
calcrete

Cacti
4 14

Found in the deserts of North and South America, cacti are succulent plants that store water in their stems and branches to survive. Most cacti have spines instead of leaves. The Saguaro cactus can live for 200 years and grow to 12m tall.

Saguaro cactus

QUESTIONS: The poles

Level 1

1. On which continent is the South Pole?
2. The explorer Robert Scott reached the South Pole. True or false?
3. LIE CRAG can be rearranged to give the name of what polar feature?
4. Icebergs are lumps of ice that have broken away from glaciers. True or false?

Level 2

5. What is a hollow formed by melting blocks of ice called: a kettle hole or a sink hole?
6. How much of an iceberg is visible above the waterline?
7. Who was the first person to reach the South Pole?
8. Why do glaciers shift?
9. Today, most Inuit use dog sleds to travel over the Arctic ice. True or false?
10. What imaginary line runs between the two poles?
11. What is a moraine?
12. What language is spoken by the Inuit?
13. What 'P' is an item of clothing worn by Arctic people?

Level 3

14. Do the Inuit live near to the North or the South Pole?
15. In which year did a person reach the South Pole for the first time?
16. Near which pole are flat-topped tabular icebergs found?
17. How far would Scott and his crew have had to travel to safety?
18. What Arctic people live in Greenland?

FIND THE ANSWER: The poles

The extreme north and south points of the world are called the poles. The polar regions of the Arctic in the north and Antarctica in the south are the coldest places on earth. At the poles themselves, the sun never sets for months in the summer, while in the winter there is complete darkness for several months.

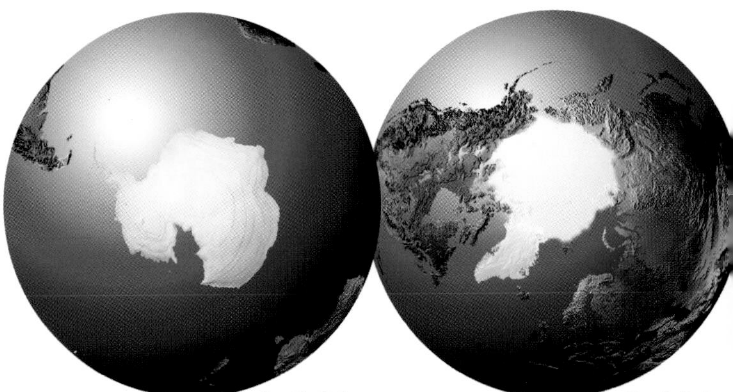

South Pole North Pole

Native peoples 12 14 18

The Inuit people live in the Arctic regions of Siberia, Alaska, Canada and Greenland. They speak Inuktitut. Other native groups include the Kalaalit of Greenland and the Yupik of the Russian Federation.

North and South 1 10

The axis on which the earth turns runs between the North and South Poles. The North Pole is on the frozen seas of the Arctic ocean. The South Pole is on the continent of Antarctica.

Living in the arctic 9 13

Arctic people were originally migrating hunters and fishermen, but most now live in modern communities. Parkas made of hide provided warmth, and dog sleds were used to travel across the ice. Snowmobiles are now used.

Scott

Robert Falcon Scott tried to become the first person to reach the South Pole. He got there on 17 January 1912, but Norwegian Roald Amundsen had already reached it on 14 December 1911. Scott and his crew starved to death in Antarctica, about 17km away from the supply depot.

traditional-style parka

dog sled

glacier

Glaciers (3) (5) (8) (11)

Glaciers are formed when fallen snow packs together over many years and crystallizes into ice. Most glaciers are found in mountainous or polar regions. Glaciers shift over time due to the weight of the ice and gravity. A melting glacier may leave behind ridges of rock called moraines. Blocks of ice that melt may form a hollow called a kettle hole.

castle iceberg

Icebergs (4) (6) (16)

Icebergs are lumps of floating ice that break away from glaciers in a process called calving. Nine-tenths of an iceberg is below water. Pinnacle, or castle, icebergs form in the Arctic. Flat-topped tabular icebergs form in the Antarctic.

QUESTIONS: Where in the world?

Level 1

1. What city is nicknamed 'The Big Apple'?
2. In which country is Rio de Janeiro?
3. What city is the biggest tourist destination in Europe?

Level 2

4. What famous event is held in Rio de Janeiro every year?
5. What did Mumbai, India, used to be called?
6. What is the oldest city in South Africa?
7. What is the biggest island in Japan?

Level 3

8. What percentage of Japan's population lives in its capital city?
9. What is a person who lives in Sydney, Australia, called?
10. Where is the biggest underground train network in the world?

FIND THE ANSWER:

Where in the world?

Cities are large settlements, bigger or more populated than towns and villages. Most cities grew from small farming or hunting settlements, although others are planned from scratch. The world's most famous cities can be larger or richer than some nations – if New York were a nation, it would be the 16th richest in the world.

Tokyo 7 8 10
Tokyo is the capital city of Japan, 'The Land of the Rising Sun'. It is on the largest of Japan's four main islands, Honshu, and is home to around 10% of the country's population. Tokyo has the biggest underground train network anywhere in the world.

New York 1
New York, 'The Big Apple', is the most populated city and the financial heart of the USA, although Washington DC is the capital.

Paris 3
Paris is the capital of France, and is the biggest tourist destination in Europe. Its famous attractions include the Eiffel Tower, the Mona Lisa and the Louvre museum.

Rio de Janeiro 2 4
Rio de Janeiro is a large city in Brazil (Brasilia is the capital). The city is famous for holding a huge carnival every year.

Cape Town 6
Cape Town is the oldest city in South Africa, and gets its name from the Cape of Good Hope, the most southwesterly point of Africa.

Mumbai 5
Mumbai, in India, used to be called Bombay. The city has a population of over 20 million. It also has the biggest port in India.

Sydney 9
Sydney is most famous for the opera house in its harbour. People who live in Sydney are known as 'Sydneysiders'.

Answers 1) New York, USA **2)**Brazil **3)**Paris, France **4)**A carnival **5)**Bombay **6)**Cape Town **7)**Honshu **8)**10% **9)**Sydneysider **10)**Tokyo, Japan

QUIZ THREE

Science and inventions

Exploring space

Solar System

Volcanoes and earthquakes

Rocks and minerals

Weather

Bones and muscles

Medicine

Trains

Early flight

Sailing

Submarines

Household inventions

Robots

Computers and gaming

Telephones

Discoveries

QUESTIONS: Exploring space

Level 1

1. The first living creature in space was a mouse. True or false?
2. Who was the first person on the Moon: Neil Armstrong, Nelly Armstrong or Norman Armstrong?
3. ENVISION OUT can be rearranged to give the name of what group of republics?
4. What 'S' is an object that orbits Earth?

Level 2

5. What 'L' was the name of the first living creature in space?
6. What 'S' was the first artificial satellite?
7. AN AIR RIG GUY can be rearranged to give the name of what astronaut, the first person to go into space?
8. In which year did people first walk on the Moon: 1959, 1969 or 1979?
9. In which year did a person first go into space: 1941, 1951 or 1961?
10. Who said 'That's one small step for man, one giant leap for mankind'?
11. VAN OR RULER can be rearranged to give the name of what vehicle used on the surface of the moon?
12. For how long did the first person to go into space stay there: 89 minutes, 89 hours or 89 days?

Level 3

13. Which was the last *Apollo* mission to land people on the Moon?
14. In what year did it reach the Moon?
15. What were Soviet astronauts called?
16. What 'V' was the first manned spacecraft?
17. What was launched on 12 April 1981?
18. Where is the Baikonur Cosmodrome: in Kazakhstan, Ukraine or the Russian Federation?

FIND THE ANSWER:

Exploring space

Sputnik

It seems strange to think that 50 years ago no one had been into space. Nowadays, an International Space Station constantly circles the Earth, manned by a crew of people from different countries. The history of space flight has happened within the lifetimes of many people alive today. It is an exciting story – and one that is far from being over.

Sputnik 3 4 6

Sputnik 1 was the world's first-ever man-made satellite (an object travelling around Earth). It was launched from Kazakhstan on 4 October 1957 by a group of republics called the Soviet Union.

Laika 1 5 18

The first living thing to enter space was Laika the dog. Laika was launched in 1957 aboard the satellite *Sputnik* 2, from Baikonur Cosmodrome in Kazakhstan.

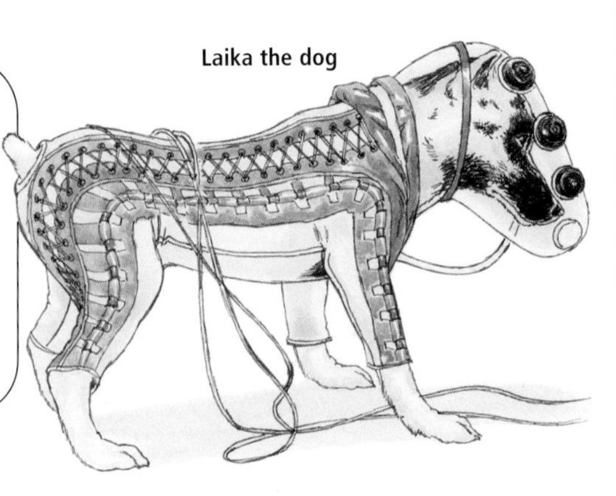
Laika the dog

Yuri Gagarin

Moon landing 2 8 10

In 1969, Neil Armstrong of the US mission *Apollo 11* became the first person to walk on the Moon, with the famous words 'That's one small step for man, one giant leap for mankind'.

rocket boosters

shuttle

USA

space shuttle launch

Man in space 7 9 12 16

On 12 April 1961, Yuri Gagarin became the first person ever to travel into space, aboard the spacecraft *Vostock 1*. A pilot from the Soviet Air Force, he travelled around the Earth for 89 minutes.

astronaut wearing an EVA (Extra Vehicular Activity) spacesuit

interior of spacesuit

external tank

Spacesuits

15

Spacesuits are designed to keep people alive in space. At first, they were worn by astronauts and cosmonauts (Soviet astronauts) inside their spacecraft. Nowadays, they are mainly used for operating outside in space itself – making repairs to a space shuttle, for instance.

Moon missions

11 13 14

In total, Americans have made six successful missions to the Moon. The fourth, *Apollo* 15, carried a vehicle called a lunar rover to drive astronauts around on the surface. The last manned mission was *Apollo* 17, which landed on 7 December 1972. Since then, no one has visited the Moon.

Space shuttle

17

Early missions into space used massive, expensive rockets, which could only be used once. On 5 January 1972, the American government announced it was going to develop a reusable spacecraft. The result was the space shuttle, which first launched on 12 April 1981. Since then, there have been over 100 launches.

QUESTIONS: Solar System

Level 1

1. Which planet do people live on?
2. How many planets are in the Solar System: seven, nine or 11?
3. MY CURER can be rearranged to give the name of what planet?

Level 2

4. On the part of a planet facing away from the Sun, is it night or day?
5. How many planets in our Solar System have names beginning with the letter 'M'?
6. Which planet is the farthest from the Sun?
7. A GANG SITS can be rearranged to give the name of what group of large planets?
8. What is the smallest planet in the Solar System?
9. The Sun is a star. True or false?
10. Are any planets in the Solar System bigger than the Sun?
11. Did the planets form at around the same time as the Sun or long before?
12. Which 'S' is a planet made mostly of hydrogen and helium?
13. How long does the Earth take to circle the Sun: a day, a month or a year?
14. What 'O' is the path planets take around the Sun?
15. Which takes longer to circle the Sun: Earth or Pluto?
16. How many planets in the Solar System have oceans of water?

Level 3

17. What 'N' is a swirling cloud of particles from which planets form?
18. Which is farther from the Sun: Uranus or Saturn?
19. Which is larger: Earth or Mars?

FIND THE ANSWER: Solar System

The Solar System is the group of planets, including Earth, that circle the Sun. Some of these planets are smaller than Earth and others are many times larger. The Solar System has existed for around 4,600 million years, first appearing about 10,400 million years after the 'Big Bang' that began the Universe.

Neptune

Uranus

Pluto

The planets 2 3 5 6 18

There are nine planets in the Solar System. The closest to the Sun is Mercury, followed by Venus, Earth, Mars, Jupiter (the largest), Saturn, Uranus, Neptune and Pluto (the farthest from the Sun).

Jupiter

Venus

Mars

Earth

Mercury

Saturn

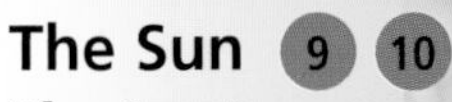

The Sun 9 10

The Sun is a star, far bigger than any of the planets. It is 1,392,000km wide and more than a million times bigger than Earth. For a star, it is relatively small.

Gas giants 7 12

Jupiter, Saturn, Uranus and Neptune are called the gas giants. Their small, rocky cores are surrounded by thick gases, mostly hydrogen and helium.

The smaller planets 8 19

The smaller planets are Mercury, Venus, Earth, Mars and Pluto. All of them have solid surfaces. Earth is the largest, and the smallest is Pluto.

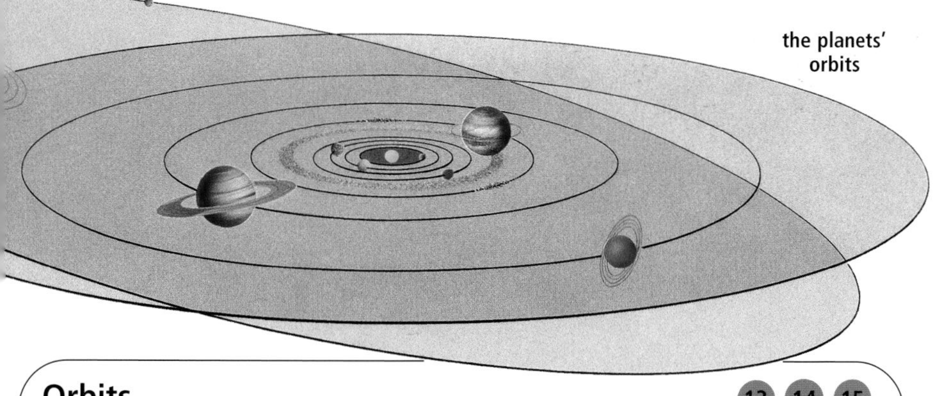

Orbits

13 14 15

All of the planets 'orbit' the Sun (travel in a circle around it). The closer the planet is to the Sun, the shorter its orbit. Earth's orbit takes exactly a year. Pluto takes more than 248 years for its orbit.

nebula

gas and dust particles drawn together

Planets forming

11 17

The planets formed at about the same time as the Sun, from a nebula (a swirling cloud of gas and dust particles). Over time, the particles of the nebula slowly gathered together to form planets, drawn together by the force of gravity.

newly formed planet

The Earth

1 4 16

People live on the planet Earth, the only one known to support life. It is the fifth largest in the Solar System, and the only one with oceans of water. As well as circling the sun once a year, Earth spins round once every 24 hours. It is day on the part of Earth facing the Sun, and night on the part facing away.

surface of the Earth

QUESTIONS: Volcanoes and earthquakes

Level 1

1. Is the surface of the earth made of solid or liquid rock?
2. What is another name for the earth's surface: the skin, crust or coat?
3. RUIN POET can be rearranged to give what word for a volcano exploding?
4. A seismologist a kind of earthquake. True or false?

Level 2

5. What 'R' is the scale used to measure strength of earthquakes?
6. Which are thicker: continental plates or oceanic plates?
7. Are most earthquakes strong enough to destroy buildings?
8. How thick is the earth's mantle: 290km or 2,900km?
9. Do ridges form where plates move together or where they move apart?
10. Earthquakes are common where plates slide past one another. True or false?
11. Japan is situated where two plates meet. True or false?
12. What 'L' is the molten rock released by a volcanic eruption?
13. What 'F' is the force produced by plates sliding past each other?
14. CUBOID NUTS can be rearranged to give the name of what plate movement?
15. Volcanoes may occur where two plates are moving apart. True or false?

Level 3

16. What is the most common substance in the earth's core?
17. Which makes up a greater proportion of the earth: the crust or mantle?
18. On which plate do volcanoes occur when an oceanic plate and a continental plate meet?

FIND THE ANSWER: Volcanoes and earthquakes

The earth's crust is in constant motion. Volcanoes and earthquakes arise as sections of crust ('plates') push together or pull apart. Volcanoes and earthquakes are more common in certain parts of the world. By monitoring ground vibrations ('seismic activity'), scientists can sometimes predict a massive earthquake or volcanic eruption and warn people.

volcano erupting

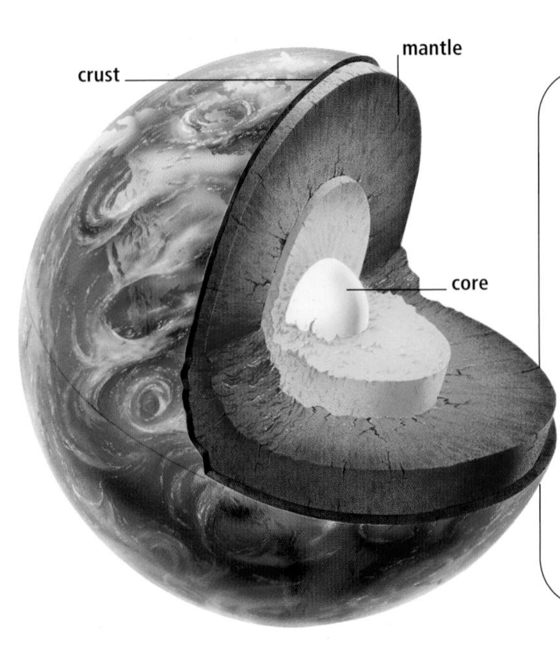

Earth
1 2 8 16 17

The solid surface layer of the earth is known as the crust, and ranges from 5km to 80km in thickness. Beneath the crust is the mantle, which is 2,900km thick and made up of molten rock. The centre of the earth, the core, is mostly made of iron. It has a liquid outer core and a solid inner core, and is around 4,500°C hot.

Volcanoes
3 12 18

Volcanoes form when molten rock is pushed up through the crust. When subduction occurs, the oceanic plate melts underground, creating a vast supply of molten rock. The rock is then released as lava in a volcanic eruption.

Moving apart
9 15

When plates move apart, ridges form. Often volcanoes occur there as molten rock moves up from the mantle to fill the gaps.

Subduction
6 14

When continental and oceanic plates move towards each other, the oceanic plate often slides underneath the thicker continental plate – this is called subduction.

oceanic plate

plates moving apart

plate melting

moving plates

Earthquakes

4 5 7 11

Earthquakes are most common where two plates meet, such as under Japan. Most earthquakes are mild, but some can destroy buildings. Special scientists called seismologists can measure the strength of earthquakes, using the Richter Scale.

Friction

10 13

Earthquakes are the result of frictional forces as two plates move side by side. The plates judder as they slide past each other, and each judder causes an earthquake.

lava

volcanoes

molten rock

continental plate

QUESTIONS: Rocks and minerals

Level 1

1. Emeralds are purple. True or false?
2. What colour are rubies?
3. Gold is a metal. True or false?
4. How many sides does a hexagon have: one, three or six?

Level 2

5. TEARING can be rearranged to give the name of what igneous rock, often used for building?
6. Crystals form underground. True or false?
7. Do sedimentary rocks form on the bottoms of seas, lakes and rivers or deep within the earth?
8. What word is used for rocks which form under great pressure or heat: metamorphic, mathematic or metaphysical?
9. Is basalt an igneous or a sedimentary rock?
10. Gems are cut and polished to make gemstones. True or false?
11. What 'C' is the substance from which diamond is formed?
12. Which are the most valuable: diamonds, emeralds or garnets?
13. HIS PAPER can be rearranged to give the name of what valuable gemstone?
14. A START can be rearranged to give what word for layers of rock?

Level 3

15. In which country is the Giant's Causeway?
16. What 'M' is molten rock, which cools to form igneous rocks?
17. What is the name for a stone which has had its edges worn smooth by the action of water?
18. What 'E' cannot be broken down into any simpler substance?

FIND THE ANSWER: Rocks and minerals

Rocks are the building blocks of earth's crust, and the substances of which they are composed are called minerals. The appearance and qualities of a rock is determined by the way it was formed. Humans use rocks and minerals to make everything from jewellery to houses.

Metamorphic rocks
8

The three main types of rock are metamorphic, sedimentary and igneous. Metamorphic rocks such as marble form underground, when existing rock is exposed to great pressure or heat.

erupting volcano

Igneous rocks
4 9 15 16

The Giant's Causeway in Northern Ireland is made up of hexagonal (six-sided) columns of basalt, an igneous rock. Like all igneous rocks, it formed from volcanic magma (melted rock), which erupted and then cooled down.

igneous rock

Sedimentary rocks
7 14

These rocks form from sediments such as sand and mud at the bottoms of seas, lakes and rivers, building up over long periods of time. Gradually, the weight of water compresses them into rock. Sedimentary rocks form in strata (layers).

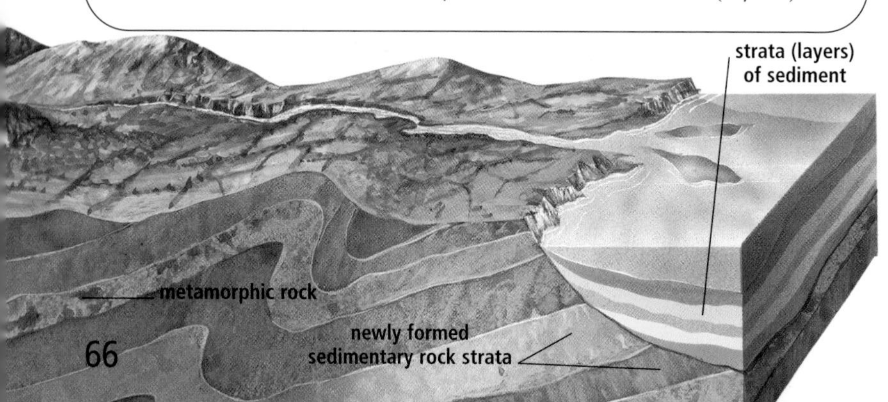

Stones

A stone is a small piece of rock, and a pebble is a stone that has had its edges smoothed over time by the action of water. The hardest stones are those from igneous rocks such as granite, or from metamorphic rocks such as slate.

granite

serpentinite

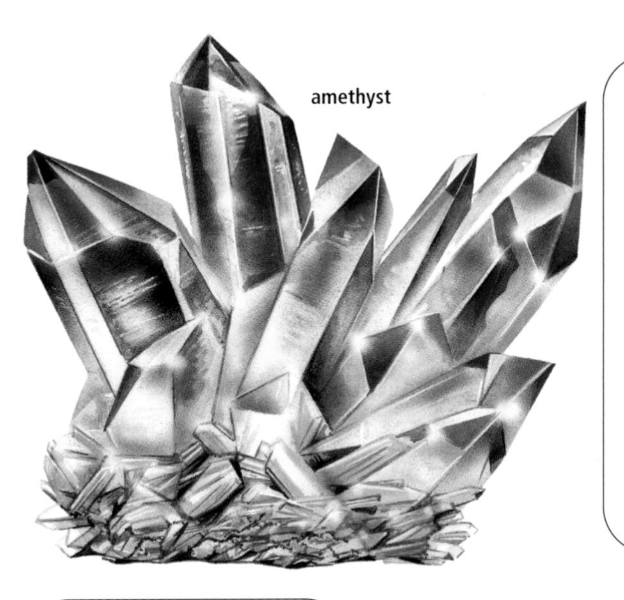

Minerals (3) (18)

There are two types of mineral: those with crystalline structures, and naturally occurring metals such as gold. These metals are elements – they cannot be broken down into any simpler substance.

Crystals (6)

Crystalline minerals form in underground rocks under great heat or pressure. Crystals have flat sides and can be extremely beautiful.

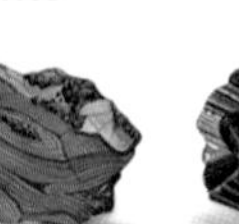

Gemstones (10)

Some crystalline minerals are known as gemstones. They are precious or semiprecious stones that can be cut and polished to make gems, which are used in jewellery. The rarest ones are considered the most valuable.

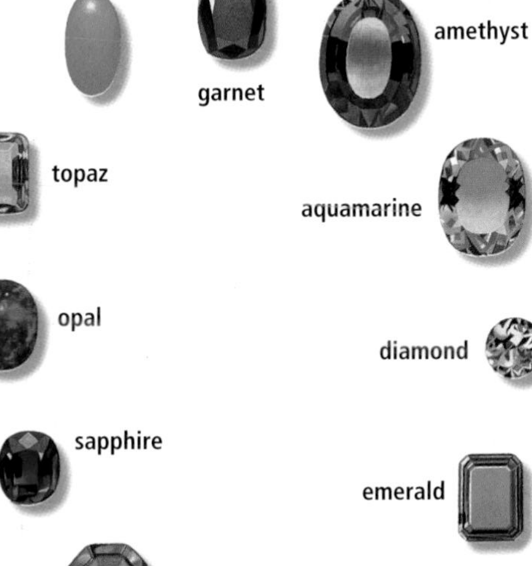

Types of gemstone (1) (2) (11) (12) (13)

The most famous and expensive gemstone is diamond. It is unusual in being a crystal made from a single element – carbon. Other very rare and precious gemstones include emeralds, which are green, rubies, which are red, and sapphires, which are blue.

QUESTIONS: Weather

Level 1

1. Does weather happen in the atmosphere or under the sea?
2. Are clouds made of cotton wool or water vapour?
3. What 'O' is the gas we must breathe in order to live?
4. What 'L' is the word for an electrical charge released from a storm cloud?
5. A weather balloon is a type of cloud. True or false?

Level 2

6. Where does the majority of the water vapour in clouds originally come from?
7. Does a weather vane measure wind speed or wind direction?
8. Which is usually associated with fine weather: high pressure or low pressure?
9. What 'R' is sometimes formed as sunlight passes through raindrops?
10. Do rainbows appear when it rains or when there is no rain?
11. Do raindrops become bigger or smaller as they fall through a cloud?
12. What 'H' is a word for frozen raindrops?
13. Do clouds become cooler or hotter as they rise?
14. REACH RUIN can be rearranged to give the name of what powerful storm?
15. RING TONE can be rearranged to give the name of what very common gas?

Level 3

16. What is a scientist who studies the weather called?
17. How many colours are there in a rainbow?
18. What 'S' do weather forecasters use to watch storms building up in the atmosphere?

FIND THE ANSWER: Weather

The weather affects all of us. It makes us decide what clothes to put on in the morning and whether we go outside or stay indoors. In some places, the weather can be very hard to predict. As we learn more about our planet, however, we are gradually getting better at working out what the weather is going to do next.

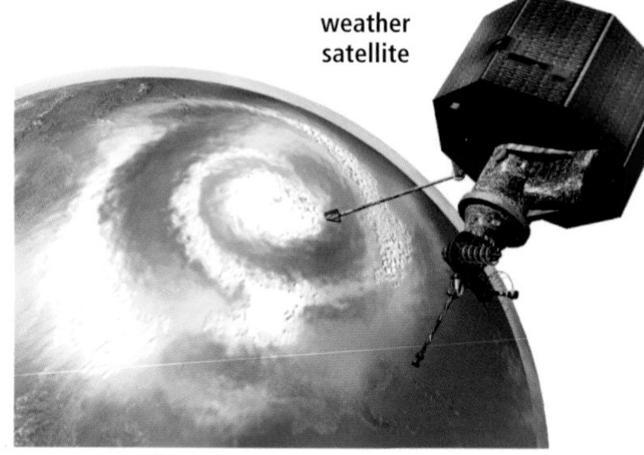

weather satellite

Watching weather (14) (18)

Nowadays, satellites watch the weather from above. They help weather forecasters to see storms building up in the atmosphere. Large storms and hurricanes appear as massive swirls of cloud.

Storm cloud (4) (13)

As clouds rise, they cool and the water vapour turns into droplets. The droplets bump into each other, causing an electric charge to build up. If the charge becomes large enough, it is released as lightning.

Atmosphere (1) (3) (15)

Weather occurs in the atmosphere – the layer of gases surrounding the earth. The most common gas is nitrogen, followed by oxygen, which we breathe in order to stay alive.

storm cloud

Clouds (2) (6)

Clouds are collections of water vapour. The vapour forms as the sun's energy evaporates liquid water, mostly from the surface of the sea.

rain

Weather research

Scientists who study the weather are known as meteorologists. Weather balloons are just one of the tools meteorologists use to gain information about the weather. The balloons carry devices that measure weather conditions far above the ground.

Measuring the weather

There are many devices for measuring the weather. Thermometers measure temperature, while barometers measure air pressure – high pressure means fine weather, and low pressure signals storms. An anemometer measures wind speed, while a weather vane shows wind direction.

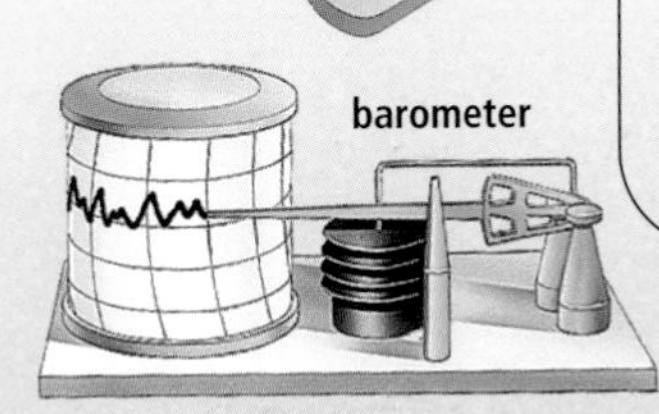

Rain

Rain falls when the droplets in clouds become too large and heavy to remain aloft. As they fall through the air, they hit other droplets and grow bigger. Sometimes they freeze and fall as hail or snow.

Rainbows

Rainbows form when it rains on sunny days. They are the result of the light from the sun being split into its seven colours as it passes through raindrops.

QUESTIONS:

Bones and muscles

Level 1

1. BELOW can be rearranged to give the name of what joint in the middle of the arm?
2. Are there muscles in the human leg?
3. What 'S' is the name for all the bones in the body put together?

Level 2

4. Do people have joints in their fingers?
5. Muscles contain millions of cells called fibres. True or false?
6. What 'B' is a muscle in the arm that helps to raise the forearm?
7. Which bones form a cage that protect the internal organs?
8. What 'C' is the proper name for the gristle in human bodies?
9. Which bone links the legs to the backbone?
10. The patella is another name for which bone?
11. The muscles in the heart work automatically. True or false?
12. When a person raises their forearm do their triceps contract or relax?
13. How many bones are there in an adult's skull: two, 12 or 22?
14. Do people have more muscles or more bones in their bodies?
15. Is the shoulder joint a hinge joint or a ball-and-socket joint?
16. What is the largest bone in the human body?
17. What is the name of the eight bones that, together, encase the brain?

Level 3

18. The mandible is another name for which part of the body?
19. In which part of the body is the smallest bone?
20. How many bones are there in the human skeleton?

FIND THE ANSWER:

Bones and muscles

The human body is an incredible natural machine. It can perform a huge variety of different movements and operations – far more than any robot or other man-made machine. Like those of other mammals, the human body is based on a complex system of muscles attached to a strong but flexible bony skeleton.

knee

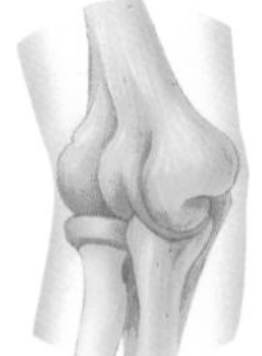

elbow

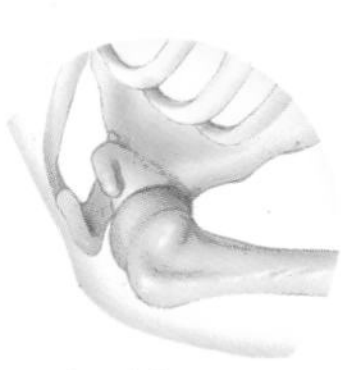

shoulder

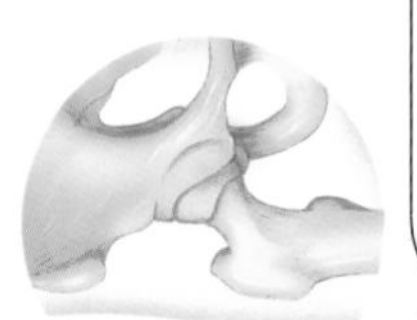

hip

Joints 1 4 15

Joints are the areas in the skeleton where different bones meet. They are what make the skeleton flexible, and allow limbs and other parts of the body to move. The shoulder and the hip joints are called ball-and-socket joints. The elbow, knee and finger joints are known as hinge joints.

kneecap (patella)

thigh bone (femur)

upper arm bone (humerus)

hip bone (pelvis)

ribcage

spine

skull

collarbone (clavicle)

shin bone (tibia)

fibula

radius

ulna

Skull 13 17 18

The skull of an adult is made up of 22 bones. Eight form the cranium, the bony box that surrounds the brain. Only the lower jaw (mandible) is able to move, allowing the person to eat and speak.

Knees 8 10

These joints separate the upper and lower halves of the legs. The ends of the bones are covered with a layer of cartilage (gristle) to stop them rubbing together. The patella (kneecap) is a small bone that protects the knee from injury.

Skeleton 3 7 9 14 16 19 20

The human skeleton is made up of 206 bones. The largest are the two thigh bones (femurs), linked to the backbone by the pelvis. The smallest are the stirrup bones, which help transmit sounds from the eardrums to the brain. The ribs mostly remain in the same position, forming a protective cage around the organs.

Muscle system 2 11 14

There are around 650 muscles in the human body powering every movement. Some, such as leg and arm muscles, work only when we want them to. Others, such as the muscles of the heart, work automatically.

triceps

biceps

uscles in the
uman body

How muscles work 6 12

Muscles have the ability to contract (shorten) and relax in a huge number of different combinations. Muscles contract when they are sent signals down nerves from the brain. The diagram above shows the arm muscles. To raise the forearm, the biceps contract, while the triceps relax. When the triceps contract, the arm is straightened out again.

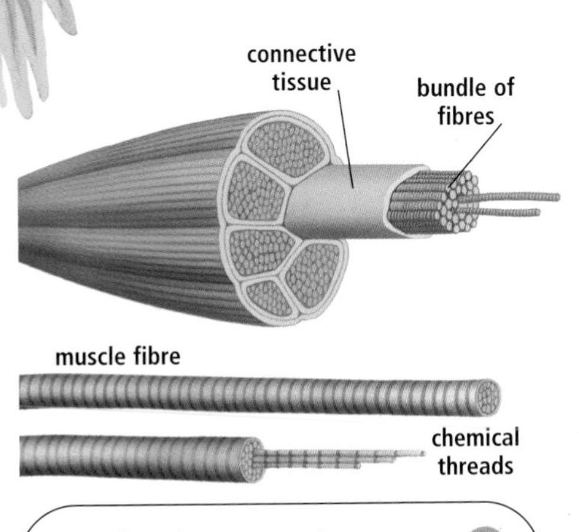

Inside the muscle 5

Muscles are made of millions of cells called fibres, which contain overlapping chemical threads. Each bundle of fibres is separated by connective tissue.

QUESTIONS: Medicine

Level 1

1. What 'D' is the person people visit when they are feeling ill?
2. What vehicles take people to hospital: ambulances, fire engines or tractors?
3. Are ambulances part of the emergency services?
4. Do nurses work in hospitals or shops?

Level 2

5. Broken bones mend themselves. True or false?
6. What 'S' is used to listen to a person's heartbeat?
7. What does a thermometer measure?
8. Is intensive care given to people who are very ill or to people who are better, just before they leave hospital?
9. What 'S' is the word for a person who carries out operations?
10. What 'T' means to replace a damaged body part with a new, healthy one?
11. Would you wear a plaster cast if you had flu or if you had a broken leg?
12. A SCARED IMP can be rearranged to give the name of what people who look after patients on the way to hospital?
13. A symptom is a kind of medicine. True or false?
14. What 'S' is a large machine that looks inside people's bodies?

Level 3

15. What 'D' means 'to work out what is wrong with a patient'?
16. What sort of injury can be treated by traction?
17. What is used to transfer nutrients straight into a person's bloodstream?
18. What 'M' is a kind of wave that scanners use to look inside a body?

FIND THE ANSWER:

Medicine

The word medicine has two meanings. When someone is ill, a doctor may give them medicine to make them feel better; but medicine is also a branch of science that studies diseases and injuries. Doctors, nurses and surgeons work in the field of medicine, and so do the pharmacists and researchers who develop new drugs and cures.

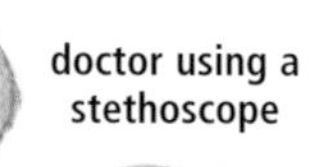

doctor using a stethoscope

Doctors 1 6 7 13 15

The doctor is the first person you go to see if you are feeling ill. Doctors look for symptoms (signs) of different illnesses and diagnose (work out) what is wrong. This doctor is using a stethoscope to listen to the boy's heartbeat. Doctors also use thermometers to measure body temperature.

the scene of an accident

Emergency services 2 3 12

Ambulances are vehicles that carry sick or injured people to hospital. They are part of the emergency services. Most ambulances have paramedics on board, who are trained to treat patients as they are taken to hospital.

Treating broken bones 5 11 16

Broken bones mend themselves, but to make sure they join back together in the right way, doctors wrap the affected limbs in rigid plaster casts. Sometimes they use 'traction' (shown below) – a system of pulleys and wires that keep the bones in the correct position.

girl with her leg in traction

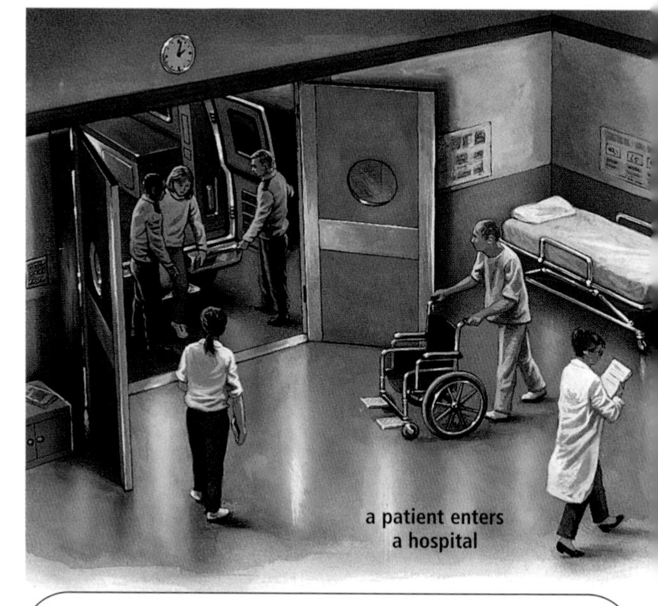

a patient enters a hospital

Hospitals 4

Hospitals are where sick and injured people go to be treated and get better. They are also the places where many doctors and most surgeons and nurses work. Most large towns and cities have at least one hospital.

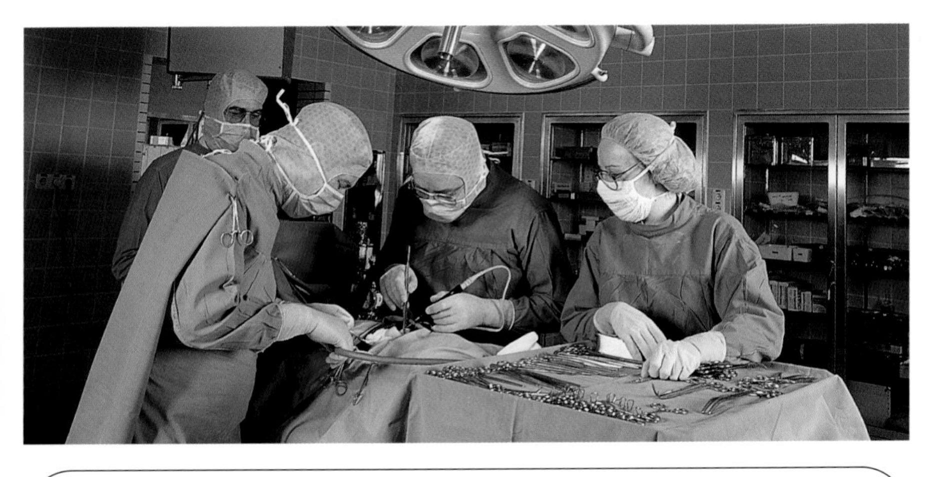

Operations

9 10

Surgeons carry out operations to make people better. Some operations involve removing diseased parts of the body. Others, known as transplants, involve taking out an old or damaged part and replacing it with a healthy new one.

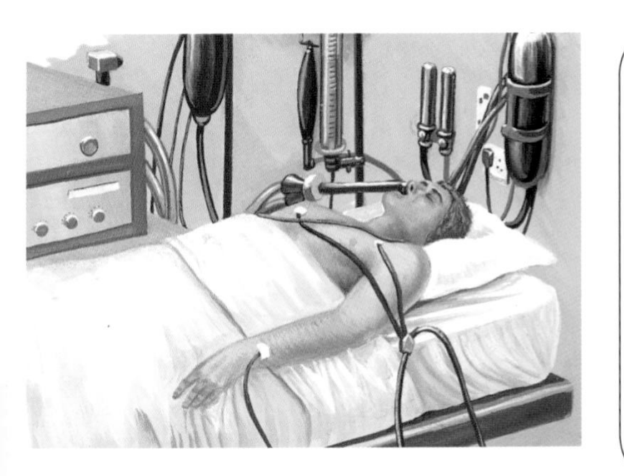

Intensive care

8 17

Very ill people need intensive care. They are watched closely by nurses and are assisted by machines. They may have a drip, which feeds nutrients through a tube straight into the blood.

Body scans

14 18

Scanners are machines that can look inside the body. They do this using X-rays or magnetic waves, which pass through the body and are picked up by sensors. The pictures generated may reveal signs of injury or disease that would otherwise be invisible.

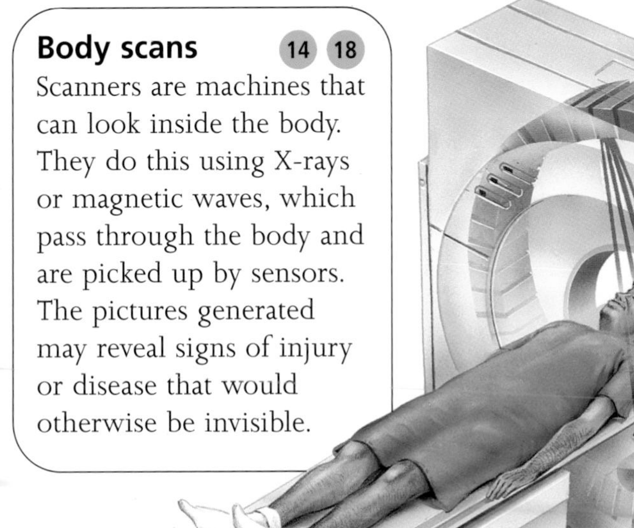

a patient has a CT (computerized tomography) scan

QUESTIONS: Trains

Level 1

1. Which came first: steam engines or electric trains?
2. Do all trains carry passengers?
3. Is diesel a type of fuel or a type of food?
4. Who built the train that ran on the first-ever steam railway: Richard Trevithick, Richard Branson or Richard the Lionheart?
5. What 'C' was burned in steam engines?

Level 2

6. Was the Wild West in Europe or in the USA?
7. Is steam created by heating water or by heating petrol?
8. Which country has bullet trains and super expresses?
9. What 'R' was a famous steam engine built by George Stephenson?
10. Which country has TGVs?
11. Are there any trains that can go faster than 200km/h?
12. What 'C' on Wild West trains was used for moving cattle off the line?
13. Were steam trains cleaner or dirtier than modern trains?

Level 3

14. In which country was the world's first-ever steam railway?
15. In which century was the first railway to cross North America built?
16. What 'F' is the word used for the goods carried by some trains?
17. How long was the world's longest ever train: 5km, 6km or 7km?
18. What 'P' were exploring settlers who travelled into the Wild West by train?

FIND THE ANSWER: Trains

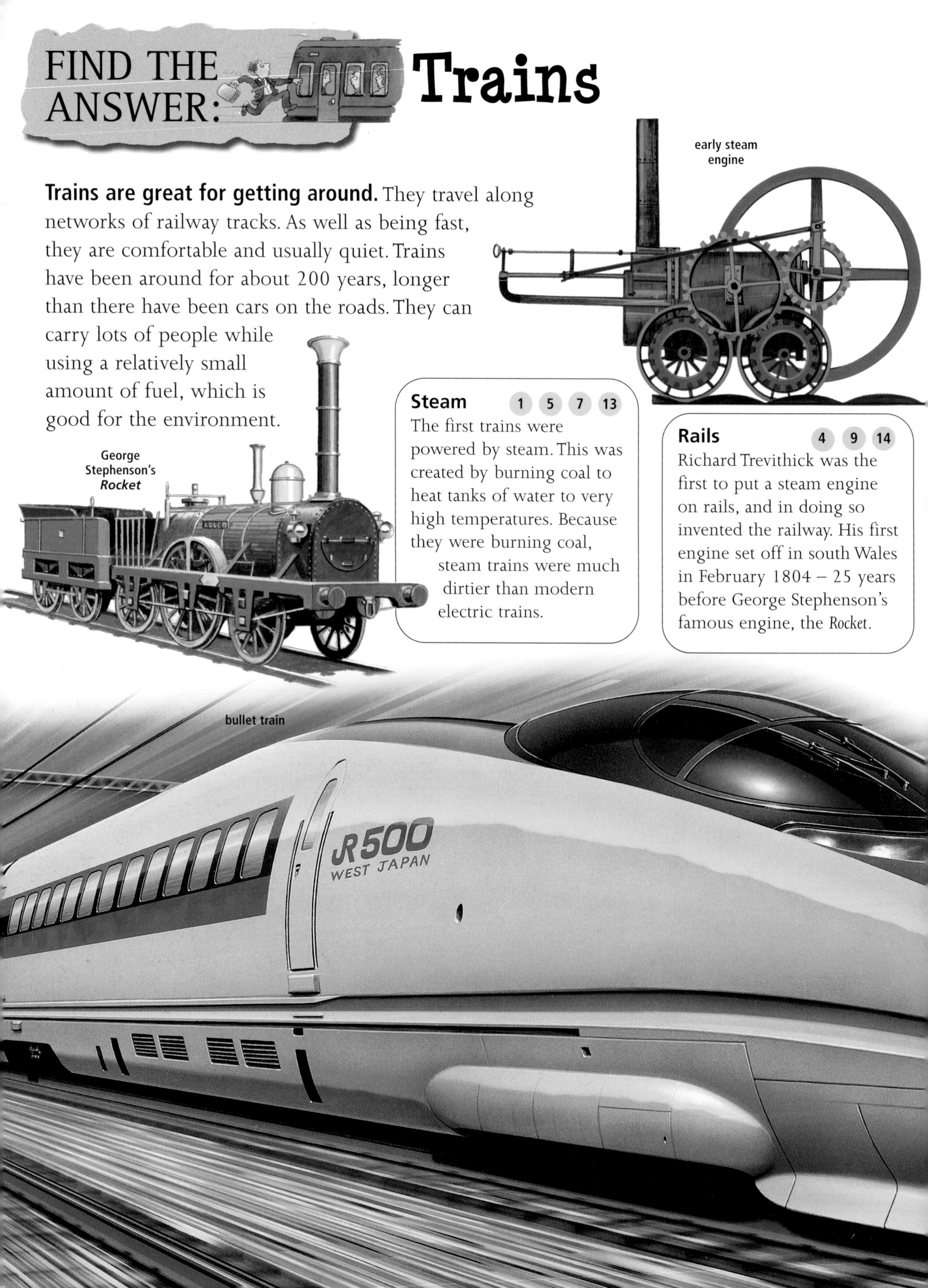

Trains are great for getting around. They travel along networks of railway tracks. As well as being fast, they are comfortable and usually quiet. Trains have been around for about 200 years, longer than there have been cars on the roads. They can carry lots of people while using a relatively small amount of fuel, which is good for the environment.

Steam (1) (5) (7) (13)

The first trains were powered by steam. This was created by burning coal to heat tanks of water to very high temperatures. Because they were burning coal, steam trains were much dirtier than modern electric trains.

Rails (4) (9) (14)

Richard Trevithick was the first to put a steam engine on rails, and in doing so invented the railway. His first engine set off in south Wales in February 1804 – 25 years before George Stephenson's famous engine, the *Rocket*.

Wild West trains

6 12 15 18

Trains helped to open up the Wild West of America to pioneers (exploring settlers). The first railway to go right across North America was finished in 1869. The trains had large chimneys and 'cowcatchers' to sweep cattle off the line.

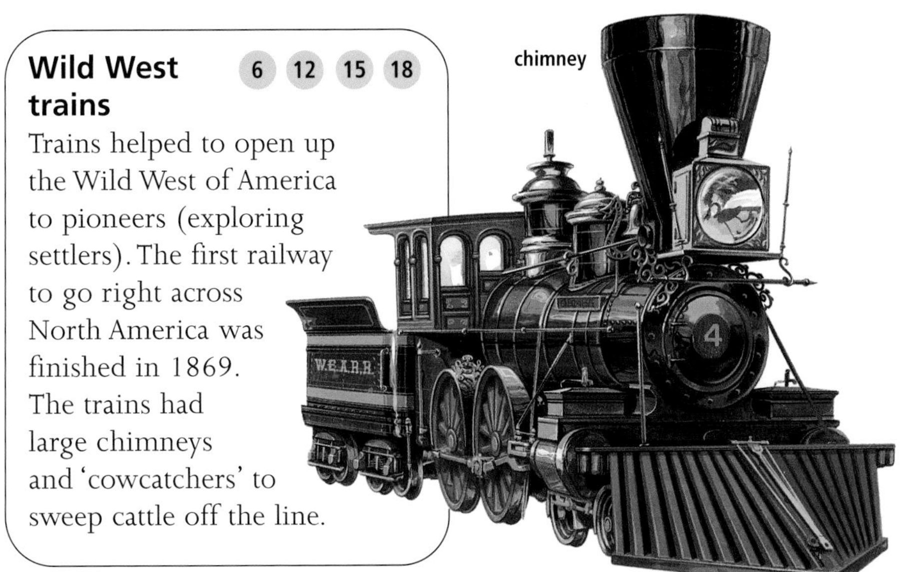

Bullet trains

8 10 11

Japan has an extremely good rail network. The fastest trains are known as bullet trains, or super expresses, and regularly run at over 300km/h. France also has very fast trains, known as TGVs.

Freight

2 3 16 17

Not all trains carry passengers. Freight trains are used to transport goods. The world's longest train carried coal across the USA. It was about 6km long and was pulled by three massive diesel-fuelled engines.

QUESTIONS: Early flight

Level 1

1. GIRDLE can be rearranged to give the name of what type of unpowered aircraft?
2. The first manned flight was in a hot-air balloon. True or false?
3. Is a dirigible a steerable airship or an Australian musical instrument?

Level 2

4. What 'H' is a type of aircraft with rotating blades?
5. Which body of water was Louis Blériot first to fly across in 1909: the English Channel or Atlantic ocean?
6. In which century did Otto Lilienthal make the first controlled glider flights: the 9th or 19th century?
7. How many wings does a monoplane have: two or four?
8. Which 'G' is a country, home to Otto Lilienthal?
9. Jean-François Pilâtre was the first man to fly. True or false?
10. Was the first powered aeroplane flight in Europe or the USA?
11. Which great 16th-century Italian artist and thinker designed a glider that was never built?
12. Which 'M' were brothers who built the first manned aircraft?

Level 3

13. What was the surname of Wilbur and Orville, who designed the first ever heavier-than-air powered aircraft?
14. What was their aircraft called?
15. What did the first heavier-than-air powered aircraft use as fuel?
16. In which century did the first-ever manned aircraft take off: the 16th, 17th or 18th century?
17. Who made the first-ever powered flight?
18. What was his nationality?

FIND THE ANSWER: Early flight

Nowadays, many people take flight for granted. Every day thousands of aeroplanes carry passengers all over the world. Yet it was only around a hundred years ago that the first petrol-driven aircraft took to the skies. The very first flights were made in hot-air balloons, airships and unpowered winged gliders.

the Montgolfier hot-air balloon

Montgolfier (2) (9) (12) (16)

The first-ever manned aircraft was a hot-air balloon built by the French Montgolfier brothers. On 15 October 1783, it lifted Jean-François Pilâtre 25m above the city of Paris, France. It was anchored with rope to stop it floating away.

da Vinci's glider

Early glider (4) (11)

People dreamed of flying long before they achieved it. The glider shown above was designed by Italian thinker and artist Leonardo da Vinci around the year 1500. He also designed a type of helicopter with rotating blades, but neither of his flying machines was actually built.

Powered flight (3) (10) (14) (17) (18)

The first heavier-than-air powered aircraft, the *Wright Flyer*, took off on 17 December 1903 in the USA. The first powered flight had already been made 50 years earlier by the Frenchman Henri Giffard in a steam-powered dirigible (steerable airship).

the *Wright Flyer*

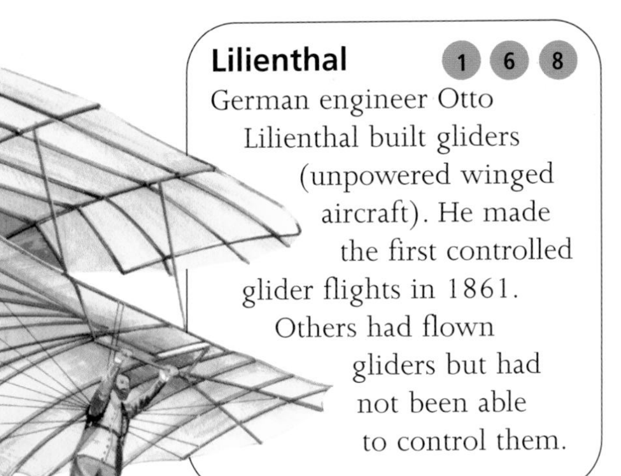

Lilienthal 1 6 8

German engineer Otto Lilienthal built gliders (unpowered winged aircraft). He made the first controlled glider flights in 1861. Others had flown gliders but had not been able to control them.

monoplane

Blériot 5 7

In 1909, Frenchman Louis Blériot became the first person to fly an aeroplane across the English Channel. Blériot also designed and built some of the world's first successful monoplanes (aeroplanes with just two wings, instead of four or six).

The Wright brothers 13 15

Wilbur and Orville Wright designed and built the first heavier-than-air powered aircraft. It had a special lightweight petrol engine. The brothers went on to build aircraft for other people.

QUESTIONS: Sailing

Level 1

1. Sailing boats use the wind to push them along. True or false?
2. Are boats kept moored in a marina, a merino or a mariner?
3. What kind of jackets do people wear to keep them afloat in the water?
4. Do any sailing boats have engines?
5. What suit keeps windsurfers warm?
6. A rudder is used to help a boat steer. True or false?
7. What 'Y' is a large sailing boat used for pleasure?

Level 2

8. Which were invented first: square sails or triangular sails?
9. What 'P' is the left-hand side of a boat and a place where ships dock?
10. What is the word for the rear of a boat?
11. BROAD ARTS can be rearranged to give what word for the right-hand side of a boat?
12. Boats with square sails can only go in the same direction as the wind. True or false?
13. How many hulls do trimarans have?
14. What is a boat with two hulls called?
15. What are small, open boats without cabins called?
16. What 'W' are people who sail standing up on a board?

Level 3

17. What part of a boat helps keep it from tipping over?
18. Which Mediterranean island was home to the sea-faring Minoans?
19. When did ancient sailing ships use their oars?

FIND THE ANSWER: Sailing

Before the 19th century, most of the world's boats and ships had sails. Sailing ships carried the explorers to America and Australia, and carried the Europeans who later settled those continents. Today, most people who sail do so for pleasure or sport, although in some parts of the world boats with sails are still used to transport goods.

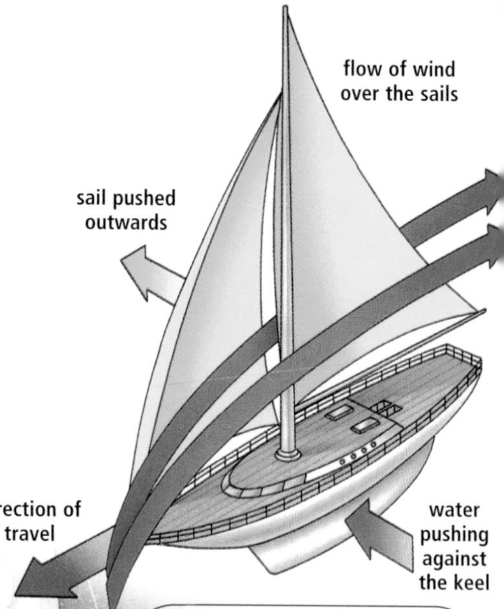

flow of wind over the sails

sail pushed outwards

direction of travel

water pushing against the keel

spinaker

cabin

How it works 1 17

The force of the wind pushes against the sails to move a boat through the water. Modern sailing boats can travel in any direction except directly into the wind. Changing direction is called 'tacking'. A keel under the boat prevents it tipping over if the wind is too strong.

The first sailing ships 8 12 18 19

Built around 2500BCE by the Minoans of Crete and the ancient Greeks, the first sailing boats had square sails, which meant that they could only sail in the same direction as the wind. They used oars to go forwards against the wind. When triangular sails appeared around 1200BCE, people could move them to sail in any direction.

Sailing for pleasure 2 4 7

Most people who own sailing boats use them for fun and keep them docked in harbours or marinas. Larger sailing boats are known as yachts. Some sailing boats also have engines for travelling when there is no wind.

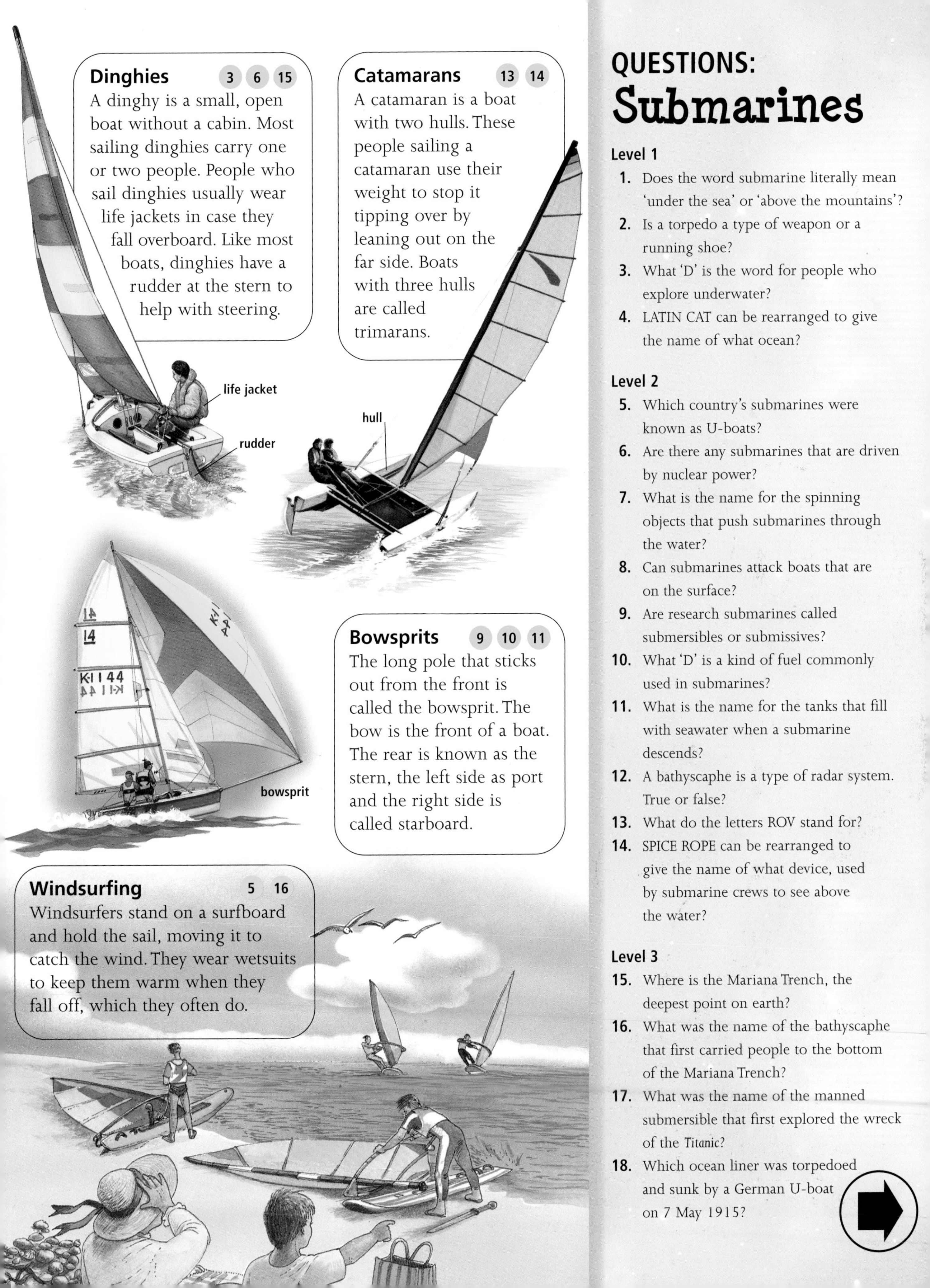

Dinghies (3) (6) (15)

A dinghy is a small, open boat without a cabin. Most sailing dinghies carry one or two people. People who sail dinghies usually wear life jackets in case they fall overboard. Like most boats, dinghies have a rudder at the stern to help with steering.

Catamarans (13) (14)

A catamaran is a boat with two hulls. These people sailing a catamaran use their weight to stop it tipping over by leaning out on the far side. Boats with three hulls are called trimarans.

Bowsprits (9) (10) (11)

The long pole that sticks out from the front is called the bowsprit. The bow is the front of a boat. The rear is known as the stern, the left side as port and the right side is called starboard.

Windsurfing (5) (16)

Windsurfers stand on a surfboard and hold the sail, moving it to catch the wind. They wear wetsuits to keep them warm when they fall off, which they often do.

QUESTIONS: Submarines

Level 1

1. Does the word submarine literally mean 'under the sea' or 'above the mountains'?
2. Is a torpedo a type of weapon or a running shoe?
3. What 'D' is the word for people who explore underwater?
4. LATIN CAT can be rearranged to give the name of what ocean?

Level 2

5. Which country's submarines were known as U-boats?
6. Are there any submarines that are driven by nuclear power?
7. What is the name for the spinning objects that push submarines through the water?
8. Can submarines attack boats that are on the surface?
9. Are research submarines called submersibles or submissives?
10. What 'D' is a kind of fuel commonly used in submarines?
11. What is the name for the tanks that fill with seawater when a submarine descends?
12. A bathyscaphe is a type of radar system. True or false?
13. What do the letters ROV stand for?
14. SPICE ROPE can be rearranged to give the name of what device, used by submarine crews to see above the water?

Level 3

15. Where is the Mariana Trench, the deepest point on earth?
16. What was the name of the bathyscaphe that first carried people to the bottom of the Mariana Trench?
17. What was the name of the manned submersible that first explored the wreck of the *Titanic*?
18. Which ocean liner was torpedoed and sunk by a German U-boat on 7 May 1915?

FIND THE ANSWER: Submarines

Submarines are used to explore the world under the sea. They are also used in the navies of some countries for defence in times of war. Although people long dreamed of voyaging under the sea, submarines have been around for less than 400 years. Today's submarines are a far cry from the earliest designs, most of which were made of wood and were powered by the people who rode in them.

Power 6 7 10

Modern submarines are driven by propellers, like most ships. These propellers are turned by massive engines. Some submarines have diesel engines, while others are driven by nuclear power.

Warfare 5 8 18

During the World Wars, the German navy made great use of their submarines, which were called U-boats. They used them to fire torpedoes at enemy warships, such as the RMS Lusitania, which was sunk on 7 May 1915.

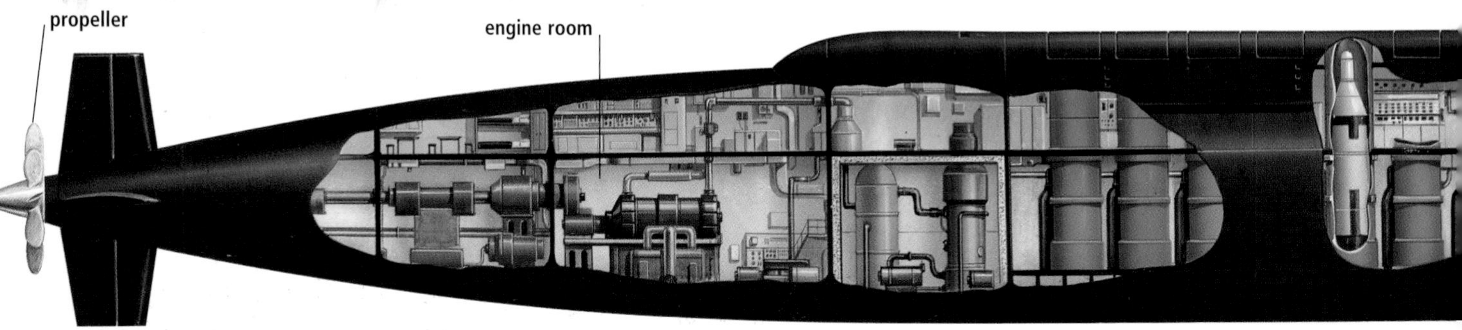

Diving and resurfacing 1 11

Submarine literally means 'under the water'. When a submarine dives, special tanks (ballast tanks) fill up with seawater. To resurface, compressed air is pumped into the tanks. This forces water out, making the submarine lighter.

Subsuits 3

Divers sometimes use subsuits like a one-person submarine for exploration in deep water. These have arms with pincers that the diver can operate, allowing him or her to pick things up and manipulate objects deep beneath the sea.

Alvin 4 9 13 17

Submarines used for research work are called submersibles. In 1986, the three-man US submersible *Alvin* explored the wreck of the great ocean liner *Titanic*, which had sunk in the Atlantic in 1912. A remotely operated vehicle (ROV) called *Jason Junior* was used to inspect the inside of the wreck.

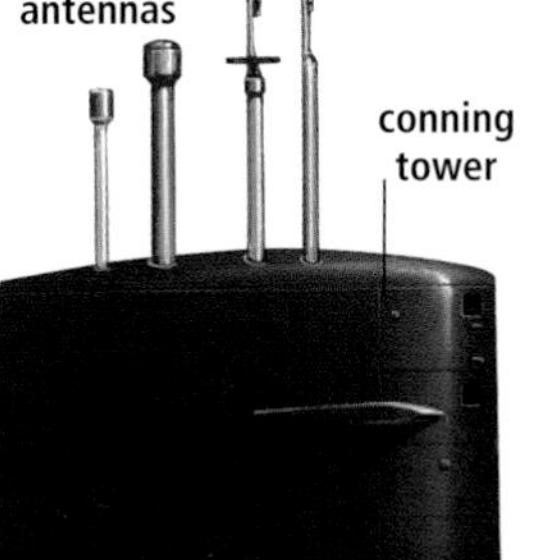

Equipment 2 14

Submarine crews use a device called a periscope to see above the water. Military submarines carry torpedoes (underwater missiles) for sinking other vessels.

Deepest dive 12 15 16

On 23 January 1960, the manned *Trieste*, a deep-diving vessel called a bathyscaphe, dived almost 11km to reach the deepest point on earth – the Mariana Trench on the bottom of the Pacific ocean. The descent took nearly five hours.

float contains petrol

steel cabin for crew members

QUESTIONS:
Household inventions

Level 1

1. Would you put bread in a toaster or a dishwasher?
2. What 'K' is used for heating water?
3. Is a Hoover a type of vacuum cleaner or a type of zip?

Level 2

4. Which invention is usually credited to John Logie Baird?
5. SHARED WISH can be rearranged to give the name of what household appliance?
6. Did the automatic cut-out on an electric kettle appear in 1890, 1930 or 1989?
7. Which was invented first: the electric washing machine or the dishwasher?
8. Which household object is usually associated with Thomas Edison?
9. People only started to use zips in the 1940s. True or false?
10. Which handy implement was invented by Laszlo Biro?
11. The aero-foam extinguisher is used on what kind of fires?
12. SCOOPS RED ROOF can be rearranged to give the name of what kitchen appliance?
13. In which decade of the 20th century did microwave ovens first go on sale?

Level 3

14. In what year was the first television picture transmitted?
15. James Murray Spangler invented the first portable what?
16. What did Alexandre Godefoy invent?
17. Which kitchen appliance was developed from an earlier invention called the magnetron?
18. Who invented the sewing machine?

FIND THE ANSWER: Household inventions

Most homes are full of man-made objects designed to make people's lives easier or get jobs done faster. Technological advances in the 20th century brought dramatic changes, with the introduction of labour-saving appliances, such as the washing machine, the dishwasher and the vacuum cleaner.

The kettle (2) (6)

The electric kettle was invented by Arthur Leslie Large in 1922. A safety device called an automatic cut-out appeared in 1930, to prevent electric shocks.

Living room (4) (8) (14) (16)

Thomas Edison made the first light bulb for sale in 1879. The first television picture was transmitted in 1925 by the engineer John Logie Baird. The electric hairdryer was invented in the 1920s by Alexandre Godefoy.

Microwave (13) (17)

The first microwave ovens went on sale in 1967. They were developed from an earlier invention called the magnetron.

In the kitchen (1) (5) (7) (12)

The electric washing machine was invented in 1908, the electric dishwasher in 1913 and the electric toaster in 1909. The food processor was invented later, in 1971.

telephone

food processor

microwave

radio

toaster

fridge-freezer

washing machine

oven

dishwasher

Fire extinguisher (11)

The first-ever fire extinguisher was patented in 1872 by Thomas Martin. The aero-foam extinguisher, for use against gas and oil fires, was invented by Dr Percy Julian, during World War II.

fire extinguisher

Ball-point pen (10)

The ball-point pen was invented in 1938 by the Hungarian journalist Laszlo Biro. He invented the ball-point so that the same quick-drying, thick ink, which was used in newspaper printing, could also be used in a pen.

ball-point pen

The zip (9) (18)

The zip was invented in 1851 by Elias Howe, who also invented the sewing machine. However, it was not until the end of the 19th century that they began to be manufactured.

zip

vacuum cleaner

The vacuum cleaner (3) (15)

Early vacuum cleaners made in the 19th century were huge. The first portable version was invented in 1907 by James Murray Spangler. The Hoover is a type of vacuum cleaner.

QUESTIONS: Robots

Level 1

1. Are there any robots that work in factories?
2. Do robots ever get tired?
3. Are there any robots that can work underwater?
4. ODD SIR can be rearranged to give what name for robots such as R2-D2?
5. Robots can only do one thing at a time. True or false?

Level 2

6. Are there any robots that can play the piano?
7. Which series of films starred the robot C-3PO?
8. What 'C' is programmed with the information that is needed to make robots operate?
9. LEWDING can be rearranged to give the name of what task performed by robots?
10. Which have travelled farthest from earth: robots or humans?
11. Solar panels are used to capture energy from which source?
12. HOW TO CORD can be rearranged to give the name of what popular TV programme?
13. Which planet is currently being explored by robots?
14. What 'M' is the word for doing more than one job at a time?
15. Can robots be programmed to detonate bombs?

Level 3

16. The word robot comes from which language?
17. Which country developed the WABOT-2 robot?
18. In what year was the animated film *Robots* released?

FIND THE ANSWER:

Robots

Robots are machines that can perform some of the physical tasks that would normally be carried out by humans. A lot of robots are now used in factories, particularly where large objects, such as cars, are made. They are also used to explore where people cannot go, such as the seabed and the surface of other planets.

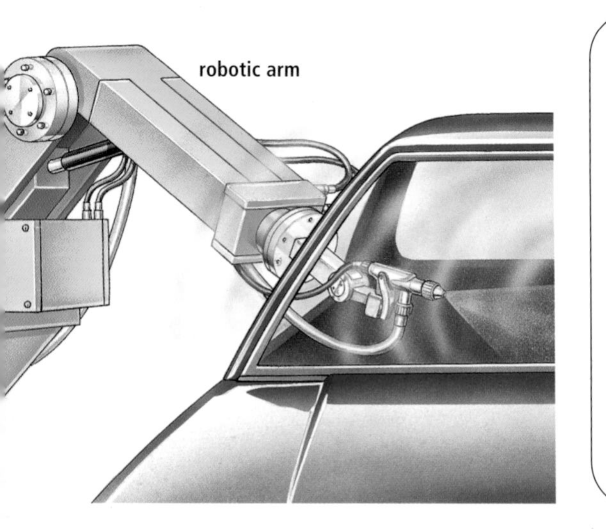

Industry 1 2 8 9

Many factories nowadays use robots for heavy, repetitive or difficult jobs. Unlike people, robots do not become tired or bored. Industrial robots are directed by computers to carry out particular tasks, such as spraying car bodywork or welding pieces together.

Multitasking 5 14

Some robots can carry out more than one job at once. They are known as multitasking robots. Each robot arm does a different job or a similar job in a different direction.

Human-like robots 6 17

The Japanese robot WABOT-2 can play the piano much faster than a human. It can either read new music, or choose a song it has played before and stored in its memory. WABOT-2 can also play gently or furiously. Other robots can perform sign language, and others can behave like pets.

UPHAUT 2 explored a narrow shaft in the Great Pyramid of Giza in 1993

Difficult access 3 15 16

The word robot comes from the Czech word *robota*, meaning 'forced labour'. Robots are very useful for doing dangerous jobs. Some are used to defuse or safely detonate bombs. Others can work deep underwater to explore shipwrecks or dangerous areas of the seabed.

Mars robots 10 11 13

Robots have travelled farther than any human being. Since January 2004, robots known as the Mars rovers have been exploring the surface of Mars. The robots, which carry cameras, are powered by solar panels, which capture energy from sunshine.

Dalek

Stars 4 7 12 18

The animated film *Robots* was released in 2005. Other screen robots include the 'droids' R2-D2 and C-3PO in *Star Wars* and the Daleks in *Doctor Who*.

QUESTIONS:
Computers and gaming

Level 1

1. What 'I' is the network that links computers all over the world?
2. Does PC stand for Perfect Computer or Personal Computer?
3. What is a computer that is small enough to fit in the hand called: a handbag, a handheld or a handshake?
4. What 'M' is a small furry animal, and a thing that attaches to a computer?
5. What is stored in MP3 files?

Level 2

6. Where were computer games played before people had home computers?
7. Can people play computer games while they are on the move?
8. What kind of computer is the word Mac short for?
9. Do most handheld gaming machines take cartridges or discs?
10. Is the information in a computer held in the hard drive, printer or mouse?
11. What 'B' is the computer equipment used to put information onto a CD?
12. Is a computer keyboard a peripheral or a profiterole?
13. What 'H' do you wear when playing a virtual-reality game?
14. What 'V' is put in front of the word 'reality' to describe lifelike situations produced by computers?
15. TOP PAL can be rearranged to give what name for a portable computer?

Level 3

16. Which would you use to store data: a CD-RAM, a CD-REM or a CD-ROM?
17. What connects a home computer to the internet?
18. What kind of files would you put on to an iPod?

FIND THE ANSWER: Computers and gaming

In the past few decades, computers have completely changed the way that people work. They have also changed the way that we play, bringing a new world of entertainment into our homes. There are now gaming machines that plug into televisions, while small, portable machines (handhelds) allow us to play games anywhere.

The internet 1 17
The internet is the network of telephone lines and servers that link home computers around the world together. The internet allows people to exchange information quickly and freely.

girl using laptop computer

Home computers 2 8 15
Many people have PCs (Personal Computers). Others have Macs, or Macintoshes, like the one shown below. Smaller, portable computers are called laptops.

Hard drive 10
The hard drive holds all the information that a computer needs to be able to work. It is the most important part of the machine.

Digital accessories 5 18
All sorts of equipment can be plugged into computers. Pictures from digital cameras can be copied on to a computer's hard drive. Music can also be stored on a computer, and can be passed to and from MP3 players such as the iPod.

hard drive

Macintosh computer

CD drive

iPod MP3 player

digital camera

keyboard

gaming handset

Peripherals 4 12
A peripheral is any device that plugs into a computer or gaming machine. Peripherals include the keyboard and mouse, as well as gaming handsets.

CD burning 11 16
CD-ROMs store data (information). Digital music files (or MP3s) can be put on to a CD using a CD burner. Most modern computers have built-in CD burners.

Handhelds

3 7 9

With small gaming machines known as handhelds, people can play video games while on the move. Most handhelds take small cartridges, which store the information for individual games.

computer graphics

Gaming

6

Every year, computer games become more and more complex and realistic, as computers become more powerful. Before home computers and gaming machines, the games were played in video arcades.

Virtual reality

13 14

Special headsets, gloves and suits can allow people to experience virtual-reality games. These are computer programs that generate situations that look and feel virtually (almost) real.

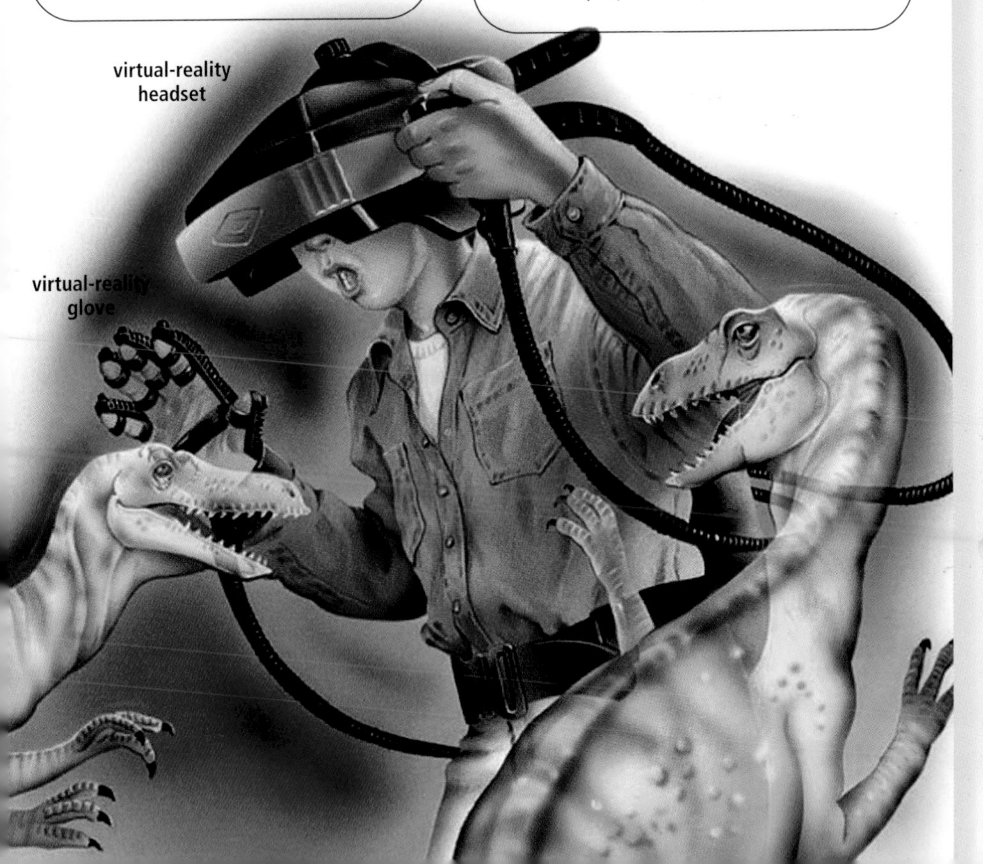

virtual-reality headset

virtual-reality glove

QUESTIONS: Telephones

Level 1

1. What 'T' is a written message sent by a mobile phone?
2. Were the first mobile phones bigger or smaller than mobile phones today?
3. Do most modern telephones have rotating dials or buttons?
4. Do mobile phones send messages using microwaves, water waves or Mexican waves?
5. Are there mobile phones that can connect to the internet?

Level 2

6. Did the world's first telephone have touch-tone dialling?
7. In what century was the telephone invented: 9th, 19th or 21st?
8. SAME CAR can be rearranged to spell what extra feature of some mobile phones?
9. HOME CUT PIE can be rearranged to spell what part of a telephone, that you speak into?
10. What 'E' is the place where telephone calls are connected?
11. What name is given to people who used to connect the calls?
12. How many names were in the first-ever telephone directory: 50, 500 or 5,000?
13. What 'T' was a kind of coded message used before telephones were invented?

Level 3

14. How did people generate the electricity to power early phones?
15. Who invented the telephone?
16. In which country was Alexander Graham Bell born?
17. Who invented the carbon-granule microphone?
18. Which was invented first: the fax or the telephone?
19. In what year did rotating dials appear: 1886, 1896 or 1906?

FIND THE ANSWER: Telephones

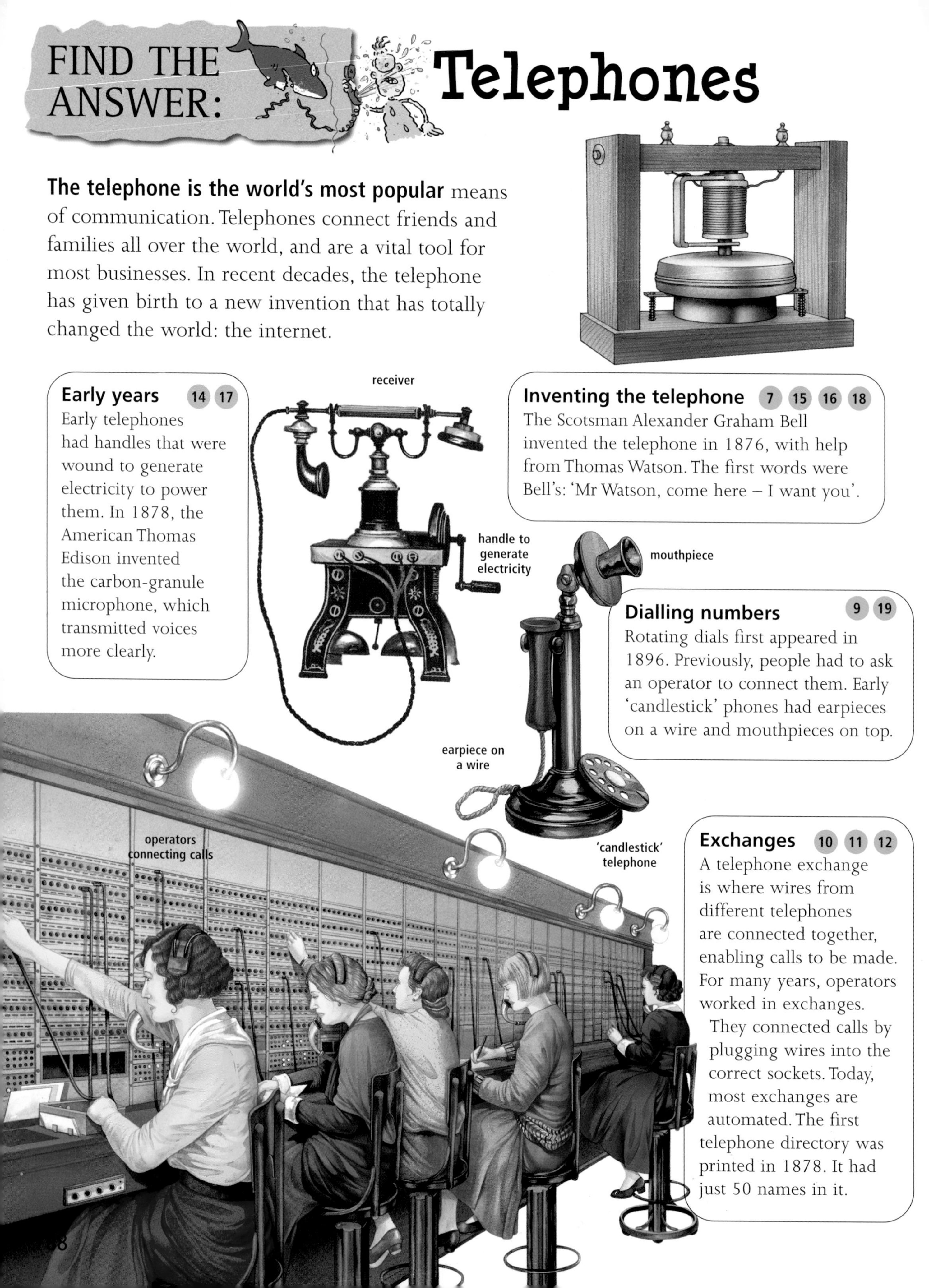

The telephone is the world's most popular means of communication. Telephones connect friends and families all over the world, and are a vital tool for most businesses. In recent decades, the telephone has given birth to a new invention that has totally changed the world: the internet.

Early years

14 17

Early telephones had handles that were wound to generate electricity to power them. In 1878, the American Thomas Edison invented the carbon-granule microphone, which transmitted voices more clearly.

Inventing the telephone

7 15 16 18

The Scotsman Alexander Graham Bell invented the telephone in 1876, with help from Thomas Watson. The first words were Bell's: 'Mr Watson, come here – I want you'.

Dialling numbers

9 19

Rotating dials first appeared in 1896. Previously, people had to ask an operator to connect them. Early 'candlestick' phones had earpieces on a wire and mouthpieces on top.

Exchanges

10 11 12

A telephone exchange is where wires from different telephones are connected together, enabling calls to be made. For many years, operators worked in exchanges. They connected calls by plugging wires into the correct sockets. Today, most exchanges are automated. The first telephone directory was printed in 1878. It had just 50 names in it.

Modern phones (3) (6)

Modern phones have 'touch-tone dialling'. Each button generates its own sound, which is recognized by computers at the telephone exchange.

buttons

number pad sensors

electronic circuit board

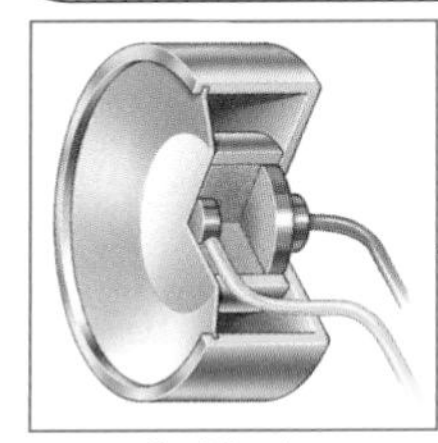

inside the mouthpiece

Telegrams (13) (18)

Before telephones, people used telegrams – coded messages which were sent down wires and then decoded. Fax was invented in 1843.

mobile telephone

Mobile phones (2) (4)

Mobile phones first became common in the 1980s. At first, they were about the size of a brick, but over time they got smaller. Mobile phones send messages through the air using microwaves. Messages are collected by special masts, and then sent on to exchanges. They can then be transmitted via the masts, or via fibre-optic cable to land-line exchanges.

'BlackBerry'

New features (1) (5) (8)

Mobile phones are changing all the time. As well as voice messages, most can transmit texts (typed messages) and even connect to the internet and send emails. Many mobile phones can be used for more than just communication. Some have built-in cameras, music and video games.

QUESTIONS: Discoveries

Level 1

1. What type of food is said to have fallen on Isaac Newton's head, giving him the idea for his most famous theory?
2. What 'W' turns around and around, allowing vehicles to move?
3. IT GRAVY can be rearranged to give the name of what force that pulls objects towards the ground?

Level 2

4. Which mathematician living in ancient Greece shouted 'Eureka' when he was in his bath?
5. What nationality was Isaac Newton?
6. In which century did the first cars with petrol engines appear?
7. Michael Faraday was an American scientist. True or false?
8. What 'S' was used to drive the earliest cars?
9. Karl Benz was a pioneer of the motor car. True or false?
10. SPICY HITS can be rearranged to give the name of what type of scientist?
11. Who came up with the theory of relativity?
12. Was the wheel invented more than 3,000 years ago?
13. What 'M' did Michael Faraday help us to understand better?
14. What nationality was Nicolas Cugnot, who built the first car?
15. By what three letters is deoxyribonucleic acid usually known?

Level 3

16. In which modern country are the ruins of the city of Uruk?
17. Which two scientists are usually credited with discovering the double helix of deoxyribonucleic acid?
18. In the formula $E = mc^2$, what does 'E' stand for?

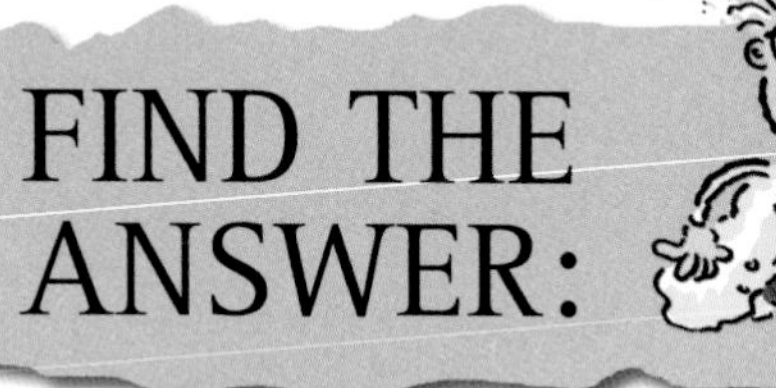

FIND THE ANSWER: Discoveries

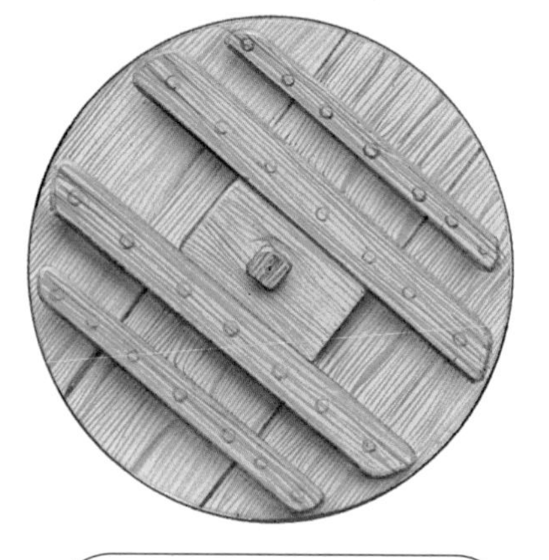

The history of science is a history of discoveries. The reason we know so much about the world is because of the great thinkers who had ideas and then tested them to see if they were true. Some of these ideas led to useful inventions. Others helped us better understand the universe around us.

Archimedes 4

The ancient Greek made an important discovery about water displacement one day, when he was in his bath and noticed water spilling out. At the moment the idea came to him, he shouted 'Eureka!'

The wheel 2 12 16

Nobody knows who invented the wheel. The earliest images of wheels come from Iraq and date back around 5,500 years. At that time, a great civilization lived there, based around the city of Uruk. It is possible that the wheel was invented before this date, however.

Sir Isaac Newton

Newton 1 3 5

The English scientist Sir Isaac Newton (1642–1727) discovered gravity. The idea came to him when he was sitting under a tree, and an apple fell on his head.

Faraday 7 13

Michael Faraday (1791–1867) was an English chemist and physicist, who helped us to understand the nature of electricity and magnetism.

Faraday demonstrates the principles of electricity

The car

6 8 9 14

The first self-propelled road vehicle was built by the Frenchman Nicolas Cugnot in 1769 and was driven by steam. In the 1880s, Karl Benz and Gottlieb Daimler worked independently to produce the first petrol engine. In 1885, Benz built his motorized three-wheel car, the first to be powered by petrol.

Relativity

10 11 18

The theory of relativity was the brainchild of the German-born physicist Albert Einstein (1879–1955). Einstein's theory showed that time, space and mass are not fixed, but change according to the position from which they are seen or measured. His theory also showed that mass and energy are interchangeable. He summed this up with a single equation: $E = mc^2$ (E is energy, m is mass and c^2 is acceleration).

the double helix

DNA

15 17

All plants and animals contain molecules of DNA (deoxyribonucleic acid) – the blueprint for life. DNA consists of chains of paired units called bases. The structure of DNA, known as the double helix, was first described in 1953 by James Watson and Francis Crick.

QUESTIONS: Where in the world?

Level 1

1. Is Cambridge in England or in Egypt?
2. Scissors were invented by Toshiba. True or false?
3. What 'A' is an American computer company and also a piece of fruit?

Level 2

4. Was gunpowder invented in China, France or Russia?
5. ARROW SLOPE can be rearranged to give the name of what form of power, used in Australia?
6. Is the company Sony from Europe, the USA or Asia?
7. In which state of the USA is Silicon Valley: Kentucky, Vermont or California?

Level 3

8. What 'E' do Brazilian cars use instead of petrol?
9. What 'S' is the plant from which this fuel is extracted?
10. In which year did the first human heart transplant take place: 1967, 1977 or 1987?

FIND THE ANSWER: Where in the world?

Advances in science and technology have caused changes all over the world. In some cases they have made countries rich. In others, they have improved all of our lives. Every year, scientists make new discoveries and inventors come up with new ideas and products. In 50 years' time, many more exciting advances will have totally changed the way that people live.

England 1
England's famous universities, Oxford and Cambridge, have been home to many ground breaking scientists, including Sir Isaac Newton and Sir Stephen Hawkins.

Japan 4 6
Asia has a long history of invention. Gunpowder, for instance, was invented in China. Today, Japan is known for high-tech companies, such as Sony, Toshiba and Hitachi. The Japanese car manufacturers Honda and Toyota are currently developing cars that use electricity instead of petrol.

Brazil 8 9
In Brazil, cars run on ethanol (alcohol) instead of petrol. This protects the environment and uses up waste sugarcane, from which the ethanol is extracted.

Egypt 2
Ancient Egypt produced many of the household objects that are common today, including paper and scissors.

The USA 3 7
California in the USA is home to Silicon Valley, where many of the world's biggest computer companies, such as Apple and Microsoft, have their headquarters.

South Africa 10
In 1967, Christian Baarnard performed the first-ever human heart transplant in South Africa, revolutionizing the field of medicine.

Australia 5
With its baked outback and deserts, Australia is one of the world's biggest users of solar power. The country hosts a giant solar-powered car race every year, with teams from all over the world competing.

Answers 1)England **2**)False (they were invented in ancient Egypt) **3**)Apple **4**)China **5**)Solar power **6**)Asia **7**)California **8**)Ethanol **9**)Sugarcane **10**)1967

QUIZ FOUR

History

Ancient Egypt

Ancient Greece

The Colosseum

Medieval life

Knights

The Renaissance

Age of exploration

World War I

QUESTIONS:

Ancient Egypt

Level 1

1. Which river flows through Egypt?
2. What did the ancient Egyptians call their leader?
3. Did Egyptians believe in life after death?
4. What was made of wool or human hair?
5. What were Egyptian clothes made from?

Level 2

6. What form of writing did the Egyptians use?
7. What was papyrus made from?
8. What was usually buried with an Egyptian's body?
9. How did the Egyptians usually decorate their coffins?
10. What was 'Opening the mouth'?
11. What is the biggest pyramid called?
12. What flower was the symbol of the Nile?

Level 3

13. Which part of the body was used to measure a cubit: the leg, the foot or the forearm?
14. How did the Egyptians transport a pharaoh's body?
15. What did Egyptians use to dry the body when embalming?
16. What animal is associated with the Egyptian god of kings?
17. What did the priest say during a death ceremony?
18. For how long did the pharaohs rule Egypt?
19. Who is buried in the Great Pyramid of Giza?

FIND THE ANSWER: Ancient Egypt

Over 5,000 years ago, a great civilization was born on the banks of the River Nile in Egypt. Egyptians were ruled by one king, obeyed one set of laws and worshipped one group of gods. Their civilization lasted for thousands of years. People's lives depended on the Nile, which overflowed each year and enriched the land.

Egyptian coffin

Art 9

The Egyptians painted their coffins and the walls of their tombs beautifully. The coffin was usually painted with a portrait of the dead person.

Afterlife 3 8

The Egyptians believed that when a person died, they would live again in a kind of heaven. There they needed the same things they needed in Egypt, including their body. A person's clothes and furniture were buried in their tomb, together with food and drink.

Writing 6 7

The Egyptians wrote on papyrus (paper made from reed). They used red or black ink and a reed pen or a brush. Their writing consisted of pictures, called hieroglyphics, that stood for objects and sounds.

Pharaohs 2 16 18

The pharaohs (powerful kings) ruled Egypt for 3,000 years. The Egyptians believed pharaohs were gods, linked with Horus (god of kings), who took the form of a hawk.

The Nile 1 12

The lotus blossom was the symbol of the River Nile in Egypt. Every year the river flooded its banks, leaving a layer of rich soil in which farmers grew crops.

symbol of Horus

Mummies (15)

After death, Egyptians preserved bodies by embalming them. They used salt to dry the body, then wrapped it in linen. The head was covered with a mask.

Tombs (10 11 14 17 19)

Pyramids were tombs for pharaohs. The largest is the Great Pyramid of Giza, built for the pharaoh Cheops. The pharaoh's body was taken to his tomb in a funeral boat. Priests then performed a ceremony called 'Opening the mouth', saying 'You live again, you live again forever.'

pharaoh's coffin on a funeral boat

Measurement (13)

A cubit is 52.5cm – the average distance between a person's middle finger and their elbow. Egyptians made special rods to measure cubits exactly.

Clothes (4 5)

Egyptians, even the pharaoh, usually walked barefoot or wore sandals made of reeds. People wore simple linen clothes and sometimes wore wigs made of wool or human hair. Egyptians wore lots of jewellery to keep away evil spirits.

wall painting of a duck

QUESTIONS: Ancient Greece

Level 1

1. What 'M' is one of the seas around Greece?
2. Who was the ruler of the Greek gods?
3. Where were the ancient Olympic games held?
4. Was the Trojan horse made of stone or wood?
5. The Greeks had slaves. True or false?

Level 2

6. A SPRAT can be rearranged to give the name of what Greek city-state?
7. What did women use to weave fabric for clothes?
8. At about what age did women marry?
9. Who hid inside the Trojan horse?
10. SNOOD PIE can be rearranged to give the name of what Greek god?
11. What material did the Greeks use to make bricks?
12. How did wealthy Greeks travel on land: by horse or by carriage?
13. The Greek empire included many islands. True or false?
14. When travelling in Greece, people slept outside. True or false?
15. Where were the gods said to live?

Level 3

16. In which modern country was the ancient city of Troy?
17. What did a winner receive at the Olympic games?
18. What was a *chiton*?
19. Where in the home did the Greeks have an altar?
20. Who was the goddess of the home?

FIND THE ANSWER:

Ancient Greece

The Greek civilization first emerged around 1200BCE, and reached its height in about 500BCE. The Greeks were the first to introduce democracy, when men in Athens were given the vote. Many people were farmers, but a middle class of merchants and craftspeople emerged in the towns. The Greeks developed forms of philosophy, art and architecture that have endured through the centuries.

Geography
1 6 13

Greece is surrounded by the Mediterranean and Aegean seas. The Greek empire included city-states in Greece itself, such as Athens (the largest) and Sparta, and many islands.

Houses
5 11 19

Greek houses were made from mud bricks and wood. They were usually built around a courtyard, which contained an altar. There were separate quarters for men, women and slaves.

Travelling
12 14

On land, wealthy citizens travelled on horseback. Others walked. People often slept outside or in the porch of a public building when away from home.

Women's lives
7 8 18

Women married at around 15. They looked after the household, and used a loom to spin and weave fabric. A single rectangle of cloth made a basic woman's dress, called a *chiton*.

Greek gods

10 15 20

Greeks believed in many different gods, who represented every aspect of their lives: from music (Apollo) to love (Aphrodite); from the sea (Poseidon) to the home (Hestia). The gods were said to live on Mount Olympus, on the mainland of Greece.

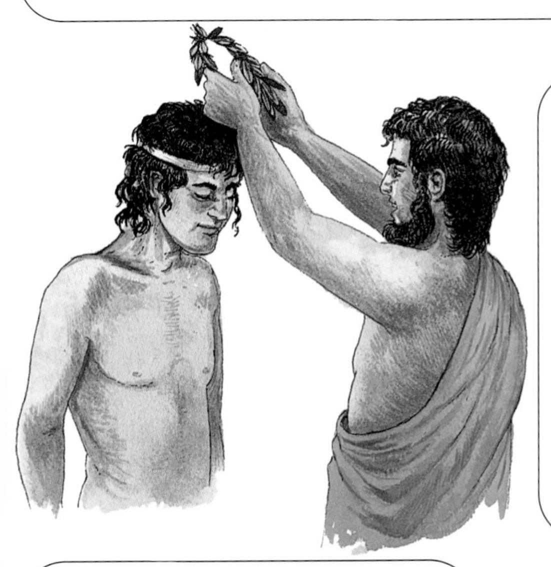

Olympic games

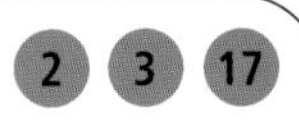

The Olympics were held every four years at Olympia to honour Zeus, the ruler of the gods. Events included running and chariot races. The winner of each event was rewarded with a crown of olive leaves.

Trojan horse

4 9 16

Troy was a city in what we now call Turkey. The Greeks wanted to capture Troy, so they presented the Trojans with a large wooden horse, in which Greek soldiers were hiding. After nightfall, the soldiers left the horse and captured the city.

QUESTIONS: The Colosseum

Level 1

1. What famous gladiator led a revolt of slaves?
2. There were elephants in the Colosseum. True or false?
3. What signal did the crowd give for a gladiator to die?
4. CUT ROSE can be rearranged to give the name of what type of gladiator?

Level 2

5. In what part of the Colosseum were the gladiators and animals kept?
6. Which emperor often fought at the Colosseum?
7. What was a *bestiarius?*
8. What did a *retiarius* use to catch his opponent?
9. Who was thrown to the animals?
10. What kind of gladiator wore a helmet decorated with a fish?
11. How many years did it take to build the Colosseum: ten, 20 or 30?
12. The *venationes* were Roman soldiers. True or false?

Level 3

13. What did a freed gladiator receive?
14. How many people could attend games at the Colosseum?
15. When were the first gladiator games held?
16. How did the Colosseum get its name?
17. How many times did Commodus fight at the Colosseum?
18. How many animals were killed in the first celebrations at the Colosseum?

FIND THE ANSWER:

The Colosseum

The ancient Romans built huge arenas called amphitheatres to stage their entertainments. The Colosseum in Rome was one of the grandest, commissioned by the Emperor Vespasian. The first ceremonies lasted for 100 days and included a mock sea battle. Romans enjoyed watching bloodthirsty games at the Colosseum for over 400 years.

Punishment (7) (9)

Christians, criminals and slaves were thrown into the arena with wild animals. The *bestiarius*, on the other hand, was trained to fight animals.

Gladiators (3) (15)

The first gladiator games were held in 264BCE. Most gladiators were prisoners, slaves or criminals who were trained to fight. If a gladiator was wounded, the crowd decided his fate by giving the thumbs up (to live) or the thumbs down (to die).

gladiator's helmet

wounded gladiator appealing to crowd

Types of gladiator (4) (8) (10)

There were several different kinds of gladiator. The *secutor* was heavily armed. The *murmillo* wore a helmet decorated with a fish. The *retiarius* tried to catch his opponent with a net and a three-pronged spear.

Commodus (6) (17)

Emperor Commodus reigned 180–192CE. During his reign, he dressed as a gladiator and fought at the Colosseum 735 times. He never lost. This behaviour shocked many Romans, who thought that gladiators were the lowest members of society. Eventually, Commodus was murdered.

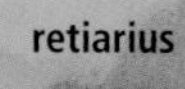

retiarius

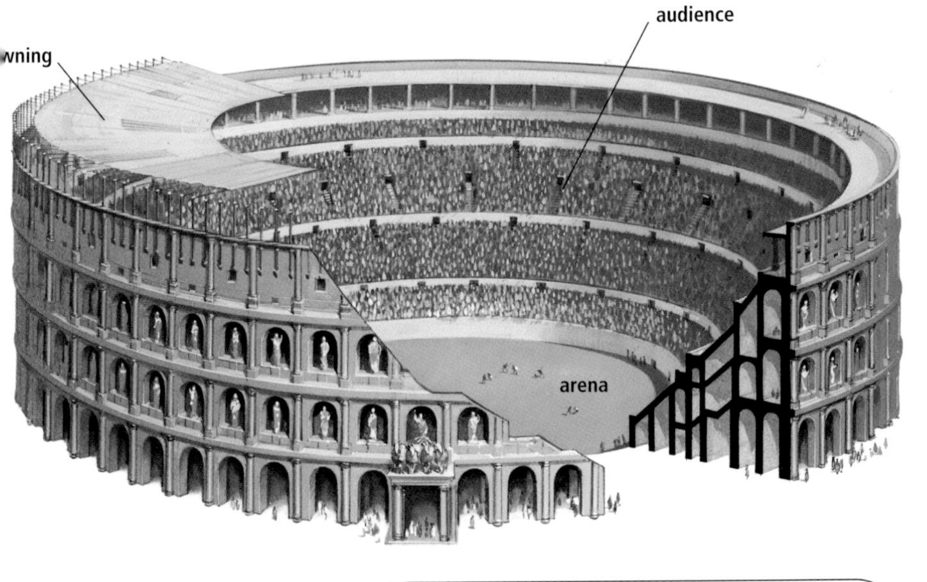

The Colosseum 5 11 14 16

It took about ten years to build the Colosseum, which got its name from the nearby colossus (statue) of Nero. It had 80 entrances and was divided into the podium, arena and *cavea* (seating area) for 50,000 people. Underground chambers held gladiators and animals.

Spartacus 1

Spartacus, a Thracian soldier, was sold into slavery and became a gladiator in Capua. In 73BCE, Spartacus led a revolt of slaves, but he was eventually defeated and killed.

Exotic animals 2 12 18

Venationes (staged hunts) were held in the morning. Exotic animals, such as elephants and tigers, were imported from overseas. During the first shows at the Colosseum, 5,000 animals were killed.

bone tablet and coins

CASSIVS

Freedom 13

If a gladiator fought well, he could be set free. His master gave him a bone tablet, inscribed with his name, and a gift of coins.

QUESTIONS: Medieval life

Level 1

1. A banquet is a type of battle. True or false?
2. People ate meals in the great hall. True or false?
3. Was a *jongleur* a person or a musical instrument?
4. Who owned the land in medieval times?
5. Who taught the children of noblemen: priests or servants?

Level 2

6. Who rented land from noblemen?
7. What were *jongleurs* called in England?
8. What was the name of the system by which land was given out?
9. What was the centre of the castle called?
10. Where did important people sit during a banquet?
11. How were castle floors kept warm?
12. Where were medieval girls taught?
13. What was the cup board for?
14. What was used to help rid the castle floor of bad smells?

Level 3

15. What language did sons of nobles learn?
16. Why did people like to hear music while they were eating?
17. Where did village boys learn trades?
18. What were trenchers?

FIND THE ANSWER: Medieval life

Society in the middle ages was strictly ordered. The king, at the head, owned all of the land but allowed certain noblemen to use it in return for their loyalties and services in war. Peasants led a hard life and had few rights. Social events were important for all medieval people – lords held banquets in their castles, while villagers attended weddings and fairs.

travelling musicians

The great hall

2 10 13 18

People dined and were entertained in the great hall. The lord and other important people sat at 'high table' near a display of cups and plates on the 'cup board' that showed off the lord's wealth. Diners ate off wooden boards called trenchers.

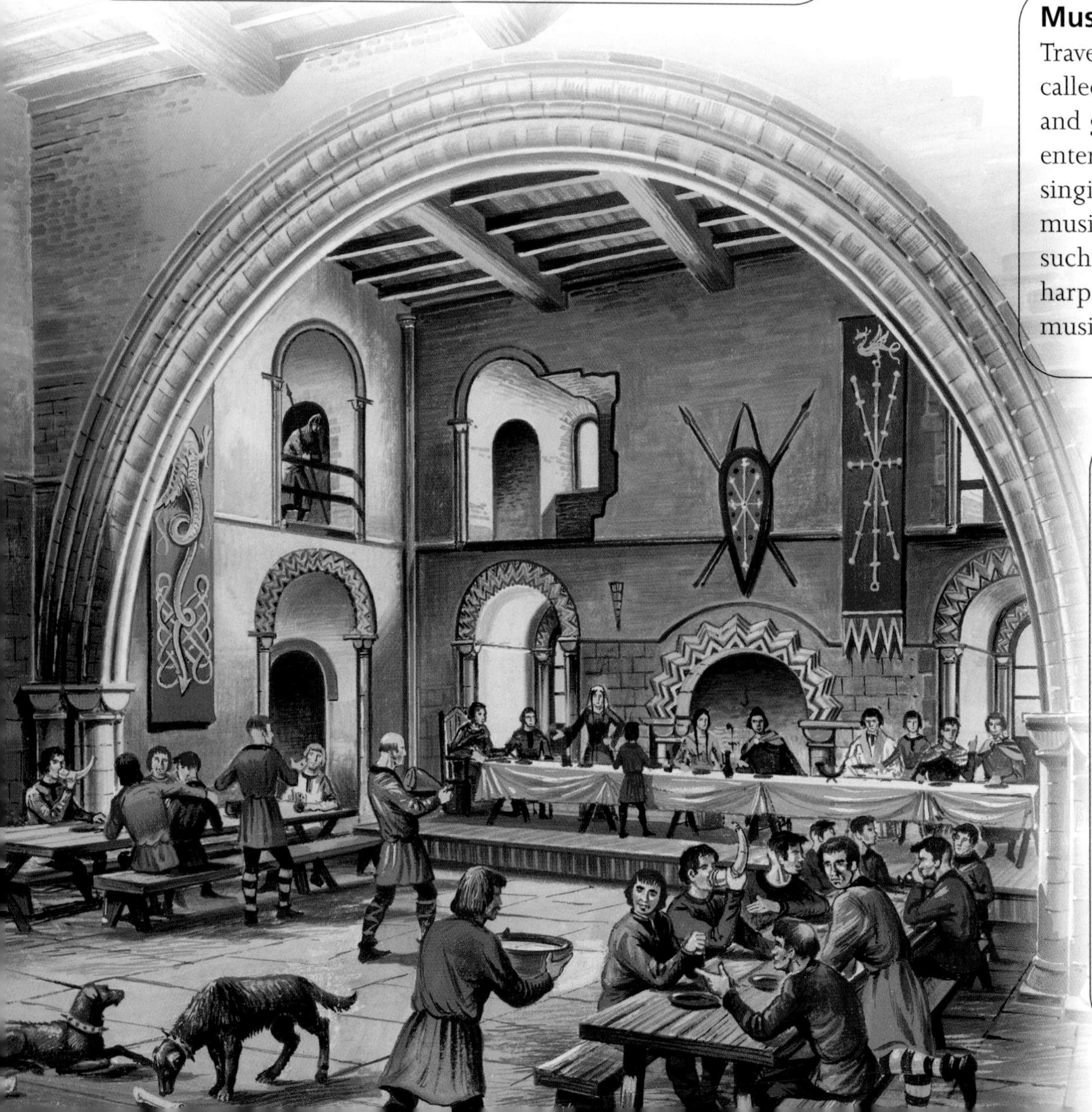

Music

3 7 16

Travelling musicians, called *jongleurs* in France and gleemen in England, entertained guests by singing and playing musical instruments, such as the lute and the harp. People believed that music aided digestion.

Banquets

1

Banquets (feasts) were held to show a lord's generosity and wealth, as well as for celebration. Food included beef, lamb, venison, fish, cheeses, eggs, bread, vegetables and fruit, as well as wines and ales. Lavish banquets included figs, dates and citrus fruit.

The castle

9 11 14

A spiral staircase led to the main tower, which was used for defence. The centre of the castle, the 'keep', held the great hall, kitchen, chapel and upstairs bed chambers. The stone floors were covered with reeds for warmth and were sprinkled with spices to reduce the stench.

Learning

5 12 15 17

Children of nobles were taught by priests. They learnt grammar, logic, Latin and mathematics. Village boys learned trades such as masonry (stone work) at local guilds, while girls were taught cooking and sewing at home.

Feudal system

4 6 8

In feudal society, the king, who owned the land, granted 'fiefs' of land to nobles. This land was then rented by knights and lords, who had peasants to farm it. The peasants, or 'serfs', were allowed to farm a small area to feed their families.

QUESTIONS: Knights

Level 1

1. What 'L' was a weapon used by knights on horseback?
2. What was a battering ram used for?
3. RED GAG can be rearranged to give the name of what weapon, used by knights?
4. Knights only ever fought on horseback. True or false?

Level 2

5. What did an esquire become during a dubbing ceremony?
6. What was a mace?
7. How did a jousting knight knock his opponent off his horse?
8. What kind of missiles did a mangonel shoot?
9. Did a knight use a crossbow or a longbow?
10. Why did jousting begin?
11. What weapon was used to shoot bolts at a castle?
12. How could knights tell each other apart in battle?
13. What is a trebuchet?
14. How could attackers force the defenders of a castle to surrender?

Level 3

15. What was the name of the fee paid by knights who did not want to fight?
16. What was a bevor?
17. How was an esquire dubbed?
18. By which century had knights begun wearing plated armour?

FIND THE ANSWER: Knights

Knights were sons of noblemen who trained to become soldiers of the king. A knight began training as a page at the age of seven. He then became an esquire, and an assistant to a knight, before finally becoming a knight himself at the age of 21. Knights were bound by the rules of chivalry, and fought to the death to protect their king and country.

Jousting

7 10

Although it began as battle training, jousting became popular entertainment to show off knights' skills at riding and fighting. Pairs of knights used blunted lances to try to knock their opponent off his horse.

Armour

16 18

By the 15th century, knights wore plated armour, which offered better protection than mail armour. Large metal plates were joined by smaller plates called 'lames'. The knight's neck was protected by a 'bevor', which was attached to the breast plate.

defenders with bows

scaling ladders

Dubbing

5 17

Esquires became knights in a ceremony called dubbing. The knight's lord tapped him on the shoulder with the flat blade of his sword.

Defence

14

Defenders shot arrows from window slits, and threw rocks, boiling water and red-hot irons at the enemy. Many sieges ended when the defenders were starved into surrendering.

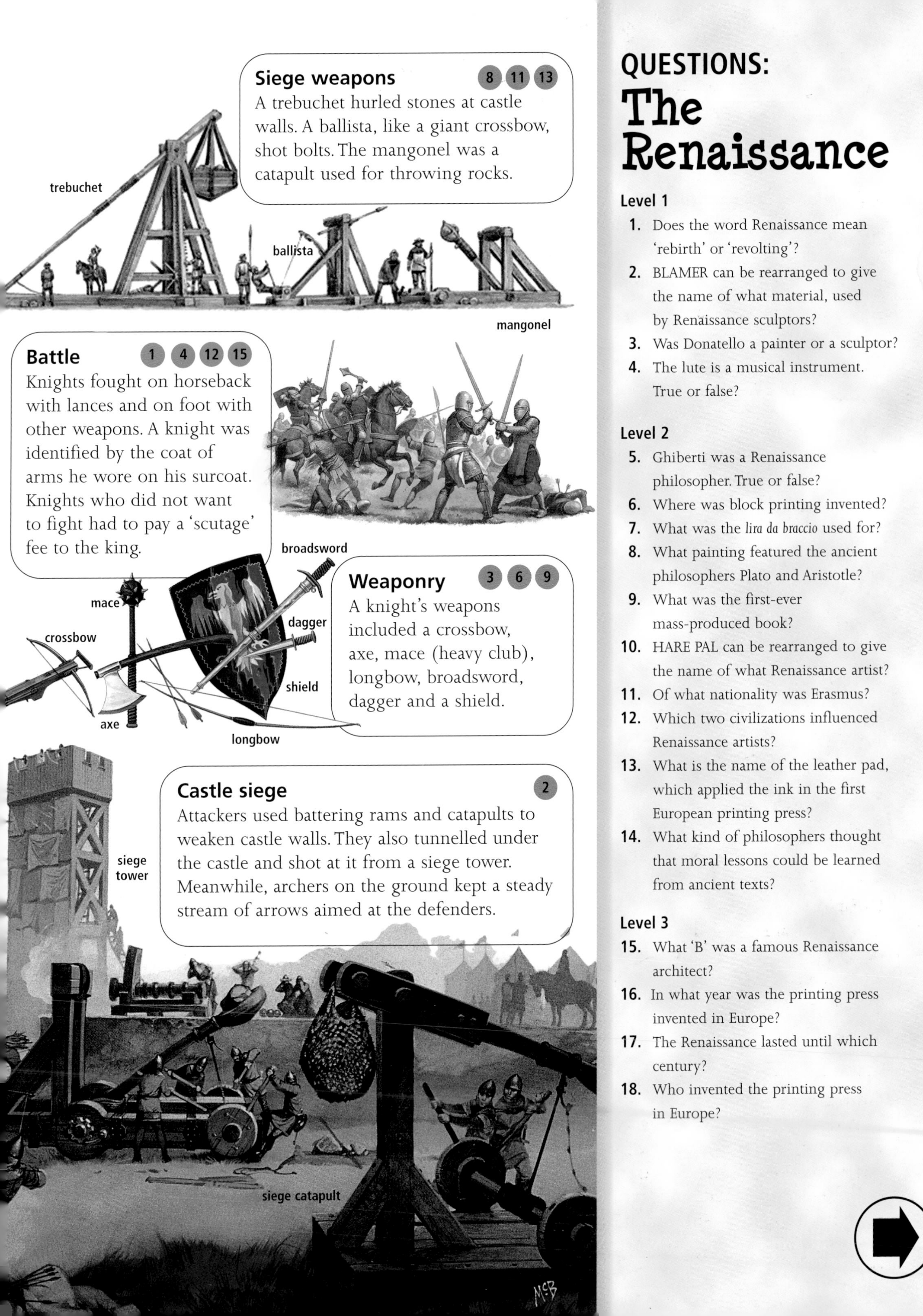

Siege weapons (8) (11) (13)

A trebuchet hurled stones at castle walls. A ballista, like a giant crossbow, shot bolts. The mangonel was a catapult used for throwing rocks.

Battle (1) (4) (12) (15)

Knights fought on horseback with lances and on foot with other weapons. A knight was identified by the coat of arms he wore on his surcoat. Knights who did not want to fight had to pay a 'scutage' fee to the king.

Weaponry (3) (6) (9)

A knight's weapons included a crossbow, axe, mace (heavy club), longbow, broadsword, dagger and a shield.

Castle siege (2)

Attackers used battering rams and catapults to weaken castle walls. They also tunnelled under the castle and shot at it from a siege tower. Meanwhile, archers on the ground kept a steady stream of arrows aimed at the defenders.

QUESTIONS: The Renaissance

Level 1

1. Does the word Renaissance mean 'rebirth' or 'revolting'?
2. BLAMER can be rearranged to give the name of what material, used by Renaissance sculptors?
3. Was Donatello a painter or a sculptor?
4. The lute is a musical instrument. True or false?

Level 2

5. Ghiberti was a Renaissance philosopher. True or false?
6. Where was block printing invented?
7. What was the *lira da braccio* used for?
8. What painting featured the ancient philosophers Plato and Aristotle?
9. What was the first-ever mass-produced book?
10. HARE PAL can be rearranged to give the name of what Renaissance artist?
11. Of what nationality was Erasmus?
12. Which two civilizations influenced Renaissance artists?
13. What is the name of the leather pad, which applied the ink in the first European printing press?
14. What kind of philosophers thought that moral lessons could be learned from ancient texts?

Level 3

15. What 'B' was a famous Renaissance architect?
16. In what year was the printing press invented in Europe?
17. The Renaissance lasted until which century?
18. Who invented the printing press in Europe?

FIND THE ANSWER: The Renaissance

The Renaissance was an era of great change that brought Europe out of the Middle, or Dark, Ages. It began in the 14th century in the Italian cities of Florence and Venice, and later spread across Europe. Artists, musicians, architects and thinkers flourished with the support of wealthy patrons, such as the Medici family. Fine libraries, academies and universities were established.

psaltery

lira da braccio

Music
4 7

Renaissance instruments included the psaltery and the *lira da braccio*, used by poets to accompany their poems. The lute, the recorder and the *organetto*, which used pipes, were also popular.

Ideas
1 11 14 17

Renaissance means 'rebirth'. There was a reawakened interest in science, art and literature. The period lasted until the 17th century. Humanism was one important movement. Humanists, such as the Dutch philosopher Erasmus, thought moral lessons could be learned from Greek and Latin texts.

Painting
8 10 12

Artists were drawn to the human form, nature and the art of ancient Greece and Rome. Raphael painted Greek philosophers like Aristotle and Plato in *The School of Athens*.

bronze sculpture

Renaissance artists

Sculpture 2 3 5

Sculptors such as Donatello and Ghiberti created amazingly realistic work that was inspired by classical sculpture, although they did not necessarily depict classical themes. Donatello carved saints and prophets clothed in Roman or Greek styles. Sculptors used materials such as bronze and marble.

classical-style arch

Architecture 15

Early Italian architects, such as Brunelleschi and Palladio, looked to classical styles for their designs, using Greek columns and Roman arches on many buildings.

Invention 6 9 13 16 18

Block printing was invented in China, but Johannes Gutenberg, a German, invented the printing press in Europe in 1440. It had moveable type held in a wooden frame, and ink was applied using a leather pad called an 'inkball'. In 1455, Gutenberg printed a Bible that became the world's first-ever mass-produced book.

Gutenberg's printing press

QUESTIONS: Age of exploration

Level 1

1. Was Sir Francis Drake an Englishman or a Spaniard?
2. What was Columbus' largest ship called: the *Santa Maria*, the *Santa Anna* or the *Santa Barbara*?
3. Francisco Pizarro conquered the Incas. True or false?
4. From which country was Bartholomew Diaz?

Level 2

5. Which did Magellan discover: the Indian ocean or the Pacific ocean?
6. How many men were in the crew of Columbus' largest ship: 30, 40 or 60?
7. Who sent Columbus to find a route to China?
8. Did Diaz or da Gama sail around the southern tip of Africa?
9. Who reached India in 1498?
10. What was Zheng He the first to do?
11. What were the names of Columbus' two caravels?
12. What was a backstaff used for?
13. Why did Ferdinand Magellan not reach his final destination?
14. What did Columbus believe he had reached?
15. What part of the world did the Incas rule?

Level 3

16. On which island did Columbus land?
17. What was discovered in 1911?
18. What is a *nao*?
19. When did a ship first sail all the way round the world?

FIND THE ANSWER: Age of exploration

During the 15th and 16th centuries, Europeans became increasingly curious about the world. Explorers made bold strides in their efforts to increase trade, find wealth and discover new worlds. By the end of this era, Portuguese, Spanish and English explorers had made their way to Africa, India, China, America and around the globe.

compass

Navigation 10 12

Compasses, star charts and a backstaff, which measured the angle of the sun, helped explorers find their way. Zheng He was the first person to use a compass on his sea voyages.

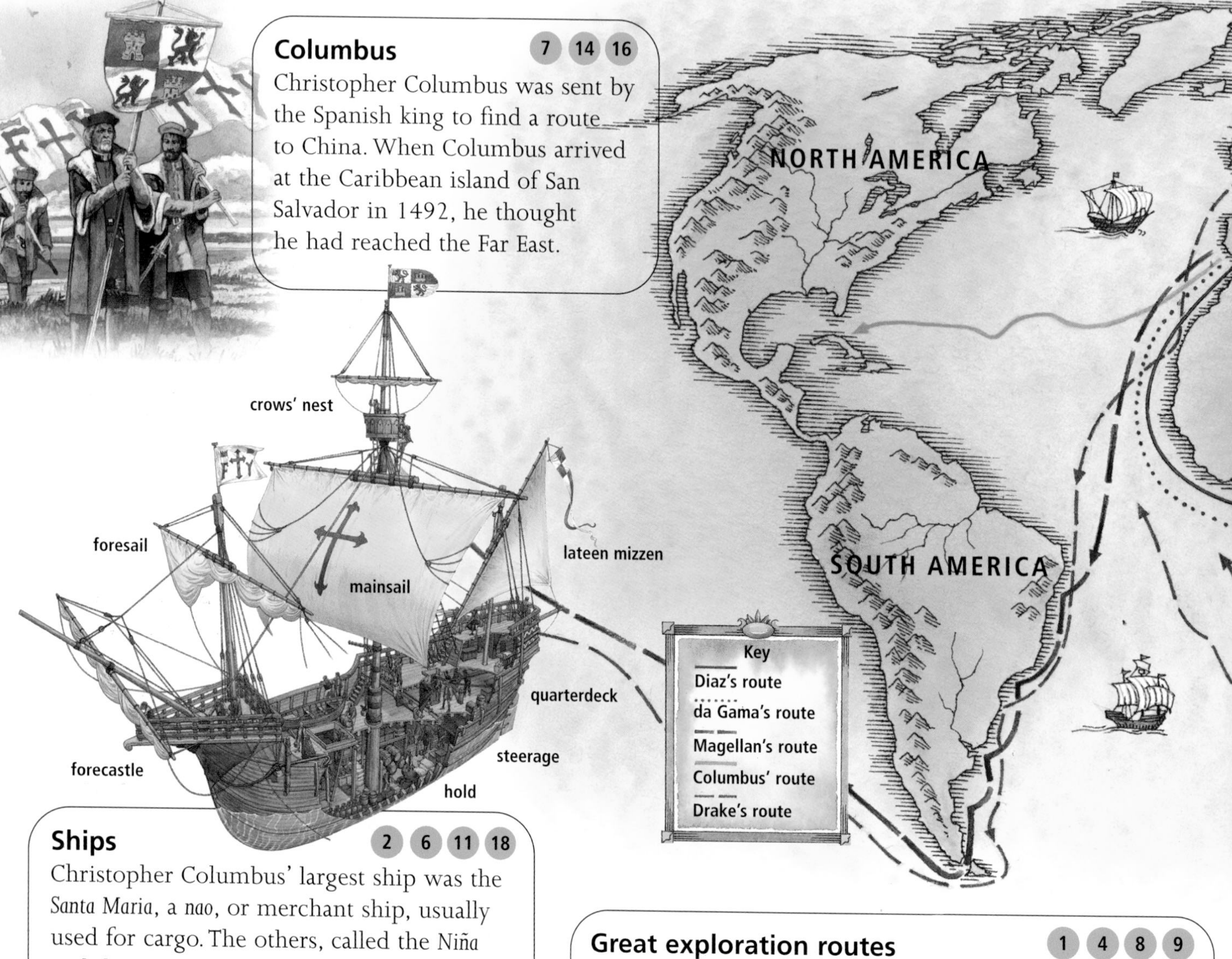

Columbus 7 14 16

Christopher Columbus was sent by the Spanish king to find a route to China. When Columbus arrived at the Caribbean island of San Salvador in 1492, he thought he had reached the Far East.

Ships 2 6 11 18

Christopher Columbus' largest ship was the *Santa Maria*, a *nao*, or merchant ship, usually used for cargo. The others, called the *Niña* and the *Pinta*, were caravels, which were much lighter ships. The *Santa Maria* held a crew of 40 men and had large square sails that gave it a lot of power at sea.

Great exploration routes 1 4 8 9

In 1488, Portuguese explorer Bartholomew Diaz sailed around the southern tip of Africa. In 1497–8, Vasco da Gama travelled to India. A century later, Sir Francis Drake, an Englishman, travelled around the world.

Pizarro (3) (15) (17)

The Spanish conquistador, Francisco Pizarro, conquered the Incas in 1532. The Incas ruled the western coast of South America, now Peru, from their capital at Cuzco. However, the Inca city of Machu Picchu, built high in the Andes mountains, was not discovered by outsiders until 1911.

EUROPE

ASIA

AFRICA

AUSTRALASIA

Magellan (5) (13) (19)

The Portuguese navigator Ferdinand Magellan discovered the Pacific ocean, but was later killed in the Philippines. His ship carried on to become the first to sail all the way round the world, in 1522.

QUESTIONS:
World War I

Level 1

1. What large machine was used for the first time in World War I?
2. What is a dogfight?
3. What was the area between enemy trenches called?
4. A grenade is a weapon. True or false?

Level 2

5. What kind of protection did soldiers have against gas?
6. For what purpose were horses used?
7. Which 'J' was a major battle fought at sea?
8. Where was the Western Front?
9. What name is used for a trained marksman who trys to pick off lone soldiers?
10. What weapon could be attached to a rifle?
11. How many lives were lost in the war: over 7.5 million, over 8.5 million or over 10 million?
12. In which country is Jutland?
13. What lined the tops of the trenches?
14. What weapons were fighter planes fitted with?

Level 3

15. In what year was poison gas first used?
16. Which model of tank was the first one strong enough to withstand anti-tank rifles?
17. What was the name given to the British soldiers who trained horses?
18. What German fighter plane was considered to be the best fighter plane of the war?

FIND THE ANSWER: World War I

World War I, often called 'The Great War', was thought to be the 'war to end all wars'. The war began with the assassination of Archduke Franz Ferdinand in 1914. The Central Powers of Germany, Bulgaria, Austro-Hungary and Turkey fought against the Allied forces, which included Britain, France and Russia, as well as a number of other countries. The war ended in 1918 when the Central Powers surrendered to the Allies.

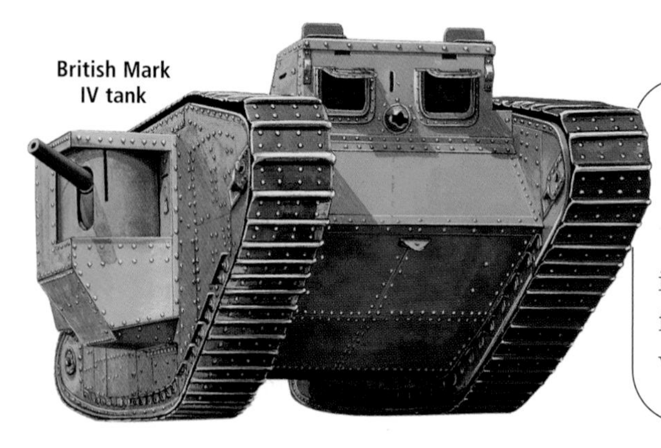

British Mark IV tank

Tanks (1) (16)

During WWI, tanks were used for the first time in battle. The British Mark IV, introduced in 1918, was the first tank strong enough to withstand anti-tank rifles.

Battle of Jutland (7) (12)

The largest sea battle fought during WWI occurred in the North sea near Jutland, Denmark. Both the Allies and the Central Powers claimed that they had won.

The Western Front (8) (11)

Fighting was fiercest in the trenches, built through Belgium and France and known as the Western Front. The war claimed over 8.5 million lives.

Trench warfare (3) (13)

Trench systems were made up of interconnecting dugouts. The land between the two opposing trenches was called 'no-man's-land'. The tops of the trenches were lined with sandbags to absorb enemy fire. Soldiers in the muddy, cold and unsanitary trenches suffered from trench foot, dysentery and body lice.

British Sopwith Camel

German Fokker D VII

War in the air

2 14 18

Dogfights were battles in the air between two or more aircraft, fitted with machine guns. The German Fokker D VII was considered to be the best fighter plane of the war.

Poison gas

5 15

Poison gas was used for the first time in 1915 at Ypres. Although soldiers had masks for protection, over 90,000 men died from the poison.

Horses

6 17

British soldiers called 'roughriders' trained tough horse breeds, such as the Australian Waler, to haul ambulances and weaponry.

soldier wearing gas mask

Snipers

9

Snipers were trained marksmen who looked for movement in the enemy trench, trying to pick off lone soldiers.

Weaponry

4 10

Grenades are bombs thrown by hand. Soldiers were also supplied with bayonets, short blades which could be attached to rifles. These were used in close combat.

QUESTIONS: Where in the world?

Level 1

1. What kind of ruler led the Chinese?
2. In which continent did the ancient Romans live?
3. What were Japanese warriors called?

Level 2

4. In which continent was the Shona empire?
5. Which European people settled in Argentina?
6. Where did the Iroquois live?
7. Which empire ruled Australia by 1829?

Level 3

8. For what is Mansa Musa famous?
9. What trading route did Chinese traders use to reach the West?
10. Which people were the first to use writing?

FIND THE ANSWER: Where in the world?

Every inhabited continent in the world has a rich history. Hunter gatherers moved from place to place in search of food and shelter until settlements were established. Great empires rose and fell. In the meantime, people lived, travelled, invented, built, fought wars and sought peace. They left behind great art, monuments and ways of thinking that are still fascinating today.

Asia
1 3 9

The Chinese were ruled by emperors. Powerful dynasties (successions of leaders from one family) were established. Chinese traders took goods along the Silk Road, a trading route to the West. In Japan, warriors called samurai ruled the land on behalf of their emperor.

North America
6

Before Europeans arrived, native American Indians like the Iroquois lived by hunting and farming. European settlers won their independence from the British in 1776 and formed the United States.

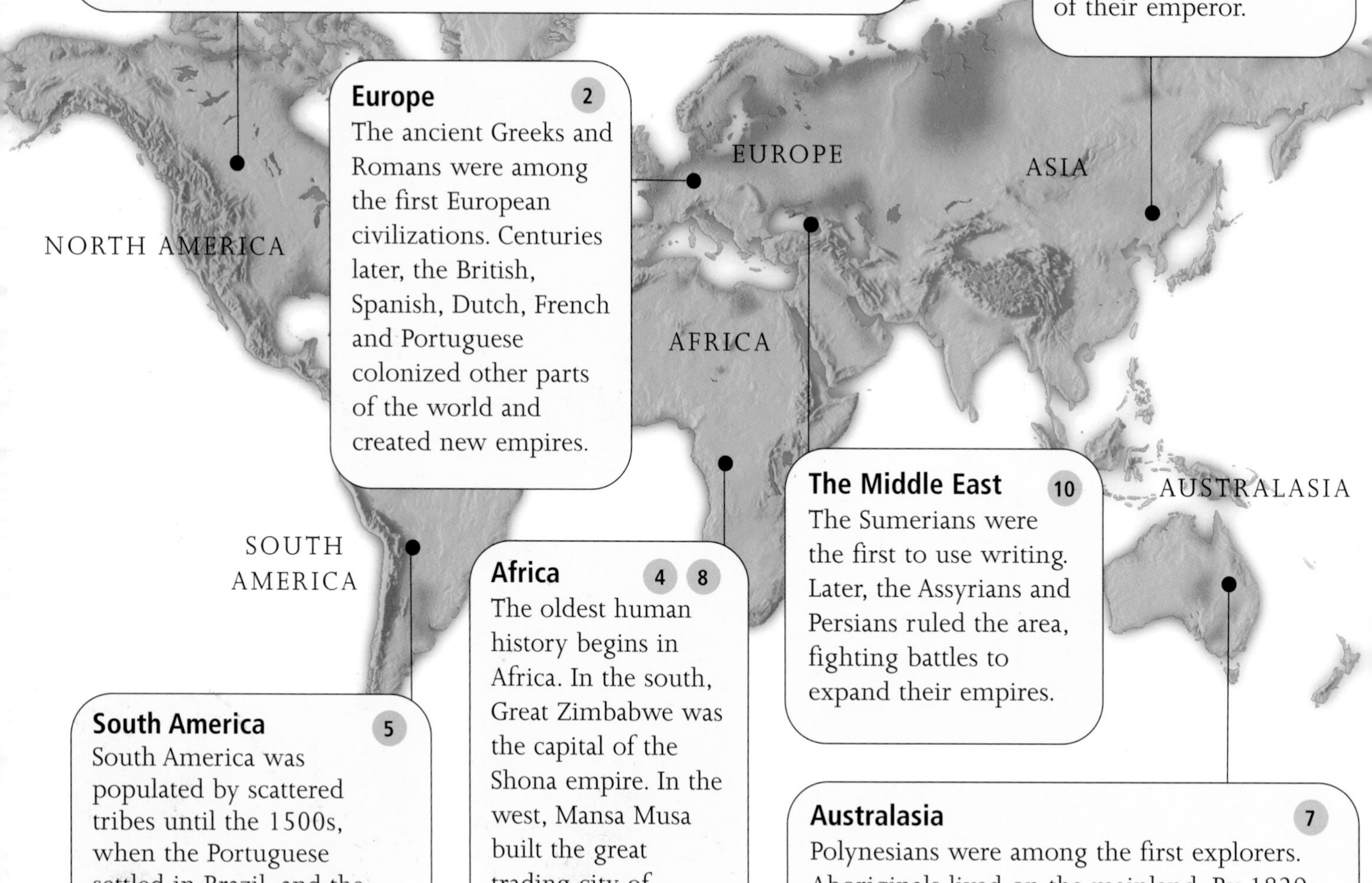

Europe
2

The ancient Greeks and Romans were among the first European civilizations. Centuries later, the British, Spanish, Dutch, French and Portuguese colonized other parts of the world and created new empires.

NORTH AMERICA

EUROPE

ASIA

AFRICA

SOUTH AMERICA

AUSTRALASIA

The Middle East
10

The Sumerians were the first to use writing. Later, the Assyrians and Persians ruled the area, fighting battles to expand their empires.

South America
5

South America was populated by scattered tribes until the 1500s, when the Portuguese settled in Brazil, and the Spaniards in Argentina.

Africa
4 8

The oldest human history begins in Africa. In the south, Great Zimbabwe was the capital of the Shona empire. In the west, Mansa Musa built the great trading city of Timbuktu in Mali.

Australasia
7

Polynesians were among the first explorers. Aboriginals lived on the mainland. By 1829, Australia was part of the British Empire.

Answers 1) An emperor **2)**Europe **3)**Samurai **4)**Africa **5)**The Spanish **6)**North America **7)**The British empire **8)**He built Timbuktu **9)**The Silk Road **10)**The Sumerians

QUIZ FIVE

Sport and art

Summer Olympics

Gymnastics

Winter sports

Football

Art and painting

Ballet

Architecture

Film and TV

QUESTIONS:

Summer Olympics

Level 1

1. How many rings are there in the Olympic symbol?
2. Which Olympic sport features a 5m-long springy pole?
3. How often are the summer Olympic games held?
4. Do equestrian events use a horse, a bicycle or a pistol?
5. Which kind of swimming race is longer: a sprint or an endurance race?

Level 2

6. Is a marathon race 20km, 42km or 50km long?
7. What is the name of a competitor in a judo fight?
8. Which horse-based sport takes three days to complete?
9. What is the name of the building in which track cyclists compete?
10. Who set a world record of 6.14m for the pole vault?
11. What is the longest distance race in track athletics at the Olympics?
12. How many Olympics has Jeannie Longo-Ciprelli appeared at: three, four or six?
13. In which sport did Mark Spitz win seven gold medals in 1972?

Level 3

14. How long is a steeplechase race at the Olympics?
15. When was judo first included in the Olympics?
16. How many lengths of the pool do swimmers in the 1,500m race have to swim?
17. How much shorter is a woman's judo bout than a man's?
18. What fraction of the total gold medals for judo did Japan win in 2004?

FIND THE ANSWER:

Summer Olympics

First held in 1896, the modern summer Olympic Games is the biggest multi-sports event in the world. The games are watched by hundreds of millions of people on television all around the world. Thousands of athletes compete in sports as varied as shooting, high diving and fencing. Their aim is to be the best in the world and win a highly prized gold medal.

Olympic flag 1

In 1913, the founder of the Olympics, Baron Pierre de Coubertin, unveiled the five-ring symbol of the Olympics.

Equestrian events 4 8

Equestrian events were introduced in 1912 for horses and riders. Horses race in show-jumping around a course of obstacles. Eventing is held over three days.

showjumping

Running 6 11 14

Track athletics includes all the running and racewalking events. The shortest is the 100m sprint. The longest are the 42km marathon and 50km racewalk. Runners jump over hurdles in 100m, 110m and 400m races. There are barriers to clear in the 3,000m steeplechase.

pistol shooting

running

swimming

Cycling 9 12

Events include mountain biking and track cycling in a velodrome. French woman Jeannie Longo-Ciprelli is famous for cycling in six Olympics.

Swimming 5 13 16

In the 50m-long Olympic swimming pool the events range from 50m sprints to 1,500m endurance races. The US swimmer Mark Spitz won seven gold medals for swimming at the 1972 games.

Hosts

(3)

Every four years, cities bid for the right to host the summer Olympics. Sydney, Australia, staged the 2000 games, and Athens, Greece, the 2004 games. In 2008, they will be held in Beijing, China, and in 2012, London, UK.

an Olympic stadium

pole vaulting

fencing

Pole vaulting

(2) (10)

Pole vaulters use a springy pole, around 5m long, to soar through the air and clear a bar. Top pole vaulters can clear over 5m. The men's world record of 6.14m is held by Ukrainian, Sergei Bubka.

Judo

(7) (15) (17) (18)

The Japanese martial art of judo, which means 'gentle way', first appeared in the Olympics in 1964. Two competitors, or judokas, fight in bouts of four (women's) or five (men's) minutes. In 2004, Japan won 8 of 16 gold medals for judo.

judo

QUESTIONS: Gymnastics

Level 1

1. When do athletes warm up?
2. What are people who perform gymnastics called?
3. How many handles does a pommel horse have?
4. Are rings used only by men, or by both men and women?
5. What do some athletes dust their hands with to help with their grip?

Level 2

6. In gymnastics, how many events do female athletes compete in?
7. Did rhythmic gymnastics first appear in the Olympics in 1932, 1968 or 1984?
8. How many items of equipment are there in rhythmic gymnastics?
9. Was the first person to get the highest possible score in artistic gymnastics at the Olympics a man or a woman?
10. What is the highest possible mark given to a competitor for one routine: 10, 15 or 20?
11. What 'H' is a piece of rhythmic gymnastics equipment?
12. What are the two hoops hanging above the ground called?
13. What kind of gymnastics is performed to music?
14. How many panels of judges mark rhythmic gymnastics?

Level 3

15. How high are the parallel bars?
16. Who was the first person to get the highest possible score in artistic gymnastics at the Olympics?
17. Who invented the parallel bars?
18. From which gymnastics apparatus would a gymnast dismount?

FIND THE ANSWER:

Gymnastics

Gymnastics is a sport in which people perform a series of movements that require strength, balance and flexibility. Artistic gymnasts perform moves on apparatus such as the parallel bars, rings and the pommel horse. Rhythmic gymnastics is a combination of gymnastics moves and dance.

Pommel horse

2 3 18

The pommel horse has two handles on top. The gymnast (someone who performs gymnastics) carries out a series of swinging moves, before leaving the pommel horse and landing. This is called the dismount.

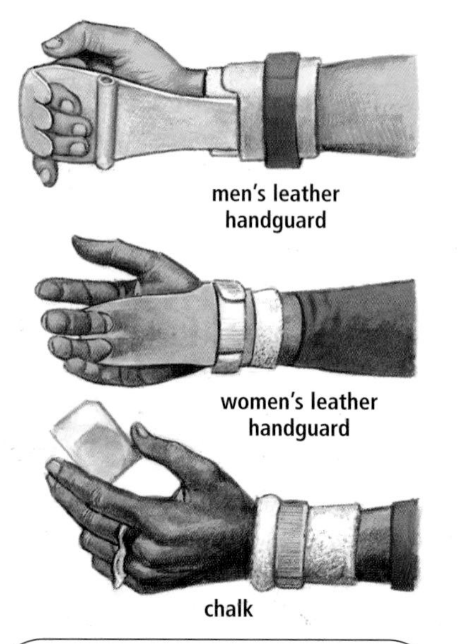

asymmetric bars
balance beam
pommel horse
floor mat
vaulting horse
horizontal bar
the rings
scoreboards
parallel bars
judges

Get a grip

5

Many gymnasts dust their hands with chalk, which helps them get a strong grip on the apparatus they are using. Some also wear leather hand protectors to prevent sprains and injuries.

Rings

4 12

This event is only for male gymnasts. The athlete swings on two rings, which hang 2.75m from a mat on the floor. They need great strength to perform their moves on the rings.

Judging

6 9 10 16

In artistic gymnastics, men are judged in six events, and women in four. In 1976, Nadia Comaneci became the first to achieve the highest score of ten.

Rhythmic gymnastics 7 13 14

Rhythmic gymnasts have been perfoming in the Olympics since 1984. Their routines are performed to music, last between 60 and 120 seconds and are marked by three panels of judges.

Equipment 8 11

Rhythmic gymnasts use five pieces of equipment in their routines: a pair of clubs, a ribbon, a rope, a ball and a hoop.

Parallel bars 15 17

Invented by Friedrich Jahn, the two flexible parallel bars stand 1.75m high and between 42–52cm apart. They are used by male gymnasts, who swing, then perform handstands and one-arm moves on them.

Warming up 1

Gymnasts always warm up before competing. The warm-up stretches their muscles so they perform their best, and helps prevent injuries from occurring.

QUESTIONS: Winter sports

Level 1

1. How many skis does a skier wear?
2. Do speed skaters race downhill, round a track or along a road?
3. Which country invented ice hockey?
4. Which is also known as cross-country skiing: Nordic or downhill?
5. What name is given to someone who teaches others to ski?

Level 2

6. In which winter sport do players try to hit a puck into a goal?
7. What is the front of a snowboard called?
8. Downhill skiing is part of the Winter Olympics. True or false?
9. What is the name of the sticks held in the hands of a skier?
10. In which winter sport can competitors reach a speed of 60km/h as they race around a track?
11. Are there six, nine or 11 players per side in ice hockey?
12. Do Nordic or slalom skiers race a zigzagging course?
13. What is the back of a snowboard called?
14. How many periods are there in an ice hockey game?
15. The biathlon involves rifle shooting and what sort of skiing?
16. In what year did snowboarding become an Olympic sport?

Level 3

17. Which can travel the fastest: speed skaters or downhill skiers?
18. What object fixes ski boots to skis?
19. Which skis are shorter and wider: Nordic skis or downhill skis?
20. What is the name of the player who guards a goal in ice hockey?

FIND THE ANSWER:

Winter sports

downhill skier in action

Winter sports all involve snow or ice, and sometimes both. They can be lots of fun to try out, and most are also competitive sports. Many winter sports, such as skiing and skating, have developed out of people's need to travel through snow and ice. People have been ice skating, for example, for over 3,000 years.

Downhill skiing

8 12 17

Downhill skiing is one of the most exciting sports in the winter Olympics. Skiers can sometimes reach speeds of over 130km/h in competition. Slalom skiing is a version of downhill skiing. Competitors must zigzag around a course as fast as possible.

Learning to ski

1 5 9 18

Millions of people learn to ski every year on gentle ski slopes or artificial dry slopes. Teachers are called ski instructors. Skiers wear special boots, which attach to their two skis with clips called bindings. They use ski poles to push themselves forwards.

Nordic skiing

4 15 19

Nordic, or cross-country, skiers travel long distances across gentle slopes and level surfaces. They use skis that are longer and narrower than downhill ones. In competitions, a top skier may complete a 15km course in less than 50 minutes. Some Nordic skiers also take part in the biathlon, which combines Nordic skiing and rifle shooting.

Nordic skiing in Finland

Snowboarding (7) (13) (16)

Snowboarding became an Olympic sport in 1998. In freestyle snowboarding riders perform tricks similar to skateboarding. They press down on the back or tail of the board to lift the front or nose, and perform jumps and other exciting moves.

a snowboarder performs a trick

Ice hockey (3) (6) (11) (14) (20)

Ice hockey was invented in Canada. The six-a-side teams skate on the ice and score points by hitting a puck past the goaltender into a goal. Ice hockey is played in three 20-minute-long periods.

Speed skating (2) (10) (17)

Skating can be fun – and a serious sport. Speed skaters race around icy tracks at speeds of 60km/h. Figure skaters are judged on their routines of skating moves.

skating in a city park

QUESTIONS: Football

Level 1

1. What is the name given to the players who try to score goals?
2. Which player is allowed to touch the ball with their hands?
3. The warning card is yellow. True or false?
4. Challenging for the ball is known as passing, throwing in or tackling?
5. What is a football pitch usually made of?

Level 2

6. For what country did Pelé play?
7. Who has scored over 100 goals for his country: Wayne Rooney, Michael Ballack or Ali Daei?
8. What is the person in charge of a football match called?
9. How often did Pelé help win the World Cup?
10. How many players are in a football team?
11. What colour is the card that means the player is sent off the pitch?
12. In which city were the first full rules of football created?
13. Did Pelé score 478, 809 or 1,281 goals in his career?
14. Does Cristiano Ronaldo play for Portugal, France or Brazil?

Level 3

15. Which of the following parts of the body can a footballer use to control the ball: head, chest, arms, thigh, hands?
16. For what country did Ali Daei play?
17. What animal's bladder was used to make early footballs?
18. Which American woman has scored 158 goals for her country?

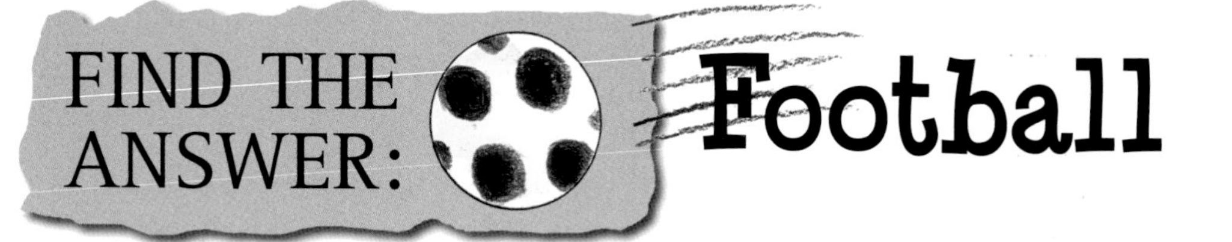

Association football (also known as soccer) is an exciting team sport played with a round ball. It is the most popular team sport in the world with tens of millions of players and fans. The sport's biggest competition is the FIFA World Cup, which is held every four years.

the opposing team's goal

attacker

defender

football pitch

midfielder

goalkeeper

footballer

First matches (12)

Games that involve kicking a ball have been played since ancient times. In some countries mob football was played between rival villages. The first full rules were drawn up in London, UK, in the 19th century.

The pitch (1) (5) (10)

Football is played on a grass pitch. The 11 players a side include defenders, midfielders, attackers (who score goals) and a goalkeeper.

Ball control (2) (15)

A player can use any part of his body, other than his hands and arms, to control the ball. Only the goalkeeper can touch the ball with his hands. Players mainly use their feet to move the ball.

The ball (14) (17)

Early footballs were made of a pig's bladder with a leather casing. Today, footballs are lighter and can be swerved in the air by players like Portugal's Cristiano Ronaldo.

Tackling (4) (11)

Tackling is when one player challenges another for the ball. If a player makes an unfair tackle, the referee shows him a red card and sends him off.

Scoring a goal

7 16 18

To score a goal, a team must get the whole of the ball over their opponent's goal line. Iran's Ali Daei was the first male player to score over 100 goals for his country. Female striker Mia Hamm scored 158 goals for the USA during her career.

attacker
goalkeeper
defender
defender
attacker

Celebrating

3 8

Players celebrate after scoring a goal. But if this goes on too long, the referee, who is in charge of the match, may show a yellow warning card for time-wasting.

Street football

6 9 13

All over the world, children enjoy games of football on the streets. The great Brazilian player, Pelé, began playing street football as a child. As an adult his team won the World Cup three times and he scored 1,281 goals himself.

QUESTIONS:
Art and painting

Level 1

1. The famous artist Michelangelo came from Italy. True or false?
2. What was Van Gogh's first name?
3. In what country are the famous Lascaux cave paintings?
4. Were sculptures, cave paintings or frescoes made on damp plaster?
5. The Lascaux cave paintings feature paintings of reindeer. True or false?

Level 2

6. What part of an egg was used by prehistoric cave painters?
7. Can you name either of the colours that were often used by the ancient Greeks to decorate their pottery?
8. Do artists painting frescoes have to work slowly or quickly?
9. Does tempera or oil paint produce richer colours?
10. Did Michelangelo paint a fresco on the doors, the walls or the ceiling of the Sistine Chapel?
11. From what was Michelangelo's sculpture of Moses carved?
12. Does oil paint or tempera paint dry more slowly?
13. What part of an egg was used to make tempera paints?

Level 3

14. *Blam!* is a famous Pop Art painting. Who painted it?
15. In what century did Michelangelo carve a sculpture of Moses?
16. How old was Van Gogh when he painted *Starry Night?*
17. In which decade did Pop Art first appear?
18. Are the prehistoric paintings in the Lascaux caves around 15,000, 16,000 or 17,000 years old?

Art and painting

Art is any piece of creative work that is used to portray images and express feelings. People have been making art for tens of thousands of years. Art is produced in many different forms, including photography, drawing and sculpture. Painting is one type of art that has been performed for at least 30,000 years.

Cave painting

3 5 18

The most famous early paintings were discovered in 1940 in the Lascaux caves in France. The lifelike animal paintings include horses, reindeer, oxen and bulls. They are about 17,000 years old.

Mixing paints

6 13

Prehistoric people made their own paints out of natural ingredients, such as earth, blood, plant juices and egg white. From about the 2nd century, artists began making 'tempera' paint by mixing pigments with egg yolk.

Oil painting

9 12

In the Renaissance (mid 1300s-1500s), painters crushed up coloured minerals and mixed them with oil to make oil paints. Oil paints produce richer colours and dry more slowly than tempera.

Decorative arts

7

Decorative arts include furniture, pottery, jewellery, metalware and glassware. Many civilizations have produced beautiful works of decorative art. The ancient Greeks, for example, were famous for their pottery. The pots were often painted in red or black with pictures of Greek heroes.

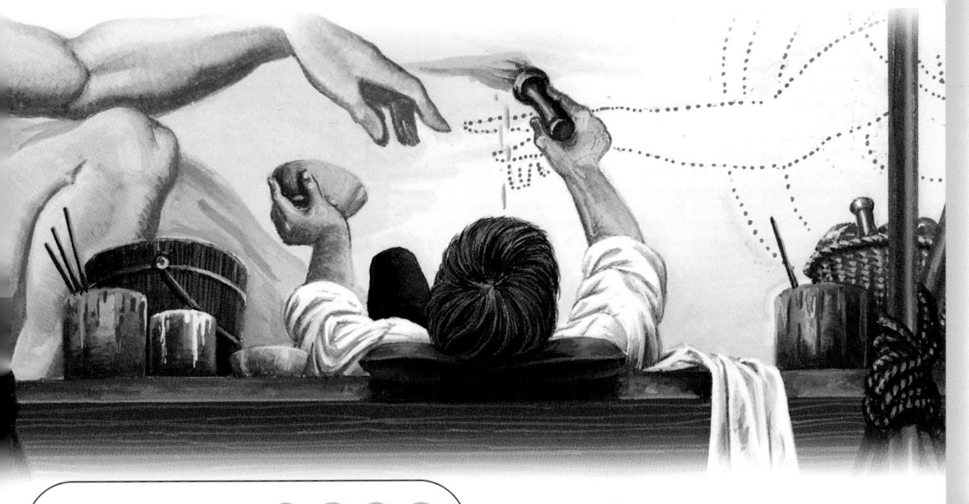

Frescoes

1 4 8 10

A fresco is a painting which is made on the damp plaster of a building. The plaster dries quickly, so the artist has to work fast. The Italian artist Michelangelo (1475–1564) painted a famous fresco on the ceiling of the Sistine Chapel in the Vatican in Rome, Italy.

Sculpture

11 15

A sculpture is a three-dimensional artistic work. Sculptures are made by carving stone, wood or other material. This marble sculpture of Moses was carved by Michelangelo in about 1513.

Van Gogh

2 16

The artist Vincent Van Gogh (1853–90) painted *Starry Night* (right) in 1889. He was famous for his expressive use of colour.

Pop Art

14 17

In the 1950s and 1960s Pop Art became fashionable. On the left is *Blam!* by the American artist Roy Lichtenstein (1923–97).

QUESTIONS: Ballet

Level 1

1. Do most ballet dancers start as children, teenagers or adults?
2. Do ballets take place in a rink, a court or in a theatre?
3. Do male ballet dancers wear make-up?
4. Is a tutu a ballet shoe, a skirt or a type of ballet move?

Level 2

5. What sort of musician often plays during ballet classes?
6. In *Swan Lake*, what part of the body does a ballerina move to look like wings?
7. Before a show, where do dancers put on their make-up?
8. A *port de bras* exercise involves the movement of what part of the body?
9. How many basic positions are there for the feet in ballet?
10. The heels touch together in which position: first, second or third?
11. ASK LAWNE can be rearranged to give the name of what ballet?
12. Why do dancers wear leg warmers when they practise?
13. What term means dancing on the tips of the toes?
14. In a ballet what is the break between acts called?
15. A major ballet may need as many as 30, 300 or 3,000 costumes?

Level 3

16. Which country does the ballet *Swan Lake* come from?
17. What term means the leading female dancer in a ballet company?
18. What 'O' is the queen of the swans in *Swan Lake*?

FIND THE ANSWER:

Ballet

Ballet is a type of dance full of graceful and artistic movements. These are usually set to music and tell a story. Ballet began in Europe in the 16th and 17th centuries. Famous ballets include *The Nutcracker* and *The Sleeping Beauty*.

leg warmers

hairspray

hair grips

wrapover cardigan

ballet shoes

The ballerina 6 11 16 17 18

Prima Ballerina means 'first dancer' in Italian. It is the name given to the leading female dancer in a ballet company. This dancer is playing the lead part in the Russian ballet, *Swan Lake*. As Odette, the queen of the swans, she stretches her neck and moves her arms to look like wings.

Clothing 12

Ballet dancers wear special clothes when they practise. Leg warmers and a wrapover cardigan help keep their muscles warm, preventing strains and injuries.

Positions 9 10

Ballet dancers are taught five basic positions for their feet. In first position, the feet are turned out, with the two heels touching.

ballerina in a tutu

Practise 1 5 8

Most ballet dancers start classes when they are children. They learn the basic steps to music. Often a class has a pianist to play the music. The students in the class (left) are practising moving their arms in a *port de bras* exercise.

Make-up 3 7

Under strong stage lights, the features of a ballet dancer's face tend to disappear. So to make sure the audience can see them, male and female dancers wear make-up. Dancers do their hair and make-up in a dressing room.

ballerina applying her make-up

modern costume

Costume 4 13 15

Costumes can be traditional or modern. Many feature a pleated skirt called a tutu. A major ballet may need up to 300 costumes. A ballerina wears pointe shoes, which allow her to do pointe-work (dancing on the tips of her toes). They are kept in place using long ribbons.

Curtain up 2 14

A major performance of a ballet takes place in a theatre. Often a full orchestra led by a conductor provides the music. A ballet is usually divided up into sections called acts, with short breaks called intervals in between each act.

QUESTIONS: Architecture

Level 1

1. Who built the Parthenon: the Greeks, Egyptians or Romans?
2. What is the name given to the giant buildings used to bury leaders (pharaohs) in ancient Egypt?
3. Were the first bricks made of mud and clay, or cement and gravel?
4. Are the pyramids of ancient Egypt made of mud, wood or stone?
5. Were the first bricks made solid by setting them on fire, letting them dry in the sun or freezing them?

Level 2

6. Which civilization invented concrete?
7. Was the Parthenon built of granite, cement or marble?
8. In which city is the Parthenon?
9. Why does Hardwick Hall have lots of windows?
10. Did the White House get water pipes or gas lighting installed first?
11. Did the Gothic style of architecture begin in Europe, Asia or Africa?
12. What is the name of the wooden strips that are filled in with daub?
13. Who built Hardwick Hall?

Level 3

14. What are the architect's detailed plans for a building called?
15. Which famous building did James Hoban rebuild?
16. The Parthenon was a temple for the worship of which goddess?
17. What is a flying buttress?
18. During which century did Gothic architecture first appear?

FIND THE ANSWER: Architecture

Egyptian pyramids

Architecture is the art of designing buildings and structures, such as bridges, houses and temples. Each building has its own purpose, but all architects aim for their buildings to last a long time, and to look good. Architects from different civilizations and historical eras have found many different ways of achieving this.

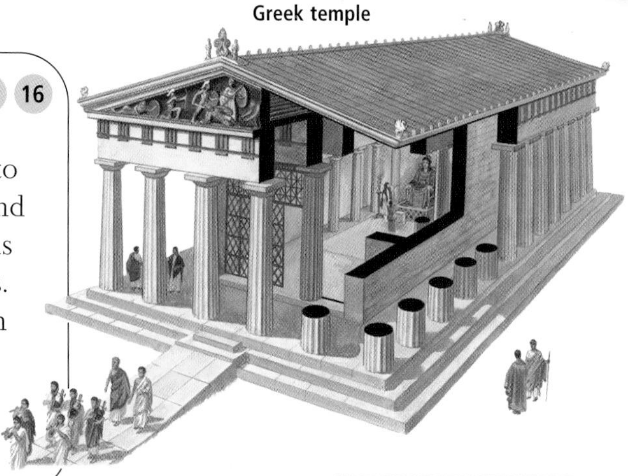

Greek temple

Parthenon 1 7 8 16

The ancient Greeks used stone and marble to build beautiful pillars and structures. An example is the Parthenon in Athens. It was built of marble in the 5th century BCE as a temple to the Greek goddess Athena.

Pyramids 2 4

The ancient Egyptians built enormous burial pyramids for their leaders (pharaohs). The largest of these, the Great Pyramid at Giza, was built over 4,500 years ago. It is made up of more than two million large stone blocks, each weighing two and a half tonnes.

Walls 12

In timber-framed buildings wooden strips called wattles formed a frame, filled in with daub – a mixture of straw, mud and dung.

Building materials 3 5

Over the years people have built with stone, wood, straw, leaves and grasses. The first bricks were made of mud and clay. These were left to dry and set hard in the sun.

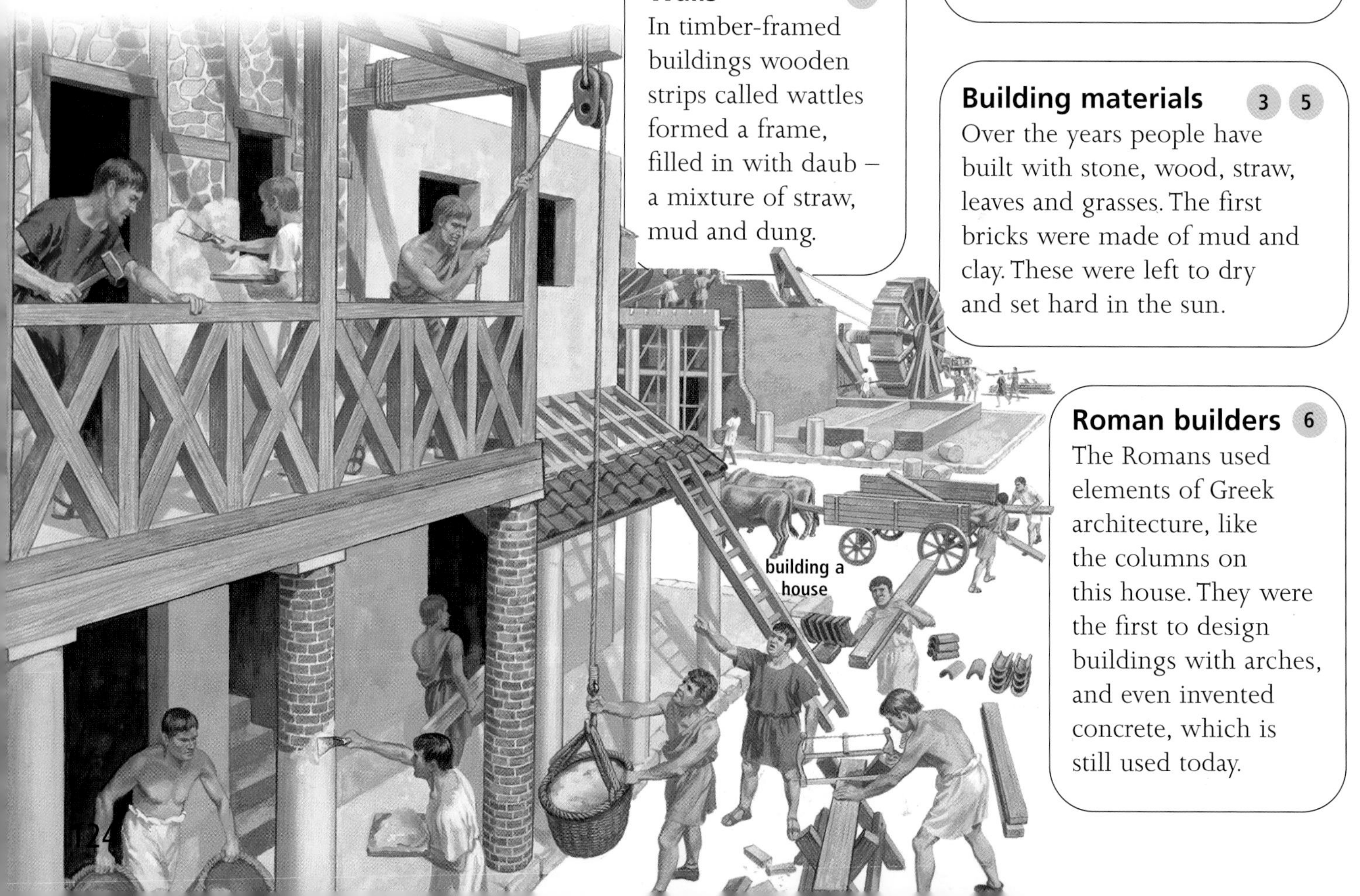

Roman builders 6

The Romans used elements of Greek architecture, like the columns on this house. They were the first to design buildings with arches, and even invented concrete, which is still used today.

building a house

Church buildings (11) (17) (18)

A style of architecture called 'Gothic' was used for many churches in Europe between 1140 and 1500. A special side-support, called a flying buttress, allowed architects to build churches with very thin walls and large windows.

Stately homes (9) (13)

A big house showed how rich and powerful a person was. Hardwick Hall in the UK, built by Bess of Hardwick, has lots of windows – a sign of wealth in the days when glass was very expensive.

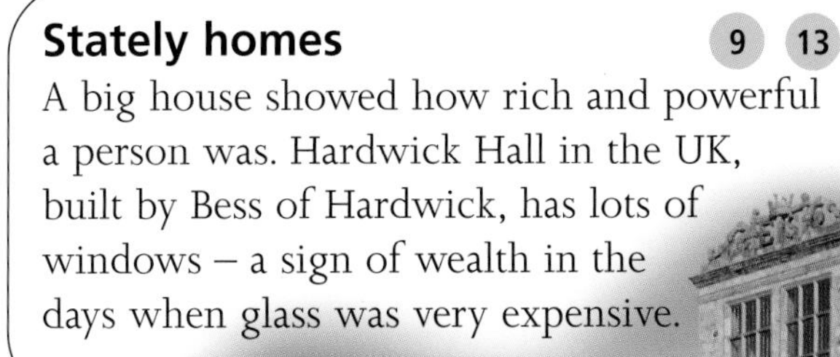

Hardwick Hall

The White House (10) (15)

The White House in Washington DC, USA, was started in 1792. It was burned down in 1814 but rebuilt by the architect James Hoban. Water pipes were fitted in 1833, followed by gas lighting (1848), a lift (1881) and electricity (1891).

Architects' plans (14)

Architects produce drawings and plans of their work to discuss with clients (the people paying them to build). Modern building plans are called blueprints.

QUESTIONS: Film and TV

Level 1

1. Were the first TV broadcasts black and white or colour?
2. What 'D' is the person in charge of the film-making process?
3. What name is given to someone who interviews people for the news?
4. What word describes people who play characters and appear in films?
5. What word describes the written-down version of a film?

Level 2

6. Who are the three people needed in a news team?
7. What word describes news reporting that is transmitted as the events unfold?
8. Was the first film with sound *Casablanca*, *The Jazz Singer* or *Snow White*?
9. WOOLY HOLD can be rearranged to give the name of what huge film industry based in the USA?
10. Near which big American city is this industry located?
11. What nickname is given to India's film industry?
12. What name is given to 24-hour news programmes?

Level 3

13. Was Telstar the name of an early television or a satellite?
14. In what year was the first 'talking' film made?
15. In 1962, what percentage of US homes had a television?
16. In what year was the first TV signal sent by satellite?
17. What word is used for sending programmes out from the TV station?
18. Which Asian country has one of the largest film industries in the world?

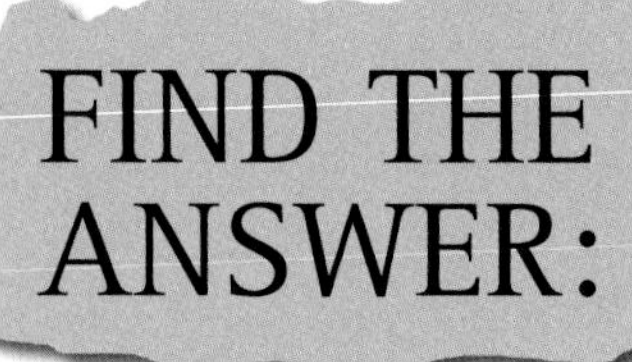

Film and TV

A film is made up of a number of photos, called frames, which are shown in a fast sequence to create moving images. Films are shown using projectors at cinemas, or they can be recorded on to videos or DVDs. Films can also be sent (transmitted) through the air or by a cable to people's television sets at home.

Film crew (8) (14)

Dozens of people work on the set of a film. Some help with the costumes, others build the scenery or operate equipment. To start with, films had no sound. The first 'talking' film with sound was *The Jazz Singer* in 1927.

Director (2) (4) (5)

The person in charge of making a film is the director. The director works with the written-down version of the film (the script) and the people who play characters in the film (the actors).

Sets (9) (10) (11) (18)

A set is where a film is shot. It can be indoors or outside. Hollywood, near Los Angeles, USA, and Mumbai, in India are home to the world's two largest film industries. India's film industry is sometimes nicknamed Bollywood.

lighting crew

cameraman

actors

News 6 7

'Live' news reporting is transmitted as the events unfold. A news team may be just three people: a reporter, a cameraman and a sound recordist.

Reporting 3 12

A reporter is the person who interviews people for the news. Some television stations offer 24-hour news programmes, known as rolling news.

Studio 17

Many TV shows are filmed in a studio. A television camera uses a sensitive electronic tube to change light into electrical signals. These are then sent out to people's homes by transmitters. Sending out a programme is known as broadcasting.

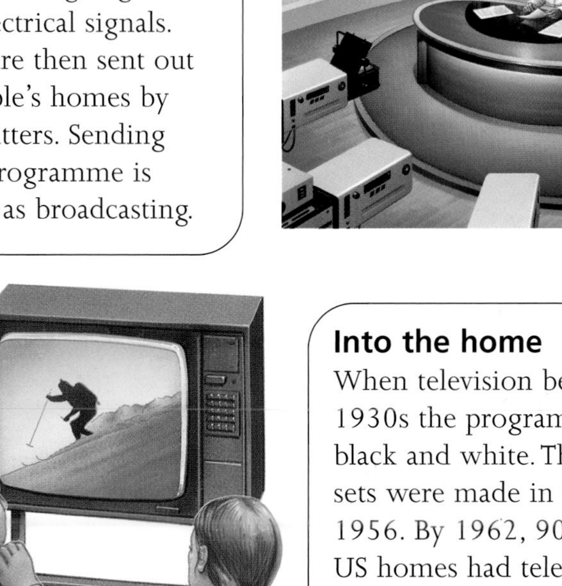

Into the home 1 13 15 16

When television began in the 1930s the programmes were in black and white. The first colour sets were made in the USA in 1956. By 1962, 90 per cent of US homes had television sets. In the same year the first TV signal was sent by a satellite called Telstar. Today, many homes have satellite or cable television.

ANSWERS

Did you get it right? Now you have finished your *Quiz Quest*, you can turn over to find the answers. Remember, with the help of a friend, you can also use the answer section for a quick quiz. Why not take it in turns, and see who gets the most right?

ANSWERS: The rainforest

Level 1

1. Are frogs reptiles or amphibians?
   Answer: Amphibians
2. Are reptiles cold-blooded or warm-blooded?
   Answer: Cold-blooded
3. What 'A' is the world's largest river?
   Answer: The Amazon
4. How often does it usually rain in the rainforest: daily, weekly or monthly?
   Answer: Daily

Level 2

5. In which continent does the cinchona tree grow?
   Answer: South America
6. What type of animal is a boa?
   Answer: A snake
7. Which plant has the largest flower in the world?
   Answer: Rafflesia
8. In which part of the rainforest do most of its animals live?
   Answer: The canopy
9. What do pitcher plants feed on?
   Answer: Insects
10. What does the flower of the rafflesia plant smell like?
    Answer: Rotten meat
11. GREEN STEM can be rearranged to give the name of which group of tall trees?
    Answer: Emergents
12. Where in the world do poison dart frogs live?
    Answer: South America
13. Is a bromeliad an animal or a plant?
    Answer: A plant
14. A poison dart frog's skin has enough poison to kill a person. True or false?
    Answer: True
15. Where does the Atlas moth live?
    Answer: Southeast Asia

Level 3

16. Are snakes more closely related to frogs or lizards?
    Answer: Lizards
17. How wide is the Amazon river at its mouth: more than 300km, more than 400km or more than 500km?
    Answer: More than 300km
18. What illness is treated with quinine?
    Answer: Malaria
19. What part of geckos' bodies gives them grip?
    Answer: Their toes
20. Where do the plants known as epiphytes grow?
    Answer: On other plants

ANSWERS: Ants

Level 1

1. Which have the stronger mandibles (jaws): worker or soldier ants?
   Answer: Soldier ants
2. What 'Q' is the large ant that lays all the eggs in a colony?
   Answer: The queen
3. Are aphids worms or insects?
   Answer: They are insects
4. Are wood ants bigger or smaller than most other ants?
   Answer: They are bigger

Level 2

5. Are there any ants that bring aphids into their nests?
   Answer: Yes
6. Most ants build nests underground. True or false?
   Answer: True
7. What do aphids feed on?
   Answer: Plant sap
8. What is the name of the sugary substance that aphids produce?
   Answer: Honeydew
9. Are honeypot ants most common in dry or wet places?
   Answer: They are most common in dry places
10. Do leaf-cutter ants live in warm or cold forests?
    Answer: They live in warm forests
11. Do wood ants ever bite people?
    Answer: Yes
12. What type of substance can some ants fire at attackers?
    Answer: Acid
13. What do wood ants build their nests from?
    Answer: Pine needles
14. Do ants ever attack birds?
    Answer: Yes

Level 3

15. Do leaf-cutter ants eat the leaves that they harvest?
    Answer: No
16. How many different types of ant are there in a colony?
    Answer: Three (queen, worker and soldier ants)
17. What does the word metamorphose mean?
    Answer: Change shape
18. In what kind of forest do most wood ants live?
    Answer: Pine forest
19. Do all of the workers in a honeypot ant colony store food in their bodies?
    Answer: No
20. Name a continent in which both honeypot and leaf-cutter ants live.
    Answer: North or South America

ANSWERS: Dinosaurs

Level 1

1. What did *Spinosaurus* have on its back: wings or a sail?
   Answer: A sail
2. What 'S' was the largest stegosaur?
   Answer: Stegosaurus
3. Which dinosaur had plates on its back: *Kentrosaurus* or *Tyrannosaurus rex?*
   Answer: Kentrosaurus
4. Which had larger teeth: plant-eating or meat-eating dinosaurs?
   Answer: Meat-eating dinosaurs

Level 2

5. *Tyrannosaurus rex* teeth could be more than 10cm long. True or false?
   Answer: True
6. Do fossils take thousands or millions of years to form?
   Answer: Millions of years
7. Did sauropods have long necks or short necks?
   Answer: They had long necks
8. Did any dinosaurs have beaks?
   Answer: Yes
9. What did *Styracosaurus* have on its nose?
   Answer: A horn
10. What did male horned dinosaurs probably use their horns for, apart from defence?
    Answer: To fight each other
11. Which are more common: scattered fossil bones or entire fossil skeletons?
    Answer: Scattered fossil bones
12. What type of dinosaur was *Kentrosaurus?*
    Answer: A stegosaur
13. How did a *Spinosaurus* cool down?
    Answer: By pumping blood into its sail
14. Where can you see dinosaur bones on display?
    Answer: At a museum

Level 3

15. What did *Tyrannosaurus rex* eat?
    Answer: Meat
16. Which was bigger: *Seismosaurus* or *Stegosaurus?*
    Answer: Seismosaurus
17. Are fossils made of bone or of minerals from rock?
    Answer: Minerals from rock
18. *Styracosaurus* ate meat. True or false?
    Answer: False
19. Is an *Apatosaurus* more closely related to a *Seismosaurus* or a *Styracosaurus?*
    Answer: Apatosaurus *and* Seismosaurus *are related*
20. How many rows of plates did most stegosaurs have?
    Answer: Two

ANSWERS: Snakes

Level 1

1. Are pythons snakes?
   Answer: Yes
2. Do snakes have legs?
   Answer: No
3. Can snakes see?
   Answer: Yes

Level 2

4. Are there any snakes that eat eggs?
   Answer: Yes
5. Which snakes have a hood that they raise when threatened?
   Answer: Cobras
6. Where is a rattlesnake's rattle: in its mouth or on the end of its tail?
   Answer: On the end of its tail
7. Are snakes vertebrates or invertebrates?
   Answer: Vertebrates
8. What are snakes' skeletons made from?
   Answer: Bone
9. Do snakes' eggs have hard or flexible shells?
   Answer: Flexible shells
10. Are there any snakes that give birth to live young?
    Answer: Yes
11. Rattlesnakes live in Africa. True or false?
    Answer: False
12. Do cobras have solid or hollow fangs?
    Answer: Hollow fangs
13. Do anacondas grow to over 50cm long, over 3m long or over 8m long?
    Answer: Over 8m long
14. Does camouflage make a snake harder or easier to see?
    Answer: Harder to see

Level 3

15. What does a baby snake have on its snout to help it hatch?
    Answer: An egg tooth
16. Why do snakes flick their tongues in and out?
    Answer: To taste the air
17. How do snakes move?
    Answer: By rippling muscles on the underside of their bodies
18. How do pythons kill their prey?
    Answer: By constriction (squeezing)
19. What does the African egg-eating snake use to break eggs?
    Answer: Spines sticking down from its backbone

ANSWERS: Sharks

Level 1

1. Are sharks fish or reptiles?
Answer: Fish
2. The whale shark is the world's biggest fish. True or false?
Answer: True
3. Do great white sharks eat lions or sea lions?
Answer: Sea lions
4. Is a shark's egg case called a mermaid's purse or a sailor's purse?
Answer: A mermaid's purse

Level 2

5. Do sharks have the same set of teeth all their lives?
Answer: No
6. Do basking sharks live in warmer or cooler waters than whale sharks?
Answer: Cooler
7. The biggest great white sharks can grow up to 6m long. True or false?
Answer: True
8. What is the name given to the tiny sea creatures that are food for whale sharks?
Answer: Plankton
9. Which is bigger: the basking or the great white shark?
Answer: The basking shark
10. HE MADE HARM can be rearranged to give the name of which type of shark?
Answer: Hammerhead
11. How heavy can a whale shark be: 11 tonnes, 21 tonnes or 31 tonnes?
Answer: 21 tonnes
12. Do all sharks lay eggs?
Answer: No, some give birth to live young
13. The teeth of an individual shark are all the same shape. True or false?
Answer: True
14. Which shark is more likely to attack people: the great white or the hammerhead?
Answer: The great white
15. Do sharks ever resort to cannibalism (eating each other)?
Answer: Yes

Level 3

16. What feature of a hammerhead makes it easier to follow a scent trail in the water?
Answer: Its widely spaced nostrils
17. What is the largest type of fish seen off the UK?
Answer: The basking shark
18. What is the largest shark to actively hunt prey?
Answer: The great white

ANSWERS: Sea creatures

Level 1

1. How many tentacles does an octopus have?
Answer: Eight
2. Most of a jellyfish's body is made up of air. True or false?
Answer: False
3. What does SCUBA equipment help people to do?
Answer: Breathe underwater
4. Are seahorses fish or molluscs?
Answer: Fish

Level 2

5. What is the world's largest species of ray?
Answer: The manta ray
6. Are there more than 100 types of shark in the world?
Answer: Yes
7. How many tentacles does a squid have?
Answer: Ten
8. What do squid eat: jellyfish, plankton or fish?
Answer: Fish
9. What do jellyfish use to attack their prey?
Answer: Stinging tentacles
10. Are squid invertebrates?
Answer: Yes
11. Which ocean habitat is home to the most types of fish?
Answer: Coral reefs
12. How long can divers stay underwater for: 10 minutes or more, 15 minutes or more or 20 minutes or more?
Answer: 20 minutes or more
13. What do the tanks in SCUBA equipment contain?
Answer: Compressed gas
14. Are sharks more closely related to squid or rays?
Answer: Rays
15. Do squid spend most of their time in open water or on the seabed?
Answer: In open water

Level 3

16. What 'P' leave behind the hard, stony cases we see in coral reefs?
Answer: Polyps
17. To which of these creatures are corals most closely related: jellyfish, giant clams or sharks?
Answer: Jellyfish
18. What word is used to describe a tail that can grip things?
Answer: Prehensile

ANSWERS: Marine mammals

Level 1

1. What is the biggest animal on earth: the elephant or the blue whale?
   Answer: The blue whale
2. Do seals eat fish or seaweed?
   Answer: Fish
3. By what name are orcas more commonly known: killer whales or seals?
   Answer: Killer whales
4. Baby harp seals are born with grey fur. True or false?
   Answer: False

Level 2

5. Which use echolocation to find their prey: dolphins or walruses?
   Answer: Dolphins
6. What 'K' are shrimp-like creatures that humpback whales eat?
   Answer: Krill
7. Seals give birth in the sea. True or false?
   Answer: False
8. Do all walruses have tusks or only the males?
   Answer: All walruses have tusks
9. What 'P' is a group of killer whales known as?
   Answer: A pod
10. Why are many large whales rare today?
    Answer: Because in the past they were hunted
11. Which marine mammals sometimes kill and eat whales that are larger than they are?
    Answer: Killer whales (orcas)
12. Do all whales eat large animals?
    Answer: No
13. Which ocean surrounds the North Pole?
    Answer: The Arctic ocean
14. What 'S' do walruses eat?
    Answer: Shellfish

Level 3

15. Where on a whale would you find its baleen?
    Answer: Inside its mouth
16. What 'C' is the name of the marine mammal group that contains whales and dolphins?
    Answer: Cetaceans
17. Near which pole do walruses live: the North or the South Pole?
    Answer: The North Pole
18. What part of a blue whale weighs as much as an elephant?
    Answer: Its tongue
19. How long was the largest blue whale ever measured?
    Answer: 33.5m long

ANSWERS: Sea birds

Level 1

1. Do puffins carry food in their mouths, their feet or their wings?
   Answer: In their mouths
2. Do seagulls ever feed inland?
   Answer: Yes
3. SNIFF UP can be rearranged to give the name of what sea birds?
   Answer: Puffins
4. An albatross is a type of sea bird. True or false?
   Answer: True
5. What 'F' is the main food of most sea birds?
   Answer: Fish

Level 2

6. Some sea birds carry food for their chicks in their stomachs. True or false?
   Answer: True
7. Why do cormorants stand with their wings open after hunting in the water?
   Answer: To dry them out
8. Do puffins use their wings or feet to swim?
   Answer: Their wings
9. Do boobies hunt by diving into the water from the air or by diving in from the surface?
   Answer: By diving in from the air
10. Is a male frigate bird's throat-pouch red, yellow or blue?
    Answer: Red
11. Do cormorants use their wings or feet to swim?
    Answer: Their feet
12. Does oil float on water or does it sink?
    Answer: It floats
13. Do frigate birds live in the tropics or near the North Pole?
    Answer: In the tropics

Level 3

14. What 'G' is a sea bird that nests near the tops of cliffs?
    Answer: The gannet
15. What does the word regurgitate mean?
    Answer: Cough up
16. How do frigate birds get food?
    Answer: By attacking other birds and stealing their food
17. Why do male frigate birds inflate their throat pouches with air?
    Answer: To attract females
18. What 'T' is a word for warm air currents that frigate birds use to lift them into the air?
    Answer: Thermals

ANSWERS: Birds

Level 1

1. Do birds have teeth?
   Answer: No
2. Birds are the only animals in the world that have feathers. True or false?
   Answer: True
3. Do birds flap their wings when they are gliding?
   Answer: No
4. Can swans fly?
   Answer: Yes

Level 2

5. A NEST FILM can be rearranged to give the name of what parts of a feather?
   Answer: Filaments
6. What is the world's largest bird?
   Answer: The ostrich
7. Birds have elbow joints. True or false?
   Answer: True
8. Are birds' bones solid or hollow?
   Answer: Hollow
9. GLEAM UP can be rearranged to give what name for the feathers that cover a bird?
   Answer: Plumage
10. Does a kestrel eat fruit, seeds or meat?
    Answer: Meat
11. Which are usually more brightly coloured: male birds or female birds?
    Answer: Male birds
12. Which 'H' means to stay still in mid-air?
    Answer: Hover
13. Which has the longer beak: a curlew or a robin?
    Answer: A curlew
14. How many times can hummingbirds flap their wings every second: seven times, 70 times or 700 times?
    Answer: 70 times

Level 3

15. What is the chamber between a bird's mouth and its stomach called?
    Answer: The crop
16. How many sections does a bird's stomach have?
    Answer: Two
17. What do hummingbirds feed on?
    Answer: Nectar
18. What 'R' is a large flightless bird?
    Answer: Rhea

ANSWERS: African herbivores

Level 1

1. Do zebras have spots or stripes?
   Answer: Stripes
2. Are rhinos larger or smaller than rabbits?
   Answer: Larger
3. Are zebras more closely related to horses or sheep?
   Answer: Horses
4. Whereabouts on an elephant's body is its trunk?
   Answer: On its face

Level 2

5. What is the world's largest land animal?
   Answer: The elephant
6. What is the world's tallest land animal?
   Answer: The giraffe
7. What 'B' is the word for a male elephant?
   Answer: Bull
8. How can an elephant use its trunk to cool itself down?
   Answer: By spraying itself with water
9. African elephants can weigh more than a tonne. True or false?
   Answer: True
10. How tall do male giraffes grow: 3m, 6m or 10m?
    Answer: 6m
11. Rhinos have excellent eyesight. True or false?
    Answer: False
12. Do giraffes feed mainly on grass, insects or leaves?
    Answer: Leaves
13. Which African predator can kill elephants?
    Answer: The lion
14. How many species (types) of zebra are there: three, five or seven?
    Answer: Three

Level 3

15. What 'P' hunts elephants for their tusks?
    Answer: Poacher
16. How many species (types) of rhino are there?
    Answer: Five
17. What 'J' is a species of rhino that lives in Asia?
    Answer: Javan
18. What are elephants' tusks made of?
    Answer: Ivory

ANSWERS: Lions

Level 1

1. What is the name for a female lion?
   Answer: Lioness
2. RIP ED can be rearranged to give what name for a group of lions?
   Answer: Pride
3. Which lions have manes: the males or the females?
   Answer: The males
4. Do male or female lions make up most of the pride?
   Answer: Females
5. Which are bigger: male or female lions?
   Answer: Male lions

Level 2

6. Which are the last members of the pride to feed at a kill?
   Answer: The cubs
7. Apart from hunting, what do the lionesses do in the pride?
   Answer: Care for the young
8. Which members of a pride of lions do most of the hunting?
   Answer: The females
9. Do female lions stay with or leave the pride when they grow up?
   Answer: They stay
10. Do lions usually hunt in groups or on their own?
    Answer: In groups
11. Do lions ever fight to the death?
    Answer: Yes
12. How long do lion cubs stay hidden from the rest of the pride: eight days, eight weeks or eight months?
    Answer: Eight weeks
13. What do lion cubs have on their coats that adult lions do not?
    Answer: Spots
14. How many male lions usually lead a pride?
    Answer: One

Level 3

15. What is the name of the area in which a pride of lions lives and hunts?
    Answer: Territory
16. What do lions use to mark the borders of this area?
    Answer: Urine, droppings and scratch marks
17. What do male lions do to keep others away?
    Answer: They roar
18. How does a male lion take over a pride?
    Answer: He challenges the established male

ANSWERS: Polar animals

Level 1

1. Can penguins fly?
   Answer: No
2. Can polar bears swim?
   Answer: Yes
3. Polar bears can weigh over a tonne. True or false?
   Answer: True
4. Do polar bears ever lie in wait for their prey?
   Answer: Yes
5. Polar bears eat seals. True or false?
   Answer: True

Level 2

6. In which season do migrating birds arrive in the polar regions?
   Answer: Spring
7. Killer whales live in polar waters. True or false?
   Answer: True
8. Why do some types of baby seal have white coats?
   Answer: To hide them in the snow
9. Do polar bears live near to the North Pole or the South Pole?
   Answer: The North Pole
10. Penguins live in the Antarctic. True or false?
    Answer: True
11. ALE BUG can be rearranged to give the name of which whale that lives in Arctic waters?
    Answer: Beluga
12. Which sense do polar bears use to find most of their prey: sight, hearing or smell?
    Answer: Smell
13. How do penguins paddle themselves through the water: with their wings or with their feet?
    Answer: With their wings
14. What is the world's largest kind of penguin?
    Answer: The emperor penguin

Level 3

15. Which bird flies all the way from the Antarctic to the Arctic and back again every year?
    Answer: The Arctic tern
16. How can people protect baby seals from humans hunting them for their fur?
    Answer: By spraying them with harmless dye
17. Do narwhals live near to the North Pole or the South Pole?
    Answer: Near to the North Pole
18. What word is used for keeping an egg warm until it hatches?
    Answer: Incubating

ANSWERS: Farm animals

Level 1

1. Are dairy cows kept for their milk or their fur?
   Answer: Their milk
2. Is a cockerel a male or a female chicken?
   Answer: Male
3. What animal do farmers keep to hunt down rats and mice?
   Answer: A cat
4. Which farm animals produce wool?
   Answer: Sheep

Level 2

5. What 'K' is a baby goat?
   Answer: Kid
6. Today, dairy cows are milked by hand. True or false?
   Answer: False
7. On which part of a cow are its teats?
   Answer: On its udder
8. How many teats does a cow have?
   Answer: Four
9. Which have larger crests on their heads: male or female chickens?
   Answer: Male chickens
10. Which animal is needed to make butter?
    Answer: A cow
11. EAGER FERN can be rearranged to give the name of what kind of chicken?
    Answer: Free-range
12. Which farm animal does gammon come from?
    Answer: Pigs
13. What 'L' is a meat from sheep?
    Answer: Lamb
14. What 'F' is removed from a sheep by shearing it?
    Answer: Fleece

Level 3

15. What is the smallest piglet in a litter called?
    Answer: A runt
16. How many teats does a goat have?
    Answer: Two
17. What is the most common kind of sheep dog in the UK?
    Answer: The border collie
18. What is a male pig called?
    Answer: A boar
19. What is the name for chickens that are kept in cages?
    Answer: Battery chickens

ANSWERS: Horses

Level 1

1. What are baby horses called?
   Answer: Foals
2. What do cowboys wear to shade them from the sun?
   Answer: Wide-brimmed hats
3. In showjumping, do riders try to jump over obstacles or crash into them?
   Answer: They try to jump over obstacles
4. Horses are used to pull ploughs. True or false?
   Answer: True
5. What 'L' is the looped rope that cowboys use to catch cattle?
   Answer: Lasso
6. Are ponies larger or smaller than horses?
   Answer: Smaller

Level 2

7. Is an Exmoor a breed of pony or a breed of horse?
   Answer: A breed of pony
8. What is the largest breed of horse?
   Answer: The shire horse
9. What is the main difference between the skeleton of a horse and the skeleton of a human?
   Answer: Horse skeletons have front legs instead of arms
10. When do male horses show their teeth and pull their lips back?
    Answer: When they smell a female horse
11. HEN CARS can be rearranged to give the name of what large farms on which cowboys work?
    Answer: Ranches
12. What is worn by jumping horses to protect their ankles from knocks?
    Answer: Bandages
13. BANDY HURDS can be rearranged to give the name of what item, used for removing dirt from a horse's coat?
    Answer: Dandy brush

Level 3

14. What 'C' is a type of pony from Iran?
    Answer: A Caspian pony
15. How does a horse show aggression?
    Answer: By holding its ears back
16. What is the name of the bones that make up a horse's spine?
    Answer: Vertebrae
17. What kind of brush is used to brush away loose hair on a horse?
    Answer: A rubber curry comb
18. What 'D' is a horse-riding sport, which tests obedience and rider control?
    Answer: Dressage

ANSWERS: Cats

Level 1

1. What are baby cats called?
Answer: Kittens

2. Is catnip a type of plant or a type of animal?
Answer: A type of plant

3. Do cats creep up and pounce on their prey or chase it round and round until it is exhausted?
Answer: They creep up and pounce

4. Do cat owners use brushes for grooming their cats or for feeding them?
Answer: For grooming them

5. Can cats climb?
Answer: Yes

6. Do young cats prefer playing with balls of wool or with knitting needles?
Answer: With balls of wool

7. Are cats good at jumping?
Answer: Yes

Level 2

8. Cats have claws. True or false?
Answer: True

9. What is a scratching post for?
Answer: Keeping the claws sharp

10. Do cats prefer to live on their own or in groups?
Answer: On their own

11. For how long do a cat's eyes stay closed after it is born?
Answer: A week

12. How often should cats be fed?
Answer: At least once a day

13. Which fight more often: male cats or female cats?
Answer: Male cats

14. What are male cats called?
Answer: Tom cats

15. Why is it a good idea to use a special dish for feeding a cat?
Answer: So that they come running when their owner approaches it

Level 3

16. What part of a cat's body can be retracted?
Answer: Its claws

17. From which animal are domestic cats descended?
Answer: The African wild cat

18. Why do cats spray and scent-mark things?
Answer: To warn other cats to stay away from their territory

ANSWERS: Dogs

Level 1

1. What is a baby dog called?
Answer: A puppy

2. Are most police dogs Alsatians or Dalmatians?
Answer: Alsatians

3. Were pit bull terriers originally bred for fighting or fetching slippers?
Answer: For fighting

4. Are most Labrador dogs friendly or aggressive?
Answer: Friendly

5. The terrier is the largest breed of dog. True or false?
Answer: False

Level 2

6. What is a group of related puppies called?
Answer: A litter

7. How long does it take for a puppy to grow into an adult: six months, a year or three years?
Answer: A year

8. Which 'S' is a kind of dog often trained to be a sniffer dog?
Answer: A spaniel

9. How might a hearing dog help a deaf owner?
Answer: By alerting them if there is a knock on the door

10. If a dog wags its tail, is it happy or angry?
Answer: Happy

11. Does a sad dog drop its tail or raise it?
Answer: It drops it

12. Which wild animal is the ancestor of all domestic dogs?
Answer: The wolf

13. EDGIER REVEL TORN can be rearranged to spell what breed of dog, often trained as guide dogs?
Answer: Golden retriever

14. Which would make a better guard dog: a Rottweiler or a Labrador?
Answer: A Rottweiler

Level 3

15. How long should you wait before giving away puppies to new owners?
Answer: A few weeks

16. During which year of a dog's life is it easiest to train?
Answer: Its first year

17. What is another word for cutting off a dog's tail?
Answer: Docking

18. How can you tell when a dog is frightened?
Answer: It holds its tail between its legs

19. What type of dog was bred to hunt large animals?
Answer: Hounds

ANSWERS: Continents

Level 1

1. Where is the Nile?
   Answer: In Africa
2. Which continent lies to the east of Europe?
   Answer: Asia
3. Is Asia the second-most populated continent?
   Answer: No (it is the most populated)
4. Is Central America part of North or South America?
   Answer: North America
5. Which is the smallest continent?
   Answer: Australasia

Level 2

6. What is the world's largest country?
   Answer: The Russian Federation
7. What divides Europe from Africa?
   Answer: The Mediterranean sea
8. What population milestone was reached in 1802?
   Answer: The world's population reached one billion
9. Is Sydney the capital city of Australia?
   Answer: No (Canberra is the capital)
10. In which continent would you find the world's highest mountains?
    Answer: Asia
11. What larger landmass encompasses Europe?
    Answer: Eurasia
12. How many billion did the world's population reach in 1999: one, five, six or 11?
    Answer: Six
13. Are the Andes on the east or west coast of South America?
    Answer: On the west coast

Level 3

14. How much of the Amazon rainforest lies outside of Brazil?
    Answer: 40%
15. What are the names of the island groups of Australasia?
    Answer: Melanesia, Micronesia and Polynesia
16. By how many million per year was the world's population increasing in 2004?
    Answer: 75 million per year
17. How many countries are in Africa: 47, 52 or 53?
    Answer: 53 countries
18. In which continent is the world's largest freshwater lake?
    Answer: In North America
19. How long is the Andes mountain range?
    Answer: 7,000km long

ANSWERS: International community

Level 1

1. The United Nations was formed during World War I. True or false?
   Answer: False
2. What does NATO stand for: the North Atlantic Treaty Organization or the North Antarctic Treaty Organization?
   Answer: The North Atlantic Treaty Organization
3. All peacekeeping units are armed. True or false?
   Answer: False
4. What is the single currency of the European Union?
   Answer: The euro
5. CRESS ROD can be rearranged to give the name of what organization that provides medical aid?
   Answer: The Red Cross

Level 2

6. Why was NATO formed?
   Answer: To ensure peace in its member states
7. What convention protects wounded soldiers and prisoners?
   Answer: The Geneva Convention
8. In what city is the UN headquarters?
   Answer: New York City
9. How many countries are in the UN?
   Answer: 191
10. What treaty marked the beginning of the European union?
    Answer: The Treaty of Paris
11. In what building do member nations of the UN meet?
    Answer: The General Assembly Building
12. For what purpose can peacekeeping units use their weapons?
    Answer: For self-defence

Level 3

13. In what year did the UN headquarters officially open?
    Answer: 1951
14. What treaty led to the formation of the European Union?
    Answer: The Maastricht Treaty
15. What is the full name of the Red Cross?
    Answer: The International Committee of the Red Cross and the Red Crescent Movement
16. How much money was donated to buy land for the UN headquarters?
    Answer: $8.5 million
17. What is the name of the central command of NATO's military forces?
    Answer: SHAPE (Supreme Headquarters Allied Powers Europe)
18. Who first used the term 'United Nations'?
    Answer: US President F D Roosevelt

ANSWERS: Flags

Level 1

1. What colours could a pirate flag be?
   Answer: Red or black
2. Where are navy flags used: at sea or in space?
   Answer: At sea
3. In what kind of sport is a black-and-white chequered flag used?
   Answer: In auto and motorcycle racing
4. What kind of flag do explorers plant on lands they have discovered?
   Answer: Their national flag
5. Which has the oldest national flag: Scotland or the USA?
   Answer: Scotland

Level 2

6. Which sport uses flags: rugby, cycling or rowing?
   Answer: All three
7. What are navy flags called?
   Answer: Signalling flags
8. What event prompted the redesign of the French flag?
   Answer: The French revolution
9. Are signalling flags used alone or together?
   Answer: Both alone and together
10. What is semaphore?
    Answer: A signalling system using flags
11. How many US flags have been placed on the moon: four, five or six?
    Answer: Six
12. Which colour is not used in navy flags: yellow, black or green?
    Answer: Green

Level 3

13. What do referees use flags to indicate in an American football game?
    Answer: An error
14. In semaphore, how is an 'R' signalled?
    Answer: By holding both arms and flags straight out
15. On a pirate flag, what does an hour glass symbolize?
    Answer: That time is running out
16. What colour flags are used in semaphore?
    Answer: Red and yellow
17. In which century were pirate flags first used?
    Answer: The 18th century
18. What displayed a US flag on Mars?
    Answer: The Viking lander

ANSWERS: Natural wonders

Level 1

1. What is the tallest mountain in the world?
   Answer: Everest
2. What is the tallest waterfall in the world?
   Answer: Angel Falls
3. K2 is in Europe. True or false?
   Answer: False
4. The Great Barrier Reef lies off the coast of which country?
   Answer: Australia
5. The Great Barrier Reef can be seen from space. True or false?
   Answer: True
6. Which is longer: the Grand Canyon or the Great Barrier Reef?
   Answer: The Great Barrier Reef

Level 2

7. Who were the first people to reach the top of Mount Everest?
   Answer: Edmund Hillary and Tenzing Norgay
8. How is the length of the Grand Canyon measured?
   Answer: By the Colorado river
9. How many times higher is Angel Falls than Niagara Falls: 10, 15 or 20?
   Answer: 15 times
10. What is the Hillary Step?
    Answer: A steep section of Mount Everest
11. How old are the rocks in the Grand Canyon?
    Answer: 2,000 million years old
12. In what continent is the widest waterfall in the world?
    Answer: Asia
13. What is another name for *aurora borealis*?
    Answer: The Northern Lights

Level 3

14. What causes the Northern Lights?
    Answer: High-speed particles from the sun colliding with gas molecules
15. How much older are the Alps than the Himalayas?
    Answer: 15 million years
16. How high is Mount Everest?
    Answer: 8,850m high
17. What is the Latin name of the Southern Lights?
    Answer: Aurora australis
18. What geographical feature is 10,783m wide?
    Answer: Khône Falls

ANSWERS: Coasts

Level 1

1. A tsunami is caused by the wind. True or false?
   Answer: False
2. ACE VASE can be rearranged to give what name for a cavern in a cliff?
   Answer: Sea cave
3. What is the wearing down of a headland called: erosion or erasure?
   Answer: Erosion
4. What two materials do waves deposit on beaches?
   Answer: Pebbles and sand
5. What 'W' causes waves?
   Answer: The wind
6. HELLO BOW can be rearranged to give the name of what coastal feature?
   Answer: Blow hole

Level 2

7. What is special about the Painted Cave?
   Answer: It is the longest sea cave in the world
8. What does the word 'tsunami' mean?
   Answer: Harbour wave
9. What causes water to gush through a blow hole?
   Answer: Built-up air pressure
10. The fetch is the material deposited on a beach. True or false?
    Answer: False
11. A stack is a mound of sand. True or false?
    Answer: False
12. Is sea water acidic or alkaline?
    Answer: Acidic

Level 3

13. Which is formed first: a cave or a blow hole?
    Answer: A cave
14. How fast do tsunami waves move?
    Answer: At over 700km/h
15. What coastal process do groynes prevent?
    Answer: Longshore drift
16. On what island is the Painted Cave?
    Answer: Santa Cruz Island, California, USA
17. How high can tsunamis be?
    Answer: Up to 30m high
18. A stack is formed from which coastal feature?
    Answer: An arch

ANSWERS: Rivers

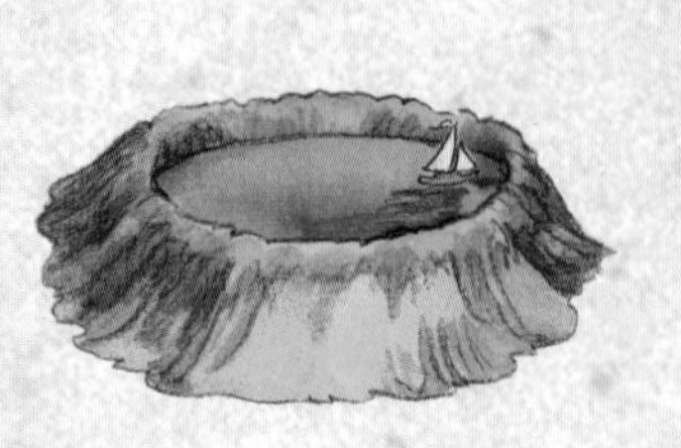

Level 1

1. What is the beginning of a river called?
   Answer: The source
2. In what continent are the Great Lakes?
   Answer: North America
3. Do waterfalls flow over a ledge of hard or soft rock?
   Answer: Hard rock
4. What is the name of the process by which water moves between the land and sea and back again?
   Answer: The water cycle
5. What is the name of the area of flat land on either side of a river?
   Answer: A flood plain

Level 2

6. What 'R' is precipitation?
   Answer: Rain
7. What kind of lakes are created by ice sheets?
   Answer: Freshwater lakes
8. What is formed when a river floods shallow lakes or ponds?
   Answer: A marsh
9. Do tributaries increase or decrease the water volume of a river?
   Answer: Increase
10. What happens to evaporated water?
    Answer: It condenses to form clouds
11. What other name is used for an estuary?
    Answer: A harbour
12. Headwaters are the top of a waterfall. True or false?
    Answer: False
13. What prevents water seepage in a marshland?
    Answer: Granite, slate or quartz beneath
14. What forms at the bottom of a waterfall?
    Answer: A plunge pool

Level 3

15. What 'Y' is a waterfall in the USA, created by a glacier?
    Answer: Yosemite Falls, California, USA
16. What name is given to fertile land formed on a flood plain?
    Answer: Alluvium
17. What can form from sediment in an estuary?
    Answer: A delta
18. How was Lake Tanganyika formed?
    Answer: By earth fault movements

ANSWERS: Deserts

Level 1

1. What 'D' is a sandy desert feature?
   Answer: Dune
2. Which animal is used to carry people and goods in the desert?
   Answer: The camel
3. Sand holds water. True or false?
   Answer: False
4. What plant with spines can survive in a desert?
   Answer: The cactus
5. What 'B' is the home of a meerkat?
   Answer: A burrow

Level 2

6. Is a Tuareg a type of sand dune or a member of a desert tribe?
   Answer: A member of a desert tribe
7. What type of sand dune forms when the wind blows in all directions?
   Answer: A star dune
8. What is a one-humped camel called?
   Answer: A dromedary
9. What is the name for wind carrying away fine sand?
   Answer: Deflation
10. What is the slope of a sand dune called?
    Answer: A slip face
11. Wind blowing in two different directions creates which type of sand dune?
    Answer: A linear dune
12. Is a hoodoo: a type of sand dune, a rock formation or a desert rodent?
    Answer: A rock formation
13. In which desert would you find a Tuareg?
    Answer: The Sahara desert

Level 3

14. What desert plant can be over 200 years old?
    Answer: The Saguaro cactus
15. What 'F' is a kind of fox that lives in the desert?
    Answer: The fennec fox
16. What is a barchan?
    Answer: A curved sand dune
17. What substance is formed by cemented sand and gravel?
    Answer: Calcrete
18. What features of a camel help it survive in deserts?
    Answer: It can go without water for several days, and has thick padded feet so that it can walk across hot sand without any pain

ANSWERS: The poles

Level 1

1. On which continent is the South Pole?
   Answer: Antarctica
2. The explorer Robert Scott reached the South Pole. True or false?
   Answer: True
3. LIE CRAG can be rearranged to give the name of what polar feature?
   Answer: Glacier
4. Icebergs are lumps of ice that have broken away from glaciers. True or false?
   Answer: True

Level 2

5. What is a hollow formed by melting blocks of ice called: a kettle hole or a sink hole?
   Answer: A kettle hole
6. How much of an iceberg is visible above the waterline?
   Answer: One-tenth
7. Who was the first person to reach the South Pole?
   Answer: Roald Amundsen
8. Why do glaciers shift?
   Answer: Because of the weight of ice and gravity
9. Today, most Inuit use dog sleds to travel over the Arctic ice. True or false?
   Answer: False
10. What imaginary line runs between the two poles?
    Answer: The axis on which the earth turns
11. What is a moraine?
    Answer: A ridge of rock left by a melting glacier
12. What language is spoken by the Inuit?
    Answer: Inuktitut
13. What 'P' is an item of clothing worn by Arctic people?
    Answer: A parka

Level 3

14. Do the Inuit live near to the North or the South Pole?
    Answer: The North Pole
15. In which year did a person reach the South Pole for the first time?
    Answer: 1911
16. Near which pole are flat-topped tabular icebergs found?
    Answer: The South Pole
17. How far would Scott and his crew have had to travel to safety?
    Answer: 17km
18. What Arctic people live in Greenland?
    Answer: The Kalaalit

ANSWERS: Exploring space

Level 1

1. The first living creature in space was a mouse. True or false?
   Answer: False
2. Who was the first person on the Moon: Neil Armstrong, Nelly Armstrong or Norman Armstrong?
   Answer: Neil Armstrong
3. ENVISION OUT can be rearranged to give the name of what group of republics?
   Answer: The Soviet Union
4. What 'S' is an object that orbits Earth?
   Answer: Satellite

Level 2

5. What 'L' was the name of the first living creature in space?
   Answer: Laika
6. What 'S' was the first artificial satellite?
   Answer: Sputnik
7. AN AIR RIG GUY can be rearranged to give the name of what astronaut, the first person to go into space?
   Answer: Yuri Gagarin
8. In which year did people first walk on the Moon: 1959, 1969 or 1979?
   Answer: 1969
9. In which year did a person first go into space: 1941, 1951 or 1961?
   Answer: 1961
10. Who said 'That's one small step for man, one giant leap for mankind'?
    Answer: Neil Armstrong
11. VAN OR RULER can be rearranged to give the name of what vehicle used on the surface of the moon?
    Answer: Lunar rover
12. For how long did the first person to go into space stay there: 89 minutes, 89 hours or 89 days?
    Answer: 89 minutes

Level 3

13. Which was the last *Apollo* mission to land people on the Moon?
    Answer: Apollo 17
14. In what year did it reach the Moon?
    Answer: 1972
15. What were Soviet astronauts called?
    Answer: Cosmonauts
16. What 'V' was the first manned spacecraft?
    Answer: Vostock 1
17. What was launched on 12 April 1981?
    Answer: The first space shuttle
18. Where is the Baikonur Cosmodrome: in Kazakhstan, Ukraine or the Russian Federation?
    Answer: Kazakhstan

ANSWERS: Solar System

Level 1

1. Which planet do people live on?
   Answer: Earth
2. How many planets are in the Solar System: seven, nine or 11?
   Answer: Nine
3. MY CURER can be rearranged to give the name of what planet?
   Answer: Mercury

Level 2

4. On the part of a planet facing away from the Sun, is it night or day?
   Answer: Night
5. How many planets in our Solar System have names beginning with the letter 'M'?
   Answer: Two
6. Which planet is the farthest from the Sun?
   Answer: Pluto
7. A GANG SITS can be rearranged to give the name of what group of large planets?
   Answer: Gas giants
8. What is the smallest planet in the Solar System?
   Answer: Pluto
9. The Sun is a star. True or false?
   Answer: True
10. Are any planets in the Solar System bigger than the Sun?
    Answer: No
11. Did the planets form at around the same time as the Sun or long before?
    Answer: Around the same time
12. Which 'S' is a planet made mostly of hydrogen and helium?
    Answer: Saturn
13. How long does the Earth take to circle the Sun: a day, a month or a year?
    Answer: A year
14. What 'O' is the path planets take around the Sun?
    Answer: Orbit
15. Which takes longer to circle the Sun: Earth or Pluto?
    Answer: Pluto
16. How many planets in the Solar System have oceans of water?
    Answer: One

Level 3

17. What 'N' is a swirling cloud of particles from which planets form?
    Answer: Nebula
18. Which is farther from the Sun: Uranus or Saturn?
    Answer: Uranus
19. Which is larger: Earth or Mars?
    Answer: Earth

ANSWERS: Volcanoes and earthquakes

Level 1

1. Is the surface of the earth made of solid or liquid rock?
   Answer: Solid rock
2. What is another name for the earth's surface: the skin, crust or coat?
   Answer: The crust
3. RUIN POET can be rearranged to give what word for a volcano exploding?
   Answer: Eruption
4. A seismologist is a kind of earthquake. True or false?
   Answer: False (a seismologist is a scientist who studies earthquakes)

Level 2

5. What 'R' is the scale used to measure strength of earthquakes?
   Answer: Richter
6. Which are thicker: continental plates or oceanic plates?
   Answer: Continental plates
7. Are most earthquakes strong enough to destroy buildings?
   Answer: No
8. How thick is the earth's mantle: 290km or 2,900km?
   Answer: 2,900km
9. Do ridges form where plates move together or where they move apart?
   Answer: Where they move apart
10. Earthquakes are common where plates slide past one another. True or false?
    Answer: True
11. Japan is situated where two plates meet. True or false?
    Answer: True
12. What 'L' is the molten rock released by a volcanic eruption?
    Answer: Lava
13. What 'F' is the force produced by plates sliding past each other?
    Answer: Friction
14. CUBOID NUTS can be rearranged to give the name of what plate movement?
    Answer: Subduction
15. Volcanoes may occur where two plates are moving apart. True or false?
    Answer: True

Level 3

16. What is the most common substance in the earth's core?
    Answer: Iron
17. Which makes up a greater proportion of the earth: the crust or mantle?
    Answer: The mantle
18. On which plate do volcanoes occur when an oceanic plate and a continental plate meet?
    Answer: On the continental plate

ANSWERS: Rocks and minerals

Level 1

1. Emeralds are purple. True or false?
   Answer: False
2. What colour are rubies?
   Answer: Red
3. Gold is a metal. True or false?
   Answer: True
4. How many sides does a hexagon have: one, three or six?
   Answer: Six

Level 2

5. TEARING can be rearranged to give the name of what igneous rock, often used for building?
   Answer: Granite
6. Crystals form underground. True or false?
   Answer: True
7. Do sedimentary rocks form on the bottoms of seas, lakes and rivers or deep within the earth?
   Answer: On the bottoms of seas, lakes and rivers
8. What word is used for rocks which form under great pressure or heat: metamorphic, mathematic or metaphysical?
   Answer: Metamorphic
9. Is basalt an igneous or a sedimentary rock?
   Answer: Igneous
10. Gems are cut and polished to make gemstones. True or false?
    Answer: False (gemstones are cut and polished to make gems)
11. What 'C' is the substance from which diamond is formed?
    Answer: Carbon
12. Which are the most valuable: diamonds, emeralds or garnets?
    Answer: Diamonds
13. HIS PAPER can be rearranged to give the name of what valuable gemstone?
    Answer: Sapphire
14. A START can be rearranged to give what word for layers of rock?
    Answer: Strata

Level 3

15. In which country is the Giant's Causeway?
    Answer: Northern Ireland
16. What 'M' is molten rock, which cools to form igneous rocks?
    Answer: Magma
17. What is the name for a stone which has had its edges worn smooth by the action of water?
    Answer: A pebble
18. What 'E' cannot be broken down into any simpler substance?
    Answer: An element

ANSWERS: Weather

Level 1

1. Does weather happen in the atmosphere or under the sea?
   Answer: In the atmosphere
2. Are clouds made of cotton wool or water vapour?
   Answer: Water vapour
3. What 'O' is the gas we must breathe in order to live?
   Answer: Oxygen
4. What 'L' is the word for an electrical charge released from a storm cloud?
   Answer: Lightning
5. A weather balloon is a type of cloud. True or false?
   Answer: False

Level 2

6. Where does the majority of the water vapour in clouds originally come from?
   Answer: The sea
7. Does a weather vane measure wind speed or wind direction?
   Answer: Wind direction
8. Which is usually associated with fine weather: high pressure or low pressure?
   Answer: High pressure
9. What 'R' is sometimes formed as sunlight passes through raindrops?
   Answer: A rainbow
10. Do rainbows appear when it rains or when there is no rain?
    Answer: When it rains
11. Do raindrops become bigger or smaller as they fall through a cloud?
    Answer: Bigger
12. What 'H' is a word for frozen raindrops?
    Answer: Hail
13. Do clouds become cooler or hotter as they rise?
    Answer: Cooler
14. REACH RUIN can be rearranged to give the name of what powerful storm?
    Answer: Hurricane
15. RING TONE can be rearranged to give the name of what very common gas?
    Answer: Nitrogen

Level 3

16. What is a scientist who studies the weather called?
    Answer: A meteorologist
17. How many colours are there in a rainbow?
    Answer: Seven
18. What 'S' do weather forecasters use to watch storms building up in the atmosphere?
    Answer: Satellites

ANSWERS: Bones and muscles

Level 1

1. BELOW can be rearranged to give the name of what joint in the middle of the arm?
   Answer: Elbow
2. Are there muscles in the human leg?
   Answer: Yes
3. What 'S' is the name for all the bones in the body put together?
   Answer: Skeleton

Level 2

4. Do people have joints in their fingers?
   Answer: Yes
5. Muscles contain millions of cells called fibres. True or false?
   Answer: True
6. What 'B' is a muscle in the arm that helps to raise the forearm?
   Answer: The biceps
7. Which bones form a cage that protect the internal organs?
   Answer: The ribs
8. What 'C' is the proper name for the gristle in human bodies?
   Answer: Cartilage
9. Which bone links the legs to the backbone?
   Answer: The pelvis
10. The patella is another name for which bone?
    Answer: The kneecap
11. The muscles in the heart work automatically. True or false?
    Answer: True
12. When a person raises their forearm do their triceps contract or relax?
    Answer: Relax
13. How many bones are there in an adult's skull: two, 12 or 22?
    Answer: 22
14. Do people have more muscles or more bones in their bodies?
    Answer: More muscles
15. Is the shoulder joint a hinge joint or a ball-and-socket joint?
    Answer: A ball-and-socket joint
16. What is the largest bone in the human body?
    Answer: The thigh bone (femur)
17. What is the name of the eight bones that, together, encase the brain?
    Answer: The cranium

Level 3

18. The mandible is another name for which part of the body?
    Answer: The lower jaw
19. In which part of the body is the smallest bone?
    Answer: The ear
20. How many bones are there in the human skeleton?
    Answer: 206

ANSWERS: Medicine

Level 1

1. What 'D' is the person people visit when they are feeling ill?
   Answer: Doctor
2. What vehicles take people to hospital: ambulances, fire engines or tractors?
   Answer: Ambulances
3. Are ambulances part of the emergency services?
   Answer: Yes
4. Do nurses work in hospitals or shops?
   Answer: In hospitals

Level 2

5. Broken bones mend themselves. True or false?
   Answer: True
6. What 'S' is used to listen to a person's heartbeat?
   Answer: Stethoscope
7. What does a thermometer measure?
   Answer: Body temperature
8. Is intensive care given to people who are very ill or to people who are better, just before they leave hospital?
   Answer: People who are very ill
9. What 'S' is the word for a person who carries out operations?
   Answer: Surgeon
10. What 'T' means to replace a damaged body part with a new, healthy one?
    Answer: Transplant
11. Would you wear a plaster cast if you had flu or if you had a broken leg?
    Answer: If you had a broken leg
12. A SCARED IMP can be rearranged to give the name of what people who look after patients on the way to hospital?
    Answer: Paramedics
13. A symptom is a kind of medicine. True or false?
    Answer: False
14. What 'S' is a large machine that looks inside people's bodies?
    Answer: Scanner

Level 3

15. What 'D' means 'to work out what is wrong with a patient'?
    Answer: Diagnose
16. What sort of injury can be treated by traction?
    Answer: A broken bone
17. What is used to transfer nutrients straight into a person's bloodstream?
    Answer: A drip
18. What 'M' is a kind of wave that scanners use to look inside a body?
    Answer: Magnetic

ANSWERS: Trains

Level 1

1. Which came first: steam engines or electric trains?
   Answer: Steam engines
2. Do all trains carry passengers?
   Answer: No
3. Is diesel a type of fuel or a type of food?
   Answer: A type of fuel
4. Who built the train that ran on the first-ever steam railway: Richard Trevithick, Richard Branson or Richard the Lionheart?
   Answer: Richard Trevithick
5. What 'C' was burned in steam engines?
   Answer: Coal

Level 2

6. Was the Wild West in Europe or in the USA?
   Answer: In America
7. Is steam created by heating water or by heating petrol?
   Answer: Heating water
8. Which country has bullet trains and super expresses?
   Answer: Japan
9. What 'R' was a famous steam engine built by George Stephenson?
   Answer: The Rocket
10. Which country has TGVs?
    Answer: France
11. Are there any trains that can go faster than 200km/h?
    Answer: Yes (Japanese bullet trains regularly run at over 300km/h)
12. What 'C' on Wild West trains was used for moving cattle off the line?
    Answer: Cowcatchers
13. Were steam trains cleaner or dirtier than modern trains?
    Answer: Dirtier

Level 3

14. In which country was the world's first-ever steam railway?
    Answer: Wales
15. In which century was the first railway to cross North America built?
    Answer: The 19th century
16. What 'F' is the word used for the goods carried by some trains?
    Answer: Freight
17. How long was the world's longest-ever train: 5km, 6km or 7km?
    Answer: 6km
18. What 'P' were exploring settlers who travelled into the Wild West by train?
    Answer: Pioneers

ANSWERS: Early flight

Level 1

1. GIRDLE can be rearranged to give the name of what type of unpowered aircraft?
   Answer: Glider
2. The first manned flight was in a hot-air balloon. True or false?
   Answer: True
3. Is a dirigible a steerable airship or an Australian musical instrument?
   Answer: A steerable airship

Level 2

4. What 'H' is a type of aircraft with rotating blades?
   Answer: Helicopter
5. Which body of water was Louis Blériot first to fly across in 1909: the English Channel or Atlantic ocean?
   Answer: The English Channel
6. In which century did Otto Lilienthal make the first controlled glider flights: the 9th or 19th century?
   Answer: The 19th century
7. How many wings does a monoplane have: two or four?
   Answer: Two
8. Which 'G' is a country, home to Otto Lilienthal?
   Answer: Germany
9. Jean-François Pilâtre was the first man to fly. True or false?
   Answer: True
10. Was the first powered flight in Europe or the USA?
    Answer: The USA
11. Which great 16th-century Italian artist and thinker designed a glider that was never built?
    Answer: Leonardo Da Vinci
12. Which 'M' were brothers who built the first manned aircraft?
    Answer: Montgolfier

Level 3

13. What was the surname of Wilbur and Orville, who designed the first ever heavier-than-air powered aircraft?
    Answer: Wright
14. What was their aircraft called?
    Answer: The Wright Flyer
15. What did the first heavier-than-air powered aircraft use as fuel?
    Answer: Petrol
16. In which century did the first-ever manned aircraft take off: the 16th, 17th or 18th century?
    Answer: The 18th century
17. Who made the first-ever powered flight?
    Answer: Henri Giffard
18. What was his nationality?
    Answer: French

ANSWERS: Sailing

Level 1

1. Sailing boats use the wind to push them along. True or false?
   Answer: True
2. Are boats kept moored in a marina, a merino or a mariner?
   Answer: A marina
3. What kind of jackets do people wear to keep them afloat in the water?
   Answer: Life jackets
4. Do any sailing boats have engines?
   Answer: Yes
5. What suit keeps windsurfers warm?
   Answer: A wetsuit
6. A rudder is used to help a boat steer. True or false?
   Answer: True
7. What 'Y' is a large sailing boat used for pleasure?
   Answer: Yacht

Level 2

8. Which were invented first: square sails or triangular sails?
   Answer: Square sails
9. What 'P' is the left-hand side of a boat and a place where ships dock?
   Answer: Port
10. What is the word for the rear of a boat?
    Answer: The stern
11. BROAD ARTS can be rearranged to give what word for the right-hand side of a boat?
    Answer: Starboard
12. Boats with square sails can only go in the same direction as the wind. True or false?
    Answer: True
13. How many hulls do trimarans have?
    Answer: Three
14. What is a boat with two hulls called?
    Answer: A catamaran
15. What are small, open boats without cabins called?
    Answer: Dinghies
16. What 'W' are people who sail standing up on a board?
    Answer: Windsurfers

Level 3

17. What part of a boat helps keep it from tipping over?
    Answer: The keel
18. Which Mediterranean island was home to the sea-faring Minoans?
    Answer: Crete
19. When did ancient sailing ships use their oars?
    Answer: When they wanted to go forward against the wind

ANSWERS: Submarines

Level 1

1. Does the word submarine literally mean 'under the sea' or 'above the mountains'?
   Answer: Under the sea
2. Is a torpedo a type of weapon or a running shoe?
   Answer: A type of weapon
3. What 'D' is the word for people who explore underwater?
   Answer: Divers
4. LATIN CAT can be rearranged to give the name of what ocean?
   Answer: Atlantic

Level 2

5. Which country's submarines were known as U-boats?
   Answer: Germany's
6. Are there any submarines that are driven by nuclear power?
   Answer: Yes
7. What is the name for the spinning objects that push submarines through the water?
   Answer: Propellers
8. Can submarines attack boats that are on the surface?
   Answer: Yes
9. Are research submarines called submersibles or submissives?
   Answer: Submersibles
10. What 'D' is a kind of fuel commonly used in submarines?
    Answer: Diesel
11. What is the name for the tanks that fill with seawater when a submarine descends?
    Answer: Ballast tanks
12. A bathyscaphe is a type of radar system. True or false?
    Answer: False
13. What do the letters ROV stand for?
    Answer: Remotely operated vehicle
14. SPICE ROPE can be rearranged to give the name of what device, used by submarine crews to see above the water?
    Answer: Periscope

Level 3

15. Where is the Mariana Trench, the deepest point on earth?
    Answer: The Pacific ocean
16. What was the name of the bathyscaphe that first carried people to the bottom of the Mariana Trench?
    Answer: Trieste
17. What was the name of the manned submersible that first explored the wreck of the *Titanic*?
    Answer: Alvin
18. Which ocean liner was torpedoed and sunk by a German U-boat on 7 May 1915?
    Answer: RMS Lusitania

ANSWERS: Household inventions

Level 1

1. Would you put bread in a toaster or a dishwasher?
   Answer: A toaster
2. What 'K' is used for heating water?
   Answer: Kettle
3. Is a Hoover a type of vacuum cleaner or a type of zip?
   Answer: A type of vacuum cleaner

Level 2

4. Which invention is usually credited to John Logie Baird?
   Answer: Television
5. SHARED WISH can be rearranged to give the name of what household appliance?
   Answer: Dishwasher
6. Did the automatic cut-out on an electric kettle appear in 1890, 1930 or 1989?
   Answer: 1930
7. Which was invented first: the electric washing machine or the dishwasher?
   Answer: The electric washing machine
8. Which household object is usually associated with Thomas Edison?
   Answer: The electric light bulb
9. People only started to use zips in the the 1940s. True or false?
   Answer: False
10. Which handy implement was invented by Laszlo Biro?
    Answer: The ball-point pen
11. The aero-foam extinguisher is used on what kind of fires?
    Answer: Gas and oil
12. SCOOPS RED ROOF can be rearranged to give the name of what kitchen appliance?
    Answer: Food processor
13. In which decade of the 20th century did microwave ovens first go on sale?
    Answer: The 1960s

Level 3

14. In what year was the first television picture transmitted?
    Answer: 1925
15. James Murray Spangler invented the first portable what?
    Answer: Vacuum cleaner
16. What did Alexandre Godefoy invent?
    Answer: The hairdryer
17. Which kitchen appliance was developed from an earlier invention called the magnetron?
    Answer: The microwave oven
18. Who invented the sewing machine?
    Answer: Elias Howe

ANSWERS: Robots

Level 1

1. Are there robots that work in factories?
   Answer: Yes
2. Do robots ever get tired?
   Answer: No
3. Are there any robots that can work underwater?
   Answer: Yes
4. ODD SIR can be rearranged to give what name for robots such as R2-D2?
   Answer: Droids
5. Robots can only do one thing at a time. True or false?
   Answer: False

Level 2

6. Are there any robots that can play the piano?
   Answer: Yes
7. Which series of films starred the robot C-3PO?
   Answer: Star Wars
8. What 'C' is programmed with the information that is needed to make robots operate?
   Answer: Computer
9. LEWDING can be rearranged to give the name of what task performed by robots?
   Answer: Welding
10. Which have travelled farthest from earth: robots or humans?
    Answer: Robots
11. Solar panels are used to capture energy from which source?
    Answer: The sun
12. HOW TO CORD can be rearranged to give the name of what popular TV programme?
    Answer: Doctor Who
13. Which planet is currently being explored by robots?
    Answer: Mars
14. What 'M' is the word for doing more than one job at a time?
    Answer: Multitasking
15. Can robots be programmed to detonate bombs?
    Answer: Yes

Level 3

16. The word robot comes from which language?
    Answer: Czech
17. Which country developed the WABOT-2 robot?
    Answer: Japan
18. In what year was the animated film *Robots* released?
    Answer: 2005

ANSWERS: Computers and gaming

Level 1

1. What 'I' is the network that links computers all over the world?
   Answer: The internet
2. Does PC stand for Perfect Computer or Personal Computer?
   Answer: Personal Computer
3. What is a computer that is small enough to fit in the hand called: a handbag, a handheld or a handshake?
   Answer: A handheld
4. What 'M' is a small furry animal, and a thing that attaches to a computer?
   Answer: A mouse
5. What is stored in MP3 files?
   Answer: Music

Level 2

6. Where were computer games played before people had home computers?
   Answer: In video arcades
7. Can people play computer games while they are on the move?
   Answer: Yes
8. What kind of computer is the word Mac short for?
   Answer: Macintosh
9. Do most handheld gaming machines take cartridges or discs?
   Answer: Cartridges
10. Is the information in a computer held in the hard drive, printer or mouse?
    Answer: In the hard drive
11. What 'B' is the computer equipment used to put information onto a CD?
    Answer: Burner
12. Is a computer keyboard a peripheral or a profiterole?
    Answer: A peripheral
13. What 'H' do you wear when playing a virtual-reality game?
    Answer: A headset
14. What 'V' is put in front of the word 'reality' to describe lifelike situations produced by computers?
    Answer: Virtual
15. TOP PAL can be rearranged to give what name for a portable computer?
    Answer: Laptop

Level 3

16. Which would you use to store data: a CD-RAM, a CD-REM or a CD-ROM?
    Answer: A CD-ROM
17. What connects a home computer to the internet?
    Answer: A telephone line
18. What kind of files would you put on to an iPod?
    Answer: MP3 files

ANSWERS: Telephones

Level 1

1. What 'T' is a written message sent by a mobile phone?
   Answer: Text
2. Were the first mobile phones bigger or smaller than mobile phones today?
   Answer: Bigger
3. Do most modern telephones have rotating dials or buttons?
   Answer: Buttons
4. Do mobile phones send messages using microwaves, water waves or Mexican waves?
   Answer: Microwaves
5. Are there mobile phones that can connect to the internet?
   Answer: Yes

Level 2

6. Did the world's first telephone have touch-tone dialling?
   Answer: No
7. In what century was the telephone invented: 9th, 19th or 21st?
   Answer: 19th
8. SAME CAR can be rearranged to spell what extra feature of some mobile phones?
   Answer: Cameras
9. HOME CUT PIE can be rearranged to spell what part of a telephone, that you speak into?
   Answer: Mouthpiece
10. What 'E' is the place where telephone calls are connected?
    Answer: Exchange
11. What name is given to people who used to connect the calls?
    Answer: Operators
12. How many names were in the first ever-telephone directory: 50, 500 or 5,000?
    Answer: 50
13. What 'T' was a kind of coded message used before telephones were invented?
    Answer: Telegram

Level 3

14. How did people generate the electricity to power early phones?
    Answer: By winding a handle on the side of the phone
15. Who invented the telephone?
    Answer: Alexander Graham Bell
16. In which country was Alexander Graham Bell born?
    Answer: Scotland
17. Who invented the carbon-granule microphone?
    Answer: Thomas Edison
18. Which was invented first: the fax or the telephone?
    Answer: The fax
19. In what year did rotating dials appear: 1886, 1896 or 1906?
    Answer: 1896

ANSWERS: Discoveries

Level 1

1. What type of food is said to have fallen on Isaac Newton's head, giving him the idea for his most famous theory?
   Answer: An apple
2. What 'W' turns around and around, allowing vehicles to move?
   Answer: A wheel
3. IT GRAVY can be rearranged to give the name of what force that pulls objects towards the ground?
   Answer: Gravity

Level 2

4. Which mathematician living in ancient Greece shouted 'Eureka' when he was in his bath?
   Answer: Archimedes
5. What nationality was Isaac Newton?
   Answer: English
6. In which century did the first cars with petrol engines appear?
   Answer: In the 19th century
7. Michael Faraday was an American scientist. True or false?
   Answer: False (he was English)
8. What 'S' was used to drive the earliest cars?
   Answer: Steam
9. Karl Benz was a pioneer of the motor car. True or false?
   Answer: True
10. SPICY HITS can be rearranged to give the name of what type of scientist?
    Answer: Physicist
11. Who came up with the theory of relativity?
    Answer: Albert Einstein
12. Was the wheel invented more than 3,000 years ago?
    Answer: Yes
13. What 'M' did Michael Faraday help us to understand better?
    Answer: Magnetism
14. What nationality was Nicolas Cugnot, who built the first car?
    Answer: French
15. By what three letters is deoxyribonucleic acid usually known?
    Answer: DNA

Level 3

16. In which modern country are the ruins of the city of Uruk?
    Answer: Iraq
17. Which two scientists are usually credited with discovering the double helix of deoxyribonucleic acid?
    Answer: Francis Crick and James Watson
18. In the formula $E = mc^2$, what does 'E' stand for?
    Answer: Energy

ANSWERS: Ancient Egypt

Level 1

1. Which river flows through Egypt?
   Answer: The Nile
2. What did the ancient Egyptians call their leader?
   Answer: The pharaoh
3. Did Egyptians believe in life after death?
   Answer: Yes
4. What was made of wool or human hair?
   Answer: Wigs
5. What were Egyptian clothes made from?
   Answer: Linen

Level 2

6. What form of writing did the Egyptians use?
   Answer: Hieroglyphics
7. What was papyrus made from?
   Answer: Reed
8. What was usually buried with an Egyptian's body?
   Answer: Their clothes and furniture, and food and drink
9. How did the Egyptians usually decorate their coffins?
   Answer: With a portrait of the dead person
10. What was 'Opening the mouth'?
    Answer: A ceremony performed by priests at a dead pharaoh's tomb
11. What is the biggest pyramid called?
    Answer: The Great Pyramid of Giza
12. What flower was the symbol of the Nile?
    Answer: The lotus

Level 3

13. Which part of the body was used to measure a cubit: the leg, the foot or the forearm?
    Answer: The forearm
14. How did the Egyptians transport a pharaoh's body?
    Answer: In a funeral boat
15. What did Egyptians use to dry the body when embalming?
    Answer: Salt
16. What animal is associated with the Egyptian god of kings?
    Answer: The hawk
17. What did the priest say during a death ceremony?
    Answer: 'You live again, you live again forever'
18. For how long did the pharaohs rule Egypt?
    Answer: For 3,000 years
19. Who is buried in the Great Pyramid of Giza?
    Answer: The pharaoh Cheops

ANSWERS: Ancient Greece

Level 1

1. What 'M' is one of the seas around Greece?
   Answer: The Mediterrean sea
2. Who was the ruler of the Greek gods?
   Answer: Zeus
3. Where were the ancient Olympic games held?
   Answer: Olympia
4. Was the Trojan horse made of stone or wood?
   Answer: Wood
5. The Greeks had slaves. True or false?
   Answer: True

Level 2

6. A SPRAT can be rearranged to give the name of what Greek city-state?
   Answer: Sparta
7. What did women use to weave fabric for clothes?
   Answer: A loom
8. At about what age did women marry?
   Answer: 15 years old
9. Who hid inside the Trojan horse?
   Answer: Greek soldiers
10. SNOOD PIE can be rearranged to give the name of what Greek god?
    Answer: Poseidon
11. What material did the Greeks use to make bricks?
    Answer: Mud
12. How did wealthy Greeks travel on land: by horse or by carriage?
    Answer: By horse
13. The Greek empire included many islands. True or false?
    Answer: True
14. When travelling in Greece, people slept outside. True or false?
    Answer: True
15. Where were the gods said to live?
    Answer: On Mount Olympus

Level 3

16. In which modern country was the ancient city of Troy?
    Answer: Turkey
17. What did a winner receive at the Olympic games?
    Answer: A crown of olive leaves
18. What was a chiton?
    Answer: A basic woman's dress made of a single rectangle of cloth
19. Where in the home did the Greeks have an altar?
    Answer: In the courtyard
20. Who was the goddess of the home?
    Answer: Hestia

ANSWERS: The Colosseum

Level 1

1. What famous gladiator led a revolt of slaves?
   Answer: Spartacus
2. There were elephants in the Colosseum. True or false?
   Answer: True
3. What signal did the crowd give for a gladiator to die?
   Answer: Thumbs down
4. CUT ROSE can be rearranged to give the name of what type of gladiator?
   Answer: Secutor

Level 2

5. In what part of the Colosseum were the gladiators and animals kept?
   Answer: In underground chambers
6. Which emperor often fought at the Colosseum?
   Answer: Commodus
7. What was a *bestiarius*?
   Answer: A man trained to fight animals
8. What did a *retiarius* use to catch his opponent?
   Answer: A net and a three-pronged spear
9. Who was thrown to the animals?
   Answer: Christians, criminals and slaves
10. What kind of gladiator wore a helmet decorated with a fish?
    Answer: A murmillo
11. How many years did it take to build the Colosseum: ten, 20 or 30?
    Answer: ten
12. The *venationes* were Roman soldiers. True or false?
    Answer: False

Level 3

13. What did a freed gladiator receive?
    Answer: A bone tablet, inscribed with his name, and a gift of coins
14. How many people could attend games at the Colosseum?
    Answer: 50,000 people
15. When were the first gladiator games held?
    Answer: In 264BCE
16. How did the Colosseum get its name?
    Answer: From the nearby colossus (statue) of Nero
17. How many times did Commodus fight at the Colosseum?
    Answer: 735 times
18. How many animals were killed in the first celebrations at the Colosseum?
    Answer: 5,000

ANSWERS: Medieval life

Level 1

1. A banquet is a type of battle. True or false?
   Answer: False (it is a feast)
2. People ate meals in the great hall. True or false?
   Answer: True
3. Was a *jongleur* a person or a musical instrument?
   Answer: A person
4. Who owned the land in medieval times?
   Answer: The king
5. Who taught the children of noblemen: priests or servants?
   Answer: Priests

Level 2

6. Who rented land from noblemen?
   Answer: Knights and lords
7. What were *jongleurs* called in England?
   Answer: Gleemen
8. What was the name of the system by which land was given out?
   Answer: The feudal system
9. What was the centre of the castle called?
   Answer: The keep
10. Where did important people sit during a banquet?
    Answer: At the high table
11. How were castle floors kept warm?
    Answer: They were covered with reeds
12. Where were medieval girls taught?
    Answer: At home
13. What was the cup board for?
    Answer: Displaying the lord's cups and plates
14. What was used to help rid the castle floor of bad smells?
    Answer: Spices

Level 3

15. What language did sons of nobles learn?
    Answer: Latin
16. Why did people like to hear music while they were eating?
    Answer: They believed it aided digestion
17. Where did village boys learn trades?
    Answer: At local guilds
18. What were trenchers?
    Answer: Wooden boards that diners ate off

ANSWERS: Knights

Level 1

1. What 'L' was a weapon used by knights on horseback?
   Answer: A lance
2. What was a battering ram used for?
   Answer: To weaken castle walls
3. RED GAG can be rearranged to give the name of what weapon, used by knights?
   Answer: Dagger
4. Knights only ever fought on horseback. True or false?
   Answer: False

Level 2

5. What did an esquire become during a dubbing ceremony?
   Answer: A knight
6. What was a mace?
   Answer: A heavy club
7. How did a jousting knight knock his opponent off his horse?
   Answer: With a blunted lance
8. What kind of missiles did a mangonel shoot?
   Answer: Rocks
9. Did a knight use a crossbow or a longbow?
   Answer: He used both
10. Why did jousting begin?
    Answer: As battle training
11. What weapon was used to shoot bolts at a castle?
    Answer: A ballista
12. How could knights tell each other apart in battle?
    Answer: By the coats of arms on their surcoats
13. What is a trebuchet?
    Answer: A siege weapon used for hurling stones at castle walls
14. How could attackers force the defenders of a castle to surrender?
    Answer: By starving them into surrender

Level 3

15. What was the name of the fee paid by knights who did not want to fight?
    Answer: Scutage
16. What was a bevor?
    Answer: A piece of armour that protected the knight's neck
17. How was an esquire dubbed?
    Answer: His lord tapped him on the shoulder with the flat blade of his sword
18. By which century had knights begun wearing plated armour?
    Answer: The 15th century

ANSWERS: The Renaissance

Level 1

1. Does the word Renaissance mean 'rebirth' or 'revolting'?
   Answer: It means 'rebirth'
2. BLAMER can be rearranged to give the name of what material, used by Renaissance sculptors?
   Answer: Marble
3. Was Donatello a painter or a sculptor?
   Answer: A sculptor
4. The lute is a musical instrument. True or false?
   Answer: True

Level 2

5. Ghiberti was a Renaissance philosopher. True or false?
   Answer: False
6. Where was block printing invented?
   Answer: China
7. What was the *lira da braccio* used for?
   Answer: For accompanying poems
8. What painting featured the ancient philosophers Plato and Aristotle?
   Answer: The School of Athens
9. What was the first-ever mass-produced book?
   Answer: A Bible
10. HARE PAL can be rearranged to give the name of what Renaissance artist?
    Answer: Raphael
11. Of what nationality was Erasmus?
    Answer: Dutch
12. Which two civilizations influenced Renaissance artists?
    Answer: Greek and Roman
13. What is the name of the leather pad, which applied the ink in the first European printing press?
    Answer: An inkball
14. What kind of philosophers thought that moral lessons could be learned from ancient texts?
    Answer: Humanists

Level 3

15. What 'B' was a famous Renaissance architect?
    Answer: Brunelleschi
16. In what year was the printing press invented in Europe?
    Answer: 1440
17. The Renaissance lasted until which century?
    Answer: The 17th century
18. Who invented the printing press in Europe?
    Answer: Johannes Gutenberg

ANSWERS: Age of exploration

Level 1

1. Was Sir Francis Drake an Englishman or a Spaniard?
   Answer: An Englishman
2. What was Columbus' largest ship called: the *Santa Maria*, the *Santa Anna* or the *Santa Barbara*?
   Answer: The Santa Maria
3. Francisco Pizarro conquered the Incas. True or false?
   Answer: True
4. From which country was Bartholomew Diaz?
   Answer: Portugal

Level 2

5. Which did Magellan discover: the Indian ocean or the Pacific ocean?
   Answer: The Pacific ocean
6. How many men were in the crew of Columbus' largest ship: 30, 40 or 60?
   Answer: 40
7. Who sent Columbus to find a route to China?
   Answer: The king of Spain
8. Did Diaz or da Gama sail around the southern tip of Africa?
   Answer: Diaz
9. Who reached India in 1498?
   Answer: Vasco da Gama
10. What was Zheng He the first to do?
    Answer: Use a compass on a sea voyage
11. What were the names of Columbus' two caravels?
    Answer: The Niña and the Pinta
12. What was a backstaff used for?
    Answer: Measuring the angle of the sun
13. Why did Ferdinand Magellan not reach his final destination?
    Answer: He was killed in the Philippines
14. What did Columbus believe he had reached?
    Answer: The Far East
15. What part of the world did the Incas rule?
    Answer: The western coast of South America (now Peru)

Level 3

16. On which island did Columbus land?
    Answer: San Salvador
17. What was discovered in 1911?
    Answer: Machu Picchu
18. What is a *nao*?
    Answer: A merchant ship
19. When did a ship first sail all the way round the world?
    Answer: 1522

ANSWERS: World War I

Level 1

1. What large machine was used for the first time in World War I?
   Answer: The tank
2. What is a dogfight?
   Answer: A battle in the air between two or more aircraft
3. What was the area between enemy trenches called?
   Answer: No-man's-land
4. A grenade is a weapon. True or false?
   Answer: True

Level 2

5. What kind of protection did soldiers have against gas?
   Answer: Gas masks
6. For what purpose were horses used?
   Answer: To haul ambulances and weaponry
7. Which 'J' was a major battle fought at sea?
   Answer: The Battle of Jutland
8. Where was the Western Front?
   Answer: In Belgium and France
9. What name is used for a trained marksman who tries to pick off lone soldiers?
   Answer: A sniper
10. What weapon could be attached to a rifle?
    Answer: A bayonet
11. How many lives were lost in the war: over 7.5 million, over 8.5 million or over 10 million?
    Answer: Over 8.5 million
12. In which country is Jutland?
    Answer: Denmark
13. What lined the tops of the trenches?
    Answer: Sandbags
14. What weapons were fighter planes fitted with?
    Answer: Machine guns

Level 3

15. In what year was poison gas first used?
    Answer: 1915
16. Which model of tank was the first one strong enough to withstand anti-tank rifles?
    Answer: The British Mark IV
17. What was the name given to the British soldiers who trained horses?
    Answer: Roughriders
18. What German fighter plane was considered to be the best fighter plane of the war?
    Answer: The Fokker DVII

ANSWERS: Summer Olympics

Level 1

1. How many rings are there in the Olympic symbol?
   Answer: Five
2. Which Olympic sport features a 5m-long springy pole?
   Answer: Pole vaulting
3. How often are the summer Olympic games held?
   Answer: Every four years
4. Do equestrian events use a horse, a bicycle or a pistol?
   Answer: A horse
5. Which kind of swimming race is longer: a sprint or an endurance race?
   Answer: An endurance race

Level 2

6. Is a marathon race 20km, 42km or 50km long?
   Answer: 42km
7. What is the name of a competitor in a judo fight?
   Answer: A judoka
8. Which horse-based sport takes three days to complete?
   Answer: Eventing
9. What is the name of the building in which track cyclists compete?
   Answer: A velodrome
10. Who set a world record of 6.14m for the pole vault?
    Answer: Sergei Bubka
11. What is the longest distance race in track athletics at the Olympics?
    Answer: The 50km racewalk
12. How many Olympics has Jeannie Longo-Ciprelli appeared at: three, four or six?
    Answer: Six
13. In which sport did Mark Spitz win seven gold medals in 1972?
    Answer: Swimming

Level 3

14. How long is a steeplechase race at the Olympics?
    Answer: 3,000m
15. When was judo first included in the Olympics?
    Answer: 1964
16. How many lengths of the pool do swimmers in the 1,500m race have to swim?
    Answer: 30
17. How much shorter is a woman's judo bout than a man's?
    Answer: One minute
18. What fraction of the total gold medals for judo did Japan win in 2004?
    Answer: Half

ANSWERS: Gymnastics

Level 1

1. When do athletes warm up?
   Answer: Before competing
2. What are people who perform gymnastics called?
   Answer: Gymnasts
3. How many handles does a pommel horse have?
   Answer: Two
4. Are rings used only by men, or by both men and women?
   Answer: Only by men
5. What do some athletes dust their hands with to help with their grip?
   Answer: Chalk

Level 2

6. In gymnastics, how many events do female athletes compete in?
   Answer: Four
7. Did rhythmic gymnastics first appear in the Olympics in 1932, 1968 or 1984?
   Answer: 1984
8. How many items of equipment are there in rhythmic gymnastics?
   Answer: Five
9. Was the first person to get the highest possible score in artistic gymnastics at the Olympics a man or a woman?
   Answer: A woman
10. What is the highest possible mark given to a competitor for one routine: 10, 15, or 20?
    Answer: 10
11. What 'H' is a piece of rhythmic gymnastics equipment?
    Answer: Hoop
12. What are the two hoops hanging above the ground called?
    Answer: Rings
13. What kind of gymnastics is performed to music?
    Answer: Rhythmic gymnastics
14. How many panels of judges mark rhythmic gymnastics?
    Answer: Three

Level 3

15. How high are the parallel bars?
    Answer: 1.75m high
16. Who was the first person to get the highest possible score in artistic gymnastics at the Olympics?
    Answer: Nadia Comaneci
17. Who invented the parallel bars?
    Answer: Friedrich Jahn
18. From which gymnastics apparatus would a gymnast dismount?
    Answer: The pommel horse

ANSWERS: Winter sports

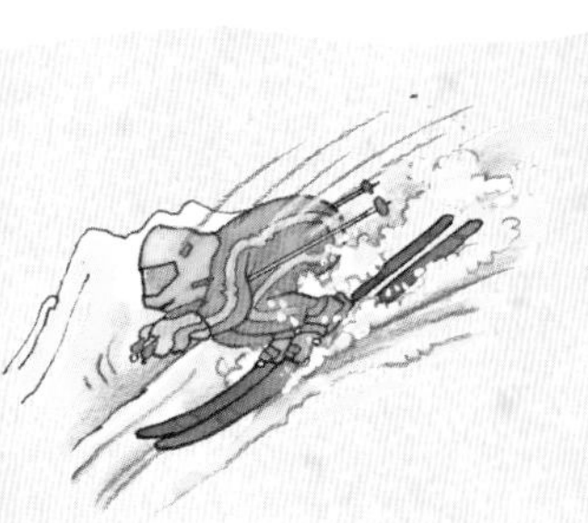

Level 1

1. How many skis does a skier wear?
   Answer: Two
2. Do speed skaters race downhill, round a track or along a road?
   Answer: Round a track
3. Which country invented ice hockey?
   Answer: Canada
4. Which is also known as cross-country skiing: Nordic or downhill?
   Answer: Nordic skiing
5. What name is given to someone who teaches others to ski?
   Answer: Ski instructor

Level 2

6. In which winter sport do players try to hit a puck into a goal?
   Answer: Ice hockey
7. What is the front of a snowboard called?
   Answer: The nose
8. Downhill skiing is part of the winter Olympics. True or false?
   Answer: True
9. What is the name of the sticks held in the hands of a skier?
   Answer: Ski poles
10. In which winter sport can competitors reach a speed of 60km/h as they race around a track?
    Answer: Speed skating
11. Are there six, nine or 11 players per side in ice hockey?
    Answer: Six
12. Do Nordic or slalom skiers race a zigzagging course?
    Answer: Slalom skiers
13. What is the back of a snowboard called?
    Answer: The tail
14. How many periods are there in an ice hockey game?
    Answer: Three
15. The biathlon involves rifle shooting and what sort of skiing?
    Answer: Nordic skiing
16. In what year did snowboarding become an Olympic sport?
    Answer: 1998

Level 3

17. Which can travel the fastest: speed skaters or downhill skiers?
    Answer: Downhill skiers
18. What object fixes ski boots to skis?
    Answer: Bindings
19. Which skis are shorter and wider: Nordic skis or downhill skis?
    Answer: Downhill skis
20. What is the name of the player who guards a goal in ice hockey?
    Answer: The goaltender

ANSWERS: Football

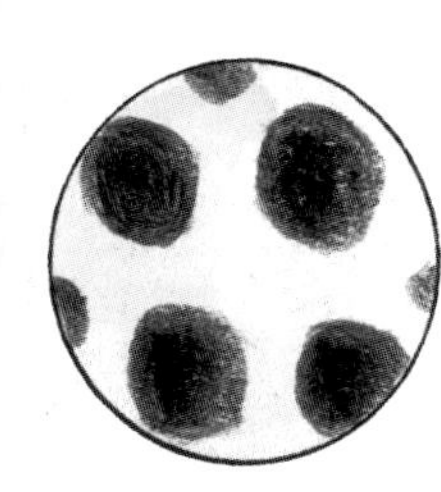

Level 1

1. What is the name given to the players who try to score goals?
   Answer: Attackers
2. Which player is allowed to touch the ball with their hands?
   Answer: The goalkeeper
3. The warning card is yellow. True or false?
   Answer: True
4. Is challenging for the ball known as passing, throwing in or tackling?
   Answer: Tackling
5. What is a football pitch usually made of?
   Answer: Grass

Level 2

6. For what country did Pelé play?
   Answer: Brazil
7. Who has scored over 100 goals for his country: Wayne Rooney, Michael Ballack or Ali Daei?
   Answer: Ali Daei
8. What is the person in charge of a football match called?
   Answer: The referee
9. How often did Pelé help win the World Cup?
   Answer: Three times
10. How many players are in a football team?
    Answer: 11
11. What colour is the card that means the player is sent off the pitch?
    Answer: Red
12. In which city were the first full rules of football created?
    Answer: London
13. Did Pelé score 478, 809 or 1,281 goals in his career?
    Answer: 1,281
14. Does Cristiano Ronaldo play for Portugal, France or Brazil?
    Answer: Portugal

Level 3

15. Which of the following parts of the body can a footballer use to control the ball: head, chest, arms, thigh, hands?
    Answer: Head, chest, thigh
16. For what country did Ali Daei play?
    Answer: Iran
17. What animal's bladder was used to make early footballs?
    Answer: A pig's
18. Which American woman has scored 158 goals for her country?
    Answer: Mia Hamm

ANSWERS: Art and painting

Level 1

1. The famous artist Michelangelo came from Italy. True or false?
   Answer: True
2. What was Van Gogh's first name?
   Answer: Vincent
3. In what country are the famous Lascaux cave paintings?
   Answer: France
4. Were sculptures, cave paintings or frescoes made on damp plaster?
   Answer: Frescoes
5. The Lascaux cave paintings feature paintings of reindeer. True or false?
   Answer: True

Level 2

6. What part of an egg was used by prehistoric cave painters?
   Answer: The white
7. Can you name either of the colours that were often used by the ancient Greeks to decorate their pottery?
   Answer: Red or black
8. Do artists painting frescoes have to work slowly or quickly?
   Answer: Quickly
9. Does tempera or oil paint produce richer colours?
   Answer: Oil paint
10. Did Michelangelo paint a fresco on the doors, the walls or the ceiling of the Sistine Chapel?
    Answer: The ceiling
11. From what was Michelangelo's sculpture of Moses carved?
    Answer: Marble
12. Does oil paint or tempera paint dry more slowly?
    Answer: Oil paint
13. What part of an egg was used to make tempera paints?
    Answer: The yolk

Level 3

14. *Blam!* is a famous Pop Art painting. Who painted it?
    Answer: Roy Lichtenstein
15. In what century did Michelangelo carve a sculpture of Moses?
    Answer: The 16th century
16. How old was Van Gogh when he painted *Starry Night*?
    Answer: 36
17. In which decade did Pop Art first appear?
    Answer: In the 1950s
18. Are the prehistoric paintings in the Lascaux caves around 15,000, 16,000 or 17,000 years old?
    Answer: Around 17,000 years old

ANSWERS: Ballet

Level 1

1. Do most ballet dancers start as children, teenagers or adults?
   Answer: As children
2. Do ballets take place in a rink, a court or in a theatre?
   Answer: A theatre
3. Do male ballet dancers wear make-up?
   Answer: Yes
4. Is a tutu a ballet shoe, a skirt or a type of ballet move?
   Answer: A skirt

Level 2

5. What sort of musician often plays during ballet classes?
   Answer: A pianist
6. In *Swan Lake*, what part of the body does a ballerina move to look like wings?
   Answer: The arms
7. Before a show, where do dancers put on their make-up?
   Answer: In the dressing room
8. A *port de bras* exercise involves the movement of what part of the body?
   Answer: The arms
9. How many basic positions are there for the feet in ballet?
   Answer: Five
10. The heels touch together in which position: first, second or third?
    Answer: First
11. ASK LAWNE can be rearranged to give the name of what ballet?
    Answer: Swan Lake
12. Why do dancers wear leg warmers when they practise?
    Answer: To keep their muscles warm and prevent strains and injuries
13. What term means dancing on the tips of the toes?
    Answer: Pointe-work
14. In a ballet what is the break between acts called?
    Answer: The interval
15. A major ballet may need as many as 30, 300 or 3,000 costumes?
    Answer: 300 costumes

Level 3

16. Which country does the ballet *Swan Lake* come from?
    Answer: Russia
17. What term means the leading female dancer in a ballet company?
    Answer: Prima Ballerina
18. What 'O' is the queen of the swans in *Swan Lake*?
    Answer: Odette

ANSWERS: Architecture

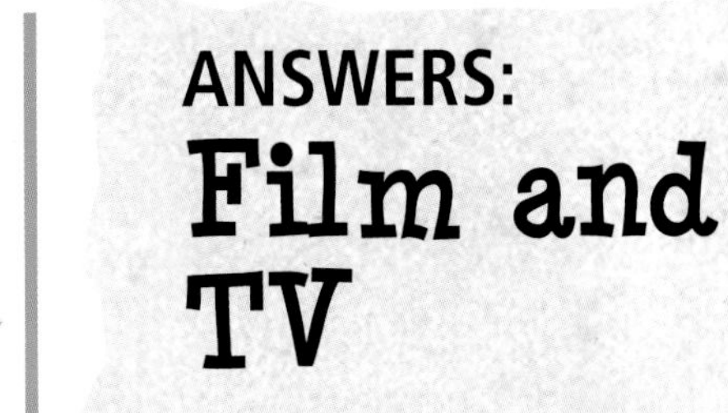

Level 1

1. Who built the Parthenon: the Greeks, Egyptians or Romans?
   Answer: The Greeks
2. What is the name given to the giant buildings used to bury leaders (pharaohs) in ancient Egypt?
   Answer: Pyramids
3. Were the first bricks made of mud and clay, or cement and gravel?
   Answer: Mud and clay
4. Are the pyramids of ancient Egypt made of mud, wood or stone?
   Answer: Stone
5. Were the first bricks made solid by setting them on fire, letting them dry in the sun or freezing them?
   Answer: Letting them dry in the sun

Level 2

6. Which civilization invented concrete?
   Answer: The Romans
7. Was the Parthenon built of granite, cement or marble?
   Answer: Marble
8. In which city is the Parthenon?
   Answer: Athens
9. Why does Hardwick Hall have lots of windows?
   Answer: As a sign of wealth
10. Did the White House get water pipes or gas lighting installed first?
    Answer: Water pipes
11. Did the Gothic style of architecture begin in Europe, Asia or Africa?
    Answer: Europe
12. What is the name of the wooden strips that are filled in with daub?
    Answer: Wattles
13. Who built Hardwick Hall?
    Answer: Bess of Hardwick

Level 3

14. What are the architect's detailed plans for a building called?
    Answer: Blueprints
15. Which famous building did James Hoban rebuild?
    Answer: The White House
16. The Parthenon was a temple for the worship of which goddess?
    Answer: Athena
17. What is a flying buttress?
    Answer: A special side-support
18. During which century did Gothic architecture first appear?
    Answer: The 12th century

ANSWERS: Film and TV

Level 1

1. Were the first TV broadcasts black and white or colour?
   Answer: Black and white
2. What 'D' is the person in charge of the film-making process?
   Answer: The director
3. What name is given to someone who interviews people for the news?
   Answer: Reporter
4. What word describes people who play characters and appear in films?
   Answer: Actors
5. What word describes the written-down version of a film?
   Answer: The script

Level 2

6. Who are the three people needed in a news team?
   Answer: Reporter, cameraman, sound recordist
7. What word describes news reporting that is transmitted as the events unfold?
   Answer: Live
8. Was the first film with sound *Casablanca*, *The Jazz Singer* or *Snow White*?
   Answer: The Jazz Singer
9. WOOLY HOLD can be rearranged to give the name of what huge film industry based in the USA?
   Answer: Hollywood
10. Near which big American city is this industry located?
    Answer: Los Angeles
11. What nickname is given to India's film industry?
    Answer: Bollywood
12. What name is given to 24-hour news programmes?
    Answer: Rolling news

Level 3

13. Was Telstar the name of an early television or a satellite?
    Answer: A satellite
14. In what year was the first 'talking' film made?
    Answer: 1927
15. In 1962, what percentage of US homes had a television?
    Answer: 90 *per cent*
16. In what year was the first TV signal sent by satellite?
    Answer: 1962
17. What word is used for sending programmes out from the TV station?
    Answer: Broadcasting
18. Which Asian country has one of the largest film industries in the world?
    Answer: India

Index

N

O

P

R

S

T

U

V

W

X

Z

Acknowledgments

The publisher would like to thank the following for permission to reproduce their material. Every care has been taken to trace copyright holders. However, if there have been unintentional omissions or failure to trace copyright holders, we apologize and will, if informed, endeavour to make corrections in any future edition.

b = bottom, c = centre, l = left, r = right, t = top

PHOTOGRAPHS

16bc Corbis/Tim Davis; 27br Corbis/Staffan Widstrand; 35cr Corbis/Kit Houghton; 60c NASA; 70bl Corbis/Frank Tusch/zefa; 73t Siemens Ltd; 86tr Corbis/Dann Tardiff; 89cl Bradbury & Williams/Roy Williams; 89br Bradbury & Williams/Roy Williams; 94tr Robert Harding; 116cr Swedish Travel and Tourism Council; 121br Corbis/KIPA; 125br Corbis/William Manning, BR; 125cr Corbis/Eric Crichton

ILLUSTRATIONS

Susanna Addario 88cr, 88bl; Lisa Alderson 4–5b, 8b; Marion Appleton 121bl; Artists Partners 83br, 127bl; Mike Atkinson 75tr; Julian Baker 64cl, 103cl; Julian Baum 62c; Owain Bell 91cr; Mark Bergin 79cl, 101tl, 102cl, 112bl; Richard Berridge (Specs Art) 35tr; Gary Bines 61cr, 85t; Brighton Illustration Agency 32c; Mike Buckley/Malcolm Parchment 118cl, 118br, 119t; Peter Bull 44tc, 69cl; John Butler 31bl; Martin Camm 21cr; Robin Carter (Wildlife Art Agency) 67tl; Jim Channell 20l, 33b, 48c; Kuo Kang Chen 82b; Harry Clow 54tr; Gino D'Achille (Artist Partners) 56–57b, 103cr; Peter Dennis (Linda Rogers) 19tr, 32tr, 46–47t, 72tr, 98tr, 101cl, 102tr, 109cl; Kay Dixey 119cl; Richard Draper 17c, 47c; Dan Escott 100bl; James Field 55t; Chris Forsey 9cr, 9br, 11cr, 12tr, 12–13b, 13t, 30b, 48tr, 49br, 52–53c, 52bc, 53tr, 59b, 60–61b, 63b, 64tr, 65t, 65cr, 66tr, 81tr, 106tr, 120cr, 120br, 124tr; Mark Franklin 46br; Oliver Frey 105tr; Luigi Galante 120bl; Tony Gibbons 80bl; Jeremy Gower 42cr, 85cr; Lindsay Graham (Linden Artists) 34tl, 35bl; Craig Greenwood (Wildlife Art Agency) 14tr; Ray Grinaway 16cl, 22–23c, 33cr, 66c, 67cr, 67bl; Nick Hall 43tr; Alan Hancock 70tr; Alan Harris 25cr; Gary Hincks 51c, 106–107c; Christian Hook (Linden Artists) 123cr, 127tl; Richard Hook 54b, 98cr; Andre Hrydziusko 69tr; Biz Hull 122cl, 122bl; Ian Jackson (Wildlife Art) 7b, 26b, 28–29b, 39c, 55b; Rob Jakeway/Bill Donohoe 64–65b; John James 76–77b, 106bl; Ron Jobson 74cl, 83tl, 83tr, 83c; Michael Johnson 51b; Peter Jones (John Martin) 106cl; Peter Kelly 43c; Roger Kent (Garden Studio) 9t; Martin Knowldon (Virgil Pomfret) 28tr, 28c; Mike Lacey (SGA) 56cr, 57tl, 107tl, 116tr, 117tl, 119b; Linden Artists 22bl, 31tr, 108tr; Bernard Long (Temple Rogers) 11t; 48b; Kevin Maddison 24cl, 50–51c, 51tl, 79tl, 79b, 97cl; Mainline Design 23br; Shirley Mallinsen 12cl; Maltings Partnership 72bl, 82c, 113tr, 87tr; John Marshall (Temple Art) 74tr; Josephine Martin 10tr; David McAllister 79tr; Angus McBride 94–95bc, 98bl, 99cl; Doreen McGuinness (Garden Studios) 48b; Jamie Medline 116bl; Chris Molan (Main) 90tr, 97br, 101br; Steve Noon (Garden Studios) 78b, 126b; Nicki Palin 9cl; Alex Pang 80tr, 90tl, 91tl; Darren Pattenden 42cl, 42bl, 43l; Andie Peck 33tl; Neil Reed 60cl; Eric Robson 18–19b, 20tr, 21tr; Eric Rowe 33cl; Michael Rowe 14c, 16–17t, 16cr, 23tr, 30cl, 38tr; Valerie Sangster 9tr; Mike Saunders (Julian Burgess) 52tr, 96tr; Nick Shewring (Garden Studio) 81b; Brian Smith 117cr; Guy Smith (Mainline Design) 70c, 71l, 71br; M Stacey 73cl; Roger Stewart 40tl, 58tl, 63cl, 63cr, 72br, 92tl, 110tl; Charlotte Styles 71br; Treve Tamblin 18tr, 20cr; Ian Thompson 84bl; Shirley Tourret 100tr; Chris Turnbull 20br; Vincent Wakerley 46bl; Helen Ward (Virgil Pomfret Agency) 38–39b, 39r; Richard Ward 70l; Ross Watton (Garden Studios) 47b; Phil Weare (Linden Artists) 15cl, 15b; Gareth Williams 127cr; Joanna Williams 113cr, 118bc; Ann Winterbotham 68–69b; Dan Wright 21c, 31c; David Wright (Kathy Jakeman) 14b; Paul Wright 49t; Jurgen Ziewe 87cl

Cartoons: Mike Davies 104; Ian Dicks 8, 16, 88, 90; Tony Kenyon (B L Kearley) 12, 18, 20, 24, 26, 36, 56, 60, 62, 64, 72, 74, 76, 78, 82, 84, 86, 96, 98, 116, 118, 120, 122, 124, 126; Anthony Lewis 30, 66; Kevin Maddison 68; Peter Wilkes (SGA) 10, 22, 28, 34, 46, 48, 50, 54, 102, 106, 108